Life in a New Language

T0398917

Life in a New Language

INGRID PILLER, DONNA BUTORAC,
EMILY FARRELL, LOY LISING,
SHIVA MOTAGHI-TABARI, AND
VERA WILLIAMS TETTEH

OXFORD
UNIVERSITY PRESS

Oxford University Press is a department of the University of Oxford. It furthers the University's objective of excellence in research, scholarship, and education by publishing worldwide. Oxford is a registered trade mark of Oxford University Press in the UK and certain other countries.

Published in the United States of America by Oxford University Press
198 Madison Avenue, New York, NY 10016, United States of America.

© Oxford University Press 2024

All rights reserved. No part of this publication may be reproduced, stored in a retrieval system, or transmitted, in any form or by any means, without the prior permission in writing of Oxford University Press, or as expressly permitted by law, by license, or under terms agreed with the appropriate reproduction rights organization. Inquiries concerning reproduction outside the scope of the above should be sent to the Rights Department, Oxford University Press, at the address above.

You must not circulate this work in any other form
and you must impose this same condition on any acquirer.

CIP data is on file at the Library of Congress

ISBN 978-0-19-008429-5 (pbk.)
ISBN 978-0-19-008428-8 (hbk.)

DOI: 10.1093/oso/9780190084288.001.0001

Paperback printed by Marquis Book Printing, Canada
Hardback printed by Bridgeport National Bindery, Inc., United States of America

Caminante, no hay camino, se hace camino al andar. (Traveler, there is no road; the road is made by traveling.)

Machado (1917), p. 229 [Ingrid's translation].

To migrants everywhere.

Contents

Acknowledgments: Or, the Story of This Book

The research behind this book started more than 20 years ago, and the book itself has been in the making for almost 5 years. During this time, we have incurred an enormous debt of gratitude to many more people than we can acknowledge. Writing an acknowledgment that does everyone justice is difficult for any book. It is even more difficult for one with such a long gestation period and one that has six authors. Therefore, we take this opportunity to tell the story of this book and ask the indulgence of anyone we might have neglected to mention.

Research on this book commenced in 2001, when the University of Sydney awarded a Sesqui Grant—so named in celebration of the one and a half centuries since the university's founding—to Ingrid to investigate success and failure in second-language learning. Emily joined the project at that time, initially as a research assistant and later as a PhD student. The first 21 participants were recruited under this project, which originally was designed as an interview study. An Australian Research Council (ARC) Discovery grant awarded to Ingrid in 2003 allowed us to add an ethnographic component involving participant observation, repeat interviews, and focus group interviews, as well as adding a further seven participants. In addition to Emily and Ingrid, Eileen Chu, Sheila Pham, and Kimie Takahashi helped with data collection at the time. Md. Rezaul Haque and Ping Tian also provided research assistance.

A second major pivot for this research occurred from 2007 onward when Ingrid took up the role of Executive Director at the Adult Migrant English Program Research Center (AMEP RC) at Macquarie University. It was there that we all first met as a group. Emily joined the AMEP RC to complete her PhD, Loy to take on a role as research coordinator, and Donna, Shiva, and Vera over the next few years to start their PhDs under the supervision of Ingrid. The AMEP RC fundamentally shaped our joint perspective on migrant language learning in Australia. The research projects we were involved with there, the professional development events we hosted for teachers in the AMEP, the teacher training we conducted around the country, the involvement in study materials development, and the policy discussions with our funder, the Immigration Department, provided us with a broad vision of the field. Two major related research projects, "Language Training and Settlement Success: Are They Related?" (Phase 1 and Phase 2: 2008–2009; 2011–2014) engaged us with close to 300 individual recent arrivals and their language learning and settlement trajectories over 7 years. These research participants are not part of this book due to restrictions on the reuse of the data collected under these two projects. Nonetheless, they have been central to shaping our thinking. We gratefully acknowledge the numerous researchers and research assistants who worked with us on these projects. They are too many to name individually, but you know who you are, and we will always treasure the time we had together in "the Cottage." We are also deeply thankful to all the AMEP training centers across the country that engaged with the AMEP RC and that we had the privilege to work with and to visit. We specifically acknowledge Adult Multicultural Education Services (AMES) NSW, AMES Victoria, AMES West Coast, Australian College of Languages, Canberra Institute of Technology, Central TAFE Western Australia, Charles Darwin University English Language Center, LM Training Specialists Adelaide, Navitas English, Technical and Further Education (TAFE) Queensland, TAFE South Australia (SA) English Language Services, and TAFE Tasmania.

The PhD scholarships of Donna, Shiva, and Vera were funded by Macquarie University through the AMEP RC, and the data they collected for their PhDs have been reanalyzed for this book. Donna worked with nine women migrants whom she had first met as an English-language teacher in an AMEP training center in Perth. Vera's PhD research focused on the language learning and settlement experiences of migrants from various African countries and included 48 participants. Shiva's research was with 19 families from Iran, and in this book we draw on the data from the 33 adults in her study. The remaining 12 participants were originally part of a workplace ethnography conducted by Loy and funded through a Macquarie University new staff grant entitled "Imported Labor, Imported English: Philippine English in the Australian Workforce."

The idea for this book started to germinate on the back of these research projects as well as several related projects undertaken by the Language on the Move research team founded by Ingrid and Kimie Takahashi in 2009. We gratefully acknowledge these other research projects related to language and migration. These include three funded projects: one about Japanese transnational migrants, funded by the Australia-Japan Foundation and awarded to Ingrid and Kimie; one about Filipino migrants' multilingual practices in Australia, funded by the Australian Linguistics Society and awarded to Loy; and one about the hidden oracies of African migrants, funded by the Linguistics Department at Macquarie University under a Chitra Fernando Early Career Award granted to Vera. Relevant research conducted by members of the Language on the Move team also includes several higher degree research projects, and we have benefited from the contributions of Tazin Abdullah, Samar Alkhalil, Awatif Alshammri, Gegentuul Baioud, Victoria Benz, Agnes Bodis, Ana Bruzon, Grace Chu-Lin Chang, Xiaoxiao Chen, Jinhyun Cho, Rahel Cramer, Sithembinkosi Dube,

Livia Gerber, Alexandra Grey, Vittoria Grossi, Jia Li, Madiha Neelam, Brynn Quick, Laura Smith-Khan, Pia Tenedero, Hanna Torsh, Yining Wang, Melanie Warnakulasuriya Fernando, Hongyan Yang, and Jie (Jenny) Zhang.

Throughout this period, our vision of migrant language learning and settlement was further shaped by our involvement with several community language schools and migrant organizations. These include the Federation of Ethnic Community Councils of Australia, Ga-Adangbe Association of NSW, German International School Sydney, NSW Federation of Community Language Schools, SBS, and the Sydney Institute for Community Languages Education (SICLE).

The idea for this book and the reanalysis of these previously collected datasets started to take shape in 2018. We are grateful to Oxford University Press, including Linguistics Commissioning Editors Hallie Stebbins and Meredith Keffer as well as three anonymous reviewers, for welcoming our book proposal so warmly. Funding from the ARC under a Discovery grant, "Communicating with People Who Have Limited English Proficiency," and from the Humboldt Foundation under an Anneliese Maier Research Award, both awarded to Ingrid, enabled us to dedicate time to the project. Even so, it got derailed by the COVID-19 pandemic and took longer than expected. Along the way, we discovered that writing a truly coauthored book with a team of six authors was more challenging than anticipated, but also much more rewarding and fun. We were never co-located during the writing period, and coordinating through in-person and virtual work meetings across Los Angeles, New York, Perth, and Sydney added spice to our project. We hope that the spirit of collaboration, engagement, dialogue, and friendship that guided our endeavor shines through the pages to follow.

During the writing period, we profited from our interactions with our colleagues and students at our home universities, Curtin University and Macquarie University, as well as Ingrid's visiting appointments at Hamburg University and Uppsala University. We had the privilege to attend more conferences and professional events than we can mention. We appreciate all the opportunities for interaction and learning that these provided. Three events at Macquarie University which we hosted deserve individual mention: a symposium devoted to linguistic diversity and social inclusion, funded by the Faculty of Human Sciences; a symposium about "Bridging Language Barriers," funded by the German Academic Exchange Service (DAAD); and a conference dedicated to sharing knowledge in the spirit of Humboldt, funded by the Humboldt Foundation. We thank all the presenters and attendees for lively debates and discussions that have extended our thinking. The Language on the Move website and associated social media feeds on Twitter and Facebook have long been inspirational sources of academic debate, interaction, and community.

The writing process was supported by Pia Tenedero, who served as minute taker during a 2-day writing retreat. We are also grateful for the proofreading support provided by Angela Turzynski-Azimi in the final stages of manuscript completion.

Our deepest gratitude must go to the participants whose stories made this book. It has been a privilege that our paths have crossed, and that we could walk a stretch of the way together. We are profoundly mindful of the responsibility that comes from having your stories entrusted to us. Some of you are still in our lives and we appreciate our connections. A few have passed away and we dedicate this book to their memory.

Our research has been conducted on Dharug, Darkinjung, Duungidjawu, Gadigal, Noongar, and Wiradjuri lands. We pay tribute to the sustenance and inspiration we have received from people and places throughout the lands on which we have traveled. We acknowledge the Traditional Custodians of Country throughout the unceded territories of Australia upon which we live and work. We pay our respects to Elders past, present, and future.

Last but not least, we express our gratitude to our families, who have been with us along the way: Çox sağol, Hvala, Nyɛyiwaladɔŋŋ, Sepas gozâram, Taospusong pasasalamat, Vageit's Good, Yɛda mo ase!

Note on Pseudonyms, Transcription, and Translation

Throughout this book we have tried to preserve the voices of our participants, as much as possible. We attribute these voices to specific speakers, all of whose names are pseudonyms. Mindful of the fact that migrant residents of small localities might be identifiable, we identify capital cities but mask regional cities, small towns, and specific organizations through descriptive pseudonyms ("Baptist Believers," "Big Beef," "Regional City," "Tiny Town," "Top Telco").

Quotes from participants come from the transcription of audio recordings, their journal entries, emails, or our fieldnotes. In representing participants' speech, we were guided by ease of readability and mostly prioritized the convenience of the reader, unless details of oral language such as hesitations and false starts were important for our analysis.

Most of the interactions reported here were in English. Some were in Akan, German, Persian, and Tagalog. In the latter case, we usually provide the English translation only. To distinguish whether a quote was originally in English or another language, we use the following conventions:

- Roman font indicates a direct quotation where the original was in English.
- Italics indicate a direct quotation where the original was in another language, and we have translated the excerpt into English. Roman font within such an excerpt indicates that a specific word was uttered in English, within an utterance that was otherwise in another language.

Participants' speech is represented in standard orthography unless conventional nonstandard forms exist (e.g., "can't" instead of "cannot"). We have avoided attempts to represent the accent of participants, as such attempts are generally not helpful to the reader and often end up stereotyping the speaker. Grammatical and lexical expressions, by contrast, are always direct quotes, even where they deviate from what might be considered correct English, to preserve the authenticity of the speakers' expression.

The following transcription conventions were used:

,	clause final intonation ("more to come")
.	clause final falling intonation
!	clause final high-fall
?	clause final rising intonation
...	long pause, i.e., more than half a second
-	truncation, i.e., incomplete word or utterance
=	one utterance latches on to another. Indicates that a speaker latches on to the previous speaker's utterance without a perceptible pause.
[...]	omission
[laughs]	analysts' comments and explanations within quotes are placed in square brackets
CAPS	emphatic stress (In keeping with standard orthography, we have capitalized "I" throughout, and the first letter of proper nouns and the first word of a new sentence. These are not to be taken to indicate emphatic stress.)
"animation"	perceptible change in voice quality when another voice is imitated or quoted
(*translation*)	In the few instances where we present expressions in a language other than English, the English translation follows in italics in brackets.

List of Participants

Pseudonym[1]	Arrival Year	Arrival Age	Gender[2]	Country of Origin	Entry Visa[3]	Highest Level of Education[4]
Abenet	2004	30–39	m	Ethiopia	Humanitarian	Bachelor
Abiba	2003	20–29	f	Sierra Leone	Humanitarian	Bachelor
Agatha	1990	30–39	f	Georgia	Tourist	≥Masters
Ahmed	2003	30–39	m	Sudan[5]	Humanitarian	≤Primary
Aiko	1997	20–29	f	Japan	Student	≥Masters
Ajara	2003	20–29	f	Sudan	Humanitarian	Year 10
Alexa	1992	20–29	f	Spain	Working holiday	Bachelor
Amin	2011	30–39	m	Iran	Skilled permanent	Bachelor
Amina	2003	40–49	f	Sierra Leone	Humanitarian	≤Primary
Amot	2004	30–39	f	Ethiopia	Humanitarian	≤Primary
Anita	2011	30–39	f	Iran	Skilled permanent, secondary	Bachelor
Anna	2007	30–39	f	Serbia	Family reunion	Bachelor
Azadeh	2006	20–29	f	Iran	Skilled permanent, secondary	Bachelor
Azim	1999	10–19	m	Pakistan	Student	Bachelor
Behnaz	2008	20–29	f	Iran	Skilled permanent, secondary	Bachelor
Benjamin	2001	40–49	m	Sudan	Humanitarian	Year 12
Bernardo	2008	30–39	m	Philippines	Skilled temporary	Bachelor
Bijan	2008	40–49	m	Iran	Skilled permanent	Bachelor
Cetareh	2010	20–29	f	Iran	Skilled permanent, secondary	Bachelor
Charity	2003	40–49	f	Sudan	Humanitarian	≤Primary
Cossette	2008	40–49	f	Philippines	Skilled temporary	Bachelor
Cyrus	2010	30–39	m	Iran	Skilled permanent	Bachelor
Dagmar	1996	30–39	f	Austria	Working holiday	Bachelor
Daisy	1999	30–39	f	Kenya	Tourist	Bachelor
Danica	1995	30–39	f	Russia	Family reunion	≥Masters
Daniel	2002	20–29	m	Sudan	Humanitarian	Bachelor
Daryoush	2009	30–39	m	Iran	Skilled permanent, secondary	Bachelor
Diba	2009	30–39	f	Iran	Skilled permanent	≥Masters

Pseudonym[1]	Arrival Year	Arrival Age	Gender[2]	Country of Origin	Entry Visa[3]	Highest Level of Education[4]
Domingo	2007	40–49	m	Philippines	Skilled temporary	Year 12
Donaldo	2006	30–39	m	Philippines	Skilled temporary	Year 10
Doris	2004	20–29	f	Sudan	Humanitarian	≤Primary
Ehsan	2012	40–49	m	Iran	Skilled permanent	≥Masters
Elham	2012	30–39	f	Iran	Skilled permanent, secondary	≥Masters
Elizabeth	2005	20–29	f	Ghana	Tourist	Year 10
Ellen	2008	30–39	f	Philippines	Skilled temporary, secondary	Year 12
Eric	2007	20–29	m	Sierra Leone	Humanitarian	Year 12
Ernestine	2006	30–39	f	Congo (DRC)	Humanitarian	Bachelor
Eva	1985	30–39	f	Chile	Humanitarian	Bachelor
Farah	2009	20–29	f	Iran	Skilled permanent	Bachelor
Farzad	2009	30–39	m	Iran	Skilled permanent, secondary	Bachelor
Fatima	2006	30–39	f	Ethiopia	Humanitarian	≤Primary
Felicia	2003	30–39	f	Sudan	Humanitarian	≤Primary
Franklin	2003	30–39	m	Sudan	Humanitarian	Bachelor
Genevieve	2002	30–39	f	Congo (DRC)	Humanitarian	Bachelor
Gesang	2000	30–39	m	Indonesia	Student	≥Masters
Golara	2010	30–39	f	Iran	Skilled permanent, secondary	Bachelor
Goran	1997	10–29	m	Yugoslavia[6]	Humanitarian	Bachelor
Goudarz	2010	30–39	m	Iran	Skilled permanent	Bachelor
Homa	2006	20–29	f	Iran	Skilled permanent, secondary	Bachelor
Iman	2006	20–29	m	Iran	Skilled permanent	Bachelor
Isabella	2001	40–49	f	Sudan	Humanitarian	≤Primary
Ishetu	2003	20–29	f	Congo (DRC)	Humanitarian	≤Primary
Jaime	1976	10–19	m	Chile	Humanitarian	Year 12
Jamileh	2007	20–29	f	Iran	Skilled permanent, secondary	Bachelor
Jane	2002	20–29	f	Sudan	Humanitarian	≤Primary
Jessie	1996	30–39	f	Taiwan	Student	≥Masters

Pseudonym[1]	Arrival Year	Arrival Age	Gender[2]	Country of Origin	Entry Visa[3]	Highest Level of Education[4]
Julie	2008	50–59	f	Singapore	Skilled permanent, secondary	Year 12
Julio	1986	10–19	m	Chile	Humanitarian	Year 12
June	2006	10–19	f	Sierra Leone	Humanitarian	≤Primary
Jutta	1970	20–29	f	Austria	Humanitarian	Year 10
Kambiz	2006	30–39	m	Iran	Skilled permanent	Bachelor
Katja	1989	40–49	f	Poland	Skilled temporary, secondary	Bachelor
Kevin	2008	20–29	m	Philippines	Skilled temporary	Bachelor
Kimia	2006	30–39	f	Iran	Skilled permanent, secondary	Bachelor
Kumiko	2008	30–39	f	Japan	Family reunion	Bachelor
Ladan	2008	30–39	f	Iran	Humanitarian	Bachelor
Laura	1995	20–29	f	Italy	Student	≥Masters
Lena	2008	40–49	f	Russia	Family reunion	Bachelor
Lewis	2005	20–29	m	Liberia	Humanitarian	Year 12
Lohrasb	2013	50–59	m	Iran	Humanitarian	Bachelor
Lou	1996	20–29	m	China	Student	≥Masters
Lucy	2001	20–29	f	Sierra Leone	Humanitarian	Year 12
Majid	2010	30–39	m	Iran	Skilled permanent	Bachelor
Majok	2001	30–39	m	Sudan	Humanitarian	Bachelor
Mamuna	2004	50–59	f	Sierra Leone	Humanitarian	≤Primary
Maria	2008	30–39	f	Brazil	Skilled permanent, secondary	Bachelor
Marina	2006	10–19	f	Sudan	Humanitarian	Year 10
Mark	2006	50–59	m	Sudan	Humanitarian	≥Masters
Marlene	2001	20–29	f	Germany	Skilled temporary	≥Masters
Mercy	2003	40–49	f	Sudan	Humanitarian	≤Primary
Michiko	2006	30–39	f	Japan	Working holiday	Bachelor
Milena	1994	10–19	f	Czech Republic	Working holiday	Bachelor
Mina	2010	30–39	f	Iran	Skilled permanent, secondary	Year 12
Mustapha	2007	20–19	m	Sudan	Humanitarian	Year 12
Nahid	2010	30–39	f	Iran	Skilled permanent	Bachelor
Nicolas	1989	40–49	m	Poland	Skilled temporary	Bachelor
Nina	2002	20–19	f	Sierra Leone	Humanitarian	Year 12
Obi	2003	30–39	m	Ethiopia	Humanitarian	Bachelor

Pseudonym[1]	Arrival Year	Arrival Age	Gender[2]	Country of Origin	Entry Visa[3]	Highest Level of Education[4]
Oldouz	2011	30–39	f	Iran	Humanitarian	Bachelor
Osman	1999	30–39	m	Ethiopia	Humanitarian	Bachelor
Parvin	2008	20–29	f	Iran	Skilled permanent	Bachelor
Paulina	2008	30–39	f	Philippines	Skilled temporary, secondary	Year 10
Paulo	1993	20–29	m	Portugal	Working holiday	≥Masters
Peter	2007	30–39	m	Sudan	Humanitarian	≤Primary
Philip	2006	30–39	m	Sudan	Humanitarian	≤Primary
Pia	1997	20–29	f	Italy	Working holiday	≥Masters
Qasem	2012	30–39	m	Iran	Skilled permanent	≥Masters
Qazal	2012	30–39	f	Iran	Skilled permanent, secondary	Bachelor
Ramin	2012	30–39	m	Iran	Skilled permanent, secondary	≥Masters
Ricardo	2006	40–49	m	Philippines	Skilled temporary	Year 10
Rita	2009	30–39	f	Philippines	Skilled temporary	Bachelor
Roberto	2007	30–39	m	Philippines	Skilled temporary	Bachelor
Rosa	2008	30–39	f	Philippines	Skilled temporary, secondary	Year 10
Rouya	2010	30–39	f	Iran	Skilled permanent	≥Masters
Roxana	2008	40–49	f	Iran	Skilled permanent, secondary	Bachelor
Ruth	2006	30–39	f	Liberia	Humanitarian	Year 12
Sally	2002	30–39	f	Zimbabwe	Family reunion	Bachelor
Saman	2009	30–39	m	Iran	Skilled permanent	≥Masters
Samuel	2006	40–49	m	Congo (DRC)	Humanitarian	Bachelor
Sarah	2006	20–29	f	Sudan	Humanitarian	≤Primary
Serena	2006	20–29	f	Sudan	Humanitarian	Year 12
Shirley	2003	30–39	f	Sudan	Humanitarian	Year 12
Sofia	1987	10–19	f	Colombia	Humanitarian	≥Masters
Soraya	2009	20–29	f	Iran	Skilled permanent, secondary	Bachelor
Suda	1999	20–29	f	Thailand	Student	≥Masters
Sylvia	2005	30–39	f	Sudan	Humanitarian	Year 10
Tania	1991	20–29	f	Spain	Working holiday	Bachelor
Thomas	2008	20–29	m	Burundi	Humanitarian	Year 12
Timothy	2006	20–29	m	Sudan	Humanitarian	≤Primary

Pseudonym[1]	Arrival Year	Arrival Age	Gender[2]	Country of Origin	Entry Visa[3]	Highest Level of Education[4]
Tina	2008	20–29	f	China	Skilled permanent, secondary	≥Masters
Torre	2006	30–39	m	Philippines	Skilled temporary	Year 10
Trinh	1991	10–19	f	Vietnam	Humanitarian	Bachelor
Venus	2004	30–39	f	Liberia	Humanitarian	Year 12
Verena	1993	30–39	f	Austria	Working holiday	≥Masters
Veronica	2007	20–29	f	Zimbabwe	Family reunion	Bachelor
Vesna	2008	50–59	f	Bulgaria	Family reunion	Bachelor
Vida	2006	40–49	f	Sudan	Humanitarian	Year 12
Violet	2005	40–49	f	Sudan	Humanitarian	≤Primary
Wang	2001	20–29	m	China	Student	≥Masters
Yumiko	1983	10–19	f	Japan	Student	≥Masters

List of Abbreviations

ALP	Australian Labor Party
AMEP	Adult Migrant English Program
AMEP RC	Adult Migrant English Program Research Center
AMES	Adult Multicultural Education Services
AMIEU	Australasian Meat Industry Employees Union
ARC	Australian Research Council
CALD	Culturally and Linguistically Diverse
CSWE	Certificates in Spoken and Written English
DAAD	German Academic Exchange Service
DOCS	Department of Community Services
DP	Displaced Person
ELICOS	English Language Intensive Courses for Overseas Students
ESL	English as a Second Language
ESOL	English for Speakers of Other Languages
IELTS	International English Language Testing System
Immigration Department	The Australian Immigration Department has changed its name several times over our research period. It was known as Department of Immigration and Multicultural Affairs (1996–2001), Department of Immigration and Multicultural and Indigenous Affairs (2001–2006), Department of Immigration and Multicultural Affairs (2006-2007), Department of Immigration and Citizenship (2007–2013), Department of Immigration and Border Protection (2013–2017), and Department of Home Affairs (since 2017) (Mence, Gangell, & Tebb, 2015). We refer to it as "Immigration Department" throughout.
KMT	Kuomintang
LOTE	Language Other Than English
MBD	Master of Business Development
MP	Member of Parliament
NESB	Non-English-Speaking Background
NSW	New South Wales
OECD	Organisation for Economic Co-operation and Development
OQU	Overseas Qualifications Unit
PRC	People's Republic of China
SA	South Australia
SBS	Special Broadcasting Service

SICLE	Sydney Institute for Community Languages Education
STEM	Science, Technology, Engineering, and Mathematics
TAFE	Technical and Further Education
TESOL	Teaching English to Speakers of Other Languages
TOEFL	Test of English as a Foreign Language
UAE	United Arab Emirates
UNHCR	United Nations High Commissioner for Refugees
USD	United States Dollar
WA	Western Australia

1

"Swimming Poor in a Raging River"

Doing Things with Words in a New Language

Adult Language Learning in Real Life

Yumiko had to drink orange juice for the first few months of her new life in Australia. Not because she wanted to, but because her attempts to order apple juice repeatedly drew a blank. When she first arrived on the Gold Coast from Japan in her late teens, she pronounced "apple" with a heavy Japanese accent that sounded a bit like "apuru." No one ever seemed to understand her, although Yumiko did not utter the word randomly but in the context of a food order in a restaurant, café, or take-away with limited choices, and followed by the word "juice." Years later, Yumiko recalled some of the responses she received. There was the waitress who shouted "WHAT?" back at her; there was the sales assistant who responded "Whaddayawan?" at rapid-fire speed; and there was more than one server who simply ignored her. This is how Yumiko discovered that "the only thing I could order was orange juice. But you know, I was sick and tired of having orange juice. I tried a few different types of juice, but they didn't understand me."

Yumiko's experience encapsulates the double challenge of adult language learning in real life. For adults, language learning is inextricably linked to having to do things with the new language. These may be banal things like ordering apple juice, but they may also be high-stakes things like finding a job, renting a house, or seeking healthcare. Furthermore, these things usually must be done in the presence of others who are confident users of the language. These fluent speakers may be uncooperative waitstaff, competitors for a job, gatekeepers for rental accommodation, or busy healthcare providers.

The responses Yumiko received neither allowed her to achieve her goal nor did they help her improve her pronunciation. Instead, she lost confidence, as she had literally been rendered incompetent, both as a speaker of English and as a customer ordering a drink. In most circumstances, the ability to order a drink is an unremarkable and mundane adult competence. Besides language learners, the only people who cannot accomplish it are those too poor to afford the desired drink. There is indeed a similarity between the experience of poverty and living one's life through a new language, as the 2009 Nobel Laureate for Literature, Herta Müller, explains when she compares the new language of the adult migrant

Life in a New Language. Ingrid Piller, Donna Butorac, Emily Farrell, Loy Lising, Shiva Motaghi-Tabari, and Vera Williams Tetteh, Oxford University Press. © Oxford University Press 2024. DOI: 10.1093/oso/9780190084288.003.0001

to pocket money: "As soon as I discovered an item I wanted, I realized my pocket money would not be enough to pay for it. What I wanted to say also needed to be paid for—in words. Many of those words I did not know, and those that I knew didn't occur to me in time."[1]

If you have never needed to achieve real-life goals in a language learned later in life, you probably imagine adult language learning to be a bit like child language learning. Child language learning seems easy, and you cannot even remember how you learned your first language. "It just happened naturally," you may think. In fact, child language learning is difficult, too, but it happens in a social world almost exclusively geared toward learning. Children's linguistic proficiency is perfectly synchronized with their social development. Newborns, for example, are taught to distinguish between sounds by people singing endless nursery rhymes to them. Their utterances, no matter how incomprehensible, are greeted with enthusiasm ("She just said, 'Daddy'!" in response to some babbling). Toddlers are simultaneously inducted into the world around them and the words we use to describe that world by pointing out the most mundane objects to them in great detail ("Look, a car! A red car. A big red car."). Preschoolers learn how to use language to manipulate the world through endless hours of play. In some cultures, caregivers simplify their speech to adapt to the level of the child; in others, children are allowed to observe and listen until they can hold their own in conversation.[2] But everywhere, child language learning is an incidental benefit of doing all the things that are part of a normal childhood, which is generally lacking in substantial responsibilities beyond learning.

Whether child or adult, for the language learner, each interlocutor becomes a language teacher. Adults interacting with children are generally supportive. Imagine a caregiver's reaction to a small child mispronouncing "apple." A conversation such as this one might unfold:

CHILD: Appou juice.
CAREGIVER: Would you like some juice, honey? What kind of juice would you like? Orange juice?
CHILD: Appou.
CAREGIVER: Uh, apple juice. You'd like some apple juice? Yummy apple juice.
CHILD: Appoul juice.
CAREGIVER: Apple juice. Here you go, here's your apple juice.
CHILD: Appal juice.
CAREGIVER: That's right, apple juice.
CHILD: Apple juice. Apple juice. Apple juice.

This conversation may be idealized, but key features will be recognizable to any parent. First, the caregiver helps the child achieve their goal (getting a drink) by cooperatively guessing the child's intent from context clues. Second, the caregiver supports the child's language development by patiently and repeatedly modeling the correct pronunciation of "apple." Third, the child gets numerous opportunities to practice, and their pronunciation increasingly approximates the target. Finally, the child repeats the newly learned pronunciation in a drill pattern that is usually perceived as cute. In countless similar examples throughout childhood, language learning and doing things with words happen in sync.

By contrast, the interlocutors of adult language learners are generally much less willing to help, as Yumiko discovered. They may become impatient, aggressive, or lose interest. It is certainly rare for them to model pronunciation slowly and repeatedly. Often, the learner gets neither what they want nor an opportunity to practice their new language. In short, adult language learning is much more difficult than child language learning because learning language and using language to do things no longer align after childhood; often they even conflict.

The language-learning experiences of migrants are different not only from those of children, but also from those of classroom language learners. Language learning in the classroom is structured to systematically progress through different linguistic skills; it is scaffolded to the level of the learner, and interactions are role-play. Language learning in the real world is the opposite. There is no structured curriculum, and the learner is challenged to speak and listen, to attend to sounds, words, grammar, textual features, and discourse conventions all at once, while sometimes also struggling with unfamiliar content. There is no scaffolded progression, and what is required of the learner at any one time may veer wildly in relation to their current level of ability. And there is definitely no role-play: every interaction is "real," and something more than teacher feedback or a grade are at stake. Sometimes, the stakes in real-life language learning may be relatively low, like having to drink orange juice instead of the desired apple juice, but they may also be extremely high, like not being attended to by emergency services.[3]

The difference between language learning in the classroom and language learning in real life can be compared to swimming in a pool versus swimming in a raging river, as Goudarz, one of our research participants, suggested. Goudarz is an engineer from Iran who migrated to Australia in his mid-30s. Looking back at his English-language learning in Tehran, through attending classes and by engaging in self-study, he described his pre-migration English language learning as "*swimming in the calm waters of a pool*." His move to Australia turned the pool into "*a raging river that does not follow a rulebook*." From an academic subject, English changed to the medium through which Goudarz—like all migrants—must live his life. This book is intended to illuminate how migrant language learners keep their head above water, a challenge that remains poorly understood, as a fictional migrant in the short story "Learning English" muses: "I think it is hard for a non-migrant to understand just how difficult it is to learn a new language while adapting to life in a new country."[4]

Migrant Speakers in Australia

Our account of life in a new language builds on ethnographic research with non-English-speaking background (NESB) migrants to Australia over a period of almost 20 years between 2000 and 2020.[5] Across the various research projects undergirding this book, we have met hundreds of people from a wide variety of linguistic backgrounds—some only for a short conversation, some as regular members of our social circles, and most as participants in research interviews and as members of institutions where we conducted fieldwork. For this book, we selected 130 core participants to inform our exploration. They are a diverse group of people—83 women and 47 men—who arrived in Australia between 1970 and 2013, with the youngest aged in their early teens on arrival and the oldest in their late 50s. They come from 34 different countries on all continents. The diversity of our core participants is reflective of Australia's highly diverse migrant intake. In 2021, 30% of the Australian population were born overseas, and an additional 20% had at least one parent born overseas. They come from all countries on earth, and 49 origin countries have sizable resident groups of at least 25,000 members in Australia.[6]

Australia's diversity is a result of the fact that immigration is central to Australian nation-building and "all non-Indigenous people are migrants and diasporic."[7] Immigrants and their descendants today make up over 96% of Australia's rapidly growing population.[8] Since the beginning of colonization in 1788, the Australian population has increased about 100-fold to close to 26 million in 2021.[9] This population explosion has been achieved through a carefully managed immigration program. Already at the time of the first countrywide census in 1891, 32% of the Australian population were born overseas. After a decline in the first half of the 20th century, their numbers have been rising rapidly again since the 1950s. During our research period from 2000 to 2020, migration added a total of 3.9 million people to the Australian population, which amounts to an average annual net intake of 200,000 people.[10]

Immigration to Australia began from 1788 onward as a British penal colony. The 19th century saw the arrival of convicts, military men, traders, laborers, free settlers, and adventurers. Voluntary migrants of the time came almost exclusively from the British Isles, but forced migrants were more diverse. Convicts, who were often transported for poverty-related crimes, came from all parts of the British Isles and included a substantial proportion of Irish Catholics. Additionally, there were Black convicts and other groups of involuntary or semi-voluntary migrants, including South Asian indentured laborers, enslaved people from the Pacific, Japanese prostitutes, and Chinese gold diggers. Upon Federation in 1901, one of the first laws passed by the young nation was the Immigration Restriction Act, also known as the "White Australia Policy." The Act was designed to curtail immigration from origin countries other than Britain. Over the following years, as the numbers of migrants fell, the history of the diversity of the pre-federation colonies was whitewashed.[11]

By the mid-20th century, Australia had established itself as a White English-speaking nation, but immigration from the British Isles alone was no longer enough to sustain the desired population growth. Therefore, Australia offered migration assistance to large numbers of continental Europeans who had been displaced and impoverished by World War II.[12] Migration assistance included not only subsidized travel, work placements, and transitional accommodation, but also English-language training. English-language classes were offered on migrant ships en route to Australia, and Australia was the first country in the world to develop a national language-teaching scheme for new arrivals, the Adult Migrant English Program (AMEP), founded in 1947.[13] The expectation that these new arrivals would assimilate into the Anglo mainstream was clear, and learning English and transitioning to using English was considered part of assimilation.

From the 1970s onward, admission was further widened, and significant numbers of people displaced by the Vietnam War and the Lebanese Civil War arrived. Around the same time, preferential admission by origin was entirely abandoned. Migration selection was replaced with a human capital approach, where prospective migrants receive points based on their skills and qualifications in relation to the needs of the Australian labor market. Economic immigration schemes have considerably expanded, as Australia competes for global talent to address labor shortages and to manage an aging population.[14]

Today's migration system is managed in three streams. While the details have varied over the years, these relate to the economy, the family, and to Australia's international humanitarian commitments.[15] The first, and by far the largest, stream comprises economic visas, both temporary and permanent,[16] issued to people for the human or financial capital they are expected to contribute to the Australian economy. The second stream is made up of family reunion visas, which constructs migrants not as economic assets but as spouses, children, or parents of Australian residents. While the number of economic migrants has increased steeply since the 1990s, the number of family reunion visas issued has steadily fallen. Admission in this stream has also become more costly and tends to involve longer wait times. The smallest visa stream allows Australia to fulfill its international humanitarian obligations by admitting refugees in resettlement programs under the auspices of the United Nations High Commissioner for Refugees (UNHCR). Overall, economic visa schemes now vastly outnumber family reunion and humanitarian admissions.[17]

In sum, from 1788 onward, the Australian continent was turned into a gigantic migrant destination to the extent that today more than 96% of the population are immigrants and their descendants.[18] The makeup of this population has been carefully engineered. Until the mid-20th century, immigration was largely restricted to migrants from the British Isles, securing the establishment of Australia as a White and English-speaking nation. During this period, English became a marker of Australian identity. Origin restrictions were progressively lifted to initially admit continental Europeans in large numbers and then were entirely abandoned so that today's migrant intake is highly diversified.

English as a Migrant Language

The eminent historian of Australia's migration program James Jupp explains that "[o]nce race had been abandoned as an official distinguishing factor, language became a central concern for policy makers."[19] In the process, the English language was transformed. In addition to serving as a means of communication and an identity marker, English also became a legal instrument of migration management and a form of human capital. All these different facets of English play out in language learning and use. Although the overwhelming majority of Australian residents are migrants or their descendants, as we showed in the previous section, not everyone is considered a migrant. The term "migrant" is, by and large, reserved for those who are not of British descent. Australia continues to have a privileged relationship with the United Kingdom. Even in the 21st century, the British monarch is the Australian head of state, and deep social, political, economic, and cultural ties between the two countries, their institutions, and people persist. The number of Australian residents who identify their ancestry as "English" (33%) still exceeds those who claim "Australian" (30%) in the most recent census of 2021. These two top ancestries are followed by Irish (10%), Scottish (9%), and Chinese (6%).[20]

Migration from the British Isles has been obscured in the act of taking possession of the continent.[21] As a result, the migrant status of people from the British Isles and their descendants remains hidden. The same is true of the English language. Referring to English as a "migrant language" sounds strange, as the term is commonly only applied to non-Indigenous languages other than English (LOTEs). This means that speaking English mediates migrant belonging. For new migrants, English therefore becomes much more than a means of communication. It is also a marker of their belonging that promises to erase their migrant status.[22]

Beyond its role as a national identity marker, the transformation of Australia's migration system from origin-based to economic-based has constructed two additional roles for English that new migrants need to navigate. English in Australia is also a legal instrument of migration management and a form of human capital. We now discuss each of these roles of English in turn.

English as a Legal Instrument of Migration Management

Since colonization in 1788, migration policy has served to engineer English as the dominant language. This was initially achieved by large population transfers from the British Isles and, later, when NESB migrants began to be admitted in significant numbers, by explicit and implicit policies of linguistic assimilation that have ensured that each new migrant group transitions to English by the second or third generation.[23]

When it became necessary to diversify countries of origin beyond the British Isles to ensure continued population growth, a tension arose between migrants as welcome additions to multicultural Australia and migrants as threats to national security.[24] Language has become a key means to managing this tension. Australia prides itself on being one of the most successful multicultural countries in the world. Governments on national, state, and local levels, on both sides of politics, regularly celebrate multicultural Australia, and this celebration is extended into a variety of public discourses, ranging from school lessons to multicultural festivals. In this narrative, migrants are smoothly and easily integrated into an Australian society that is welcoming, diverse, and egalitarian. Moreover, welcoming migrants is constructed as beneficial to all, as diversity is seen to foster innovation in a harmonious mingling of different people and their cuisines, cultures, and customs.

This bright vision of migration coexists with a more troubling one in which Australia is under threat from migrants. This discourse has deep roots, too. As we explained above, the 1901 Immigration Restriction Act was motivated by the perceived Asian threat to this British outpost in the Pacific.[25] Although this abated somewhat in the second half of the 20th century, events in 2001 breathed new life into the "migrants as threat" discourse internationally. In addition to the securitization of migration following the 9/11 terrorist attacks in the United States, a local Australian event, the "Children Overboard Affair," further contributed to the politicization of a specific form of migration, namely asylum seeking.[26] In the aftermath, asylum seeking in Australia came to be seen predominantly through the lens of national security. Both major political parties have sought to win elections by brandishing their credentials on their "tough" stance on illegal immigration. While economic immigration has soared, the much smaller number of asylum seekers arriving by boat have been subjected to mandatory detention. As a rule, they have also been barred from ever achieving permanent residency.[27]

In the 21st century, then, Australia has paradoxically run one of the world's largest and most generous legal migration programs for skilled and business entrants, side by side with one of the world's harshest exclusion schemes of asylum seekers. Simultaneously, English-language proficiency, as measured through language testing, has come to be seen as a sensible way to distinguish between "good" and "bad" migrants. The use of language testing as a legal instrument to determine eligibility for admission to Australia goes back to the Immigration Restriction Act of 1901. When the Act was considered by the parliament of the young nation, Britain expressed concern that overtly racist legislation with "color" as an admission criterion might offend citizens of the British Empire in India and elsewhere, as well as citizens of some of its allies, such as Japan. To cover the racist intent of the legislation, an English-language test for would-be immigrants was proposed. However, it was quickly dismissed when parliamentarians realized that the English language could be learned:

> The education test proposed will not shut out the Japanese if they desire to come to Australia. It will not shut out the Indian "toff" who becomes a human parasite preying upon the people of the country. It will not shut out the intellectual Afghan. We have more to fear from the educated colored people than from the ignorant colored people, because the latter will not attempt to mingle or associate with the white race.[28]

Eventually, the linguistic fig leaf that was adopted to cover racist legislation was a dictation test in any European language (changed to any language at all in 1905). This way, any undesirable person could be refused admission by making them take a dictation test in a language it had been determined in advance that they did not know. The most famous exclusion based on the dictation test is probably that of the Jewish German-Czech communist Egon Erwin Kisch. Although he was fleeing Nazi persecution in 1934, the decision not to admit him was made based on anticipated "subversive activities" while he was still en route to Australia. When Kisch jumped ship in Sydney to physically enter the country, he was denied legal status on the grounds that this accomplished multilingual—Kisch wrote in Czech, German, French, Spanish, and English—had failed a language test in Scottish Gaelic. Despite challenging the ruling in court, he was ultimately forced to leave Australia and return to Europe.[29]

Adult language learning in Australia today continues to be affected by the Act's construction of language proficiency as a proxy for race and a pseudo-objective criterion for admissibility. The requirement to pass a language test was resurrected in 2007 with the introduction of a formal citizenship test. Since then, permanent residents who wish to become citizens need to undertake a computerized multiple-choice test about Australian institutions, customs, history, and values. Although not an explicit language test, the test, which can only be taken in English, in fact requires relatively high levels of English-language proficiency.[30]

The 2007 Australian Citizenship Act constituted a major milestone, turning English-language proficiency into a legal instrument of migrant sorting. This milestone had followed years of public debate about the English-language proficiency of new arrivals, but it did not end it. The claim that an increasing number of new migrants did not speak English and refused to learn it has been a matter of considerable public debate in the 21st century. After one flare-up of the debate in 2017–2018, the Australian parliament legislated, ultimately unsuccessfully, for the introduction of a formal English-language proficiency test as a citizenship requirement. The proposed level of performance on that language test was the same as the level required for university admission.[31]

These ongoing debates about supposed low levels of English-language proficiency among some migrant groups—including not only asylum seekers, but also international students, humanitarian entrants, and Muslim women—have established a solid link between English and national security.[32] These debates have firmly placed migrants' English-language proficiency in the court of public opinion. There, the supposedly large numbers of migrants with "poor English" are seen not only as a threat to national security, but also as a liability for the Australian economy.

English as Human Capital

To understand how English has come to function as an economic asset—and, conversely, its absence as a liability—we need to return to economic migration. As we explained above, since the 1990s, most migrants to Australia have arrived under a skilled or business visa. These economic visa schemes construct migrants not as (prospective) citizens in the Australian nation, but as bundles of human and financial resources that constitute assets for the Australian economy. The recasting of migrants as the purveyors of capital, both human and financial, has gone hand in hand with a proliferation of temporary visa schemes which may no longer have clear and relatively short pathways to citizenship, or even permanent residency, as used to be the case in the past.[33]

Most economic visa categories are based on a points system. Applicants are selected based on the points they score for education, professional qualifications, sponsorship by an Australian employer, age, and/or willingness to settle in regional Australia. Additionally, points may be awarded for a high level of

English-language proficiency. This means that English literally becomes an asset for prospective migrants. It also means that English-language learning has been frontloaded into the pre-migration period. Pre-migration screening for English-language proficiency has shifted the cost of English-language learning from the host society onto the individual migrant. In Australia, this has been a monumental shift. As explained above, Australia has long incentivized immigrants and subsidized their passages and early settlement, including through free English-language training in the AMEP. This has changed in the past decades, and economic migrants are now specifically excluded from most forms of government assistance during the first few years after arrival in Australia, a fact that caused hardship to many new migrants when they were not allowed to access federal disaster relief payments during the COVID-19 pandemic.[34]

By excluding new arrivals from settlement support in Australia, the cost of and responsibility for their migration, including their English-language learning, has been transferred from the receiving society to individual migrants and their sending societies. From these, Australia is creaming off individuals with high levels of human and financial capital by "selecting for success," or "picking winners."[35] In the process, migrants have been reconceptualized as bundles of skills and assets which they need to entrepreneurially manage to achieve their goals.[36] Within these bundles, knowing English is the trait of winners and, conversely, not knowing English is the sign of losers.

In the conceptualizations of English that we have discussed in this chapter—English as a marker of national identity, as a legal instrument to determine admissibility, and as a form of human capital—English-language proficiency is a binary where a clear line divides the acceptable English of immigrants from the British Isles from the unacceptable English of others, the legitimate English of those who pass a test from the illegitimate English of those who fail the test, and the valuable English of those with the right credentials from the worthless English of those without those credentials.

Language learning and use in real life, however, is not black and white. When it comes to doing things with words on a daily basis, the binaries discussed here are often relatively meaningless. Yet, the constant scrutiny of NESB residents' English that these relentless debates about migration and language invite adds a heavy burden to the dual task of language learning and doing things with words. It is like placing additional weights on the swimmers in the raging river.

The Lived Experience of Life in a New Language

It is the aim of this book to illuminate the lived experience of life in a new language. As such it is not primarily about language, but about how language intersects with what it means to be a citizen, a worker, or a parent. Migration is transformative, and adults must re-establish their identities in a new neighborhood, a new workplace, a new friendship group. For NESB migrants, available social positions are circumscribed by a language that may not roll off their tongue easily and that always signals difference.

The lived experience of life in a new language is highly diverse. Country of origin, level of education, occupation, visa stream, and prior level of English-language proficiency are just some of the factors behind the diversity of experiences that we have already alluded to in this introductory chapter. There are many more. And diversity stems not only from the range of new arrivals themselves, but also from the variety of their interlocutors and the ever-changing diversity of the contexts in which their interactions take place.

To capture the diversity of the lived experience of life in a new language, we have chosen an ethnographic research method. That means that we spent time with our research participants and acted as participant observers in their lives. The institutions where we conducted fieldwork fall broadly into three groups: adult education centers, community language schools, and workplaces. Additionally, we conducted audio-recorded interviews and conversations, both with individuals and groups, in informal contexts such as coffee shops, quiet corners in their or our workplaces, and participants' homes. We also collected emails, journal entries, and photos of relevant artifacts, and we filled many notebooks with fieldnotes. Reusing data from six distinct research projects conducted over a period of 20 years and pooling our data offer a unique opportunity to explore the lived experience of migrant language learning and settlement across an exceptionally large ethnographic dataset.

Our observations and interviews did not follow one single observational grid or interview guide because they were part of different research projects with different focusses. All datasets do include accounts of language-learning experiences, migration trajectories, and observations or accounts of intercultural interactions. Beyond this common core, data relate to education, employment, parenting, gender performance, discrimination, citizenship, and sense of belonging. Sometimes, emphasis on a specific topic came from the researcher. Shiva's data collection, for instance, focused on parenting experiences, and Donna's on gendered experiences of migration. Sometimes, the emphasis came from the participants. Finding employment, for instance, is a topic that was often brought up by participants without prompting from the researcher, as we discuss in Chapter 3.

Our data take the form of field notes, transcripts of audio recordings, journal entries, emails, and some other textual artifacts. They constitute an extensive corpus of observations, reflections, and stories about migrant language learning in Australia in the first two decades of the 21st century. We analyzed these data by first determining the key areas where language learning and settlement intersect: education, employment, workplace interactions, parenting, experiences of discrimination, and sense of belonging.[37] We then coded our data for key patterns within each of these topics. Coding was undertaken both individually and as a team, with each author taking the lead in producing a draft analysis of one of the main chapters. Overall, our aim was to produce a rich, holistic, and credible account of the lived experience of life in a new language.[38]

For us, life in a new language is not only an academic research topic.[39] Beyond our academic expertise, we share with our participants the experience of being migrant speakers. Like our participants, our group of authors reflects the diversity of 21st-century Australia. All of us are settlers on Indigenous land. We or our ancestors have come to Australia from Germany, Ghana, Iran, Ireland, the Philippines, and Yugoslavia. Those four of us who came to Australia as adults share with our participants the experience of settling in a new country through the medium of a new language. Our experience as English-language teachers and teacher trainers also informs our account. We hope that the way we have pooled our lived experiences in a unique intercultural team to write this book will add richness and depth to our account.

We started this chapter with the metaphors of poverty and of swimming in a raging river to capture the experience of simultaneously learning and using a new language. Swimming in a raging river can be scary, exhausting, and overpowering. It can also be exhilarating when the learner takes some rapids in their stride, when the turbulences become fewer, and when language proficiency has improved to the point where swimming in the river begins to resemble swimming in the pool. It is the aim of this book to illuminate the experience of language learning in real life during the early years of migrants' settlement journeys. By making visible the struggles of adult language learning as they are inextricably enmeshed in going about the business of daily life, this book is also a plea to help smooth the turbulent waters so that new migrants do not sink or fall back right at the start. The stories in this book demonstrate that full and equitable social inclusion has a linguistic dimension, which requires institutional arrangements that accommodate to the diverse linguistic resources and needs of all its members, including new arrivals.

2
"English Opens All the Doors in the World"
Arriving in a New Language

Bringing English to Australia

When Franklin was a primary school child in South Sudan in the 1970s, an opportunity came up for a place in the British school in Juba. At that time, he knew only two words of English, "yes" and "no." His first language was Bari and the first few years of his schooling had been through the medium of Arabic.[1] Even so, his father decided that he must change schools—and languages. He did not like the idea and tried to reason with his father. Looking back, as an adult in Australia, Franklin recounted his boyhood arguments. He had not wanted to change to an English-medium school because he did not even know how to write his name in English, because starting a new school with a different language of instruction would place such a heavy burden on him, and because, after all, English was the language of White people. None of this cut any ice with Franklin's father. English, his father advised him, "is the one ruling the world now," and English "opens all the doors in the world."

Thanks to his father's insistence on an English-medium education for his son all those years back, Franklin arrived in Australia as a fluent speaker of English. However, as he was to discover almost immediately, the English he brought was quite different from the English he encountered. Franklin described the English he brought as "pure English" and the English he encountered as "Australian slang." It was not only the form of English that changed, but also its value. Franklin's English had indeed opened doors for him back home and on his long flight from South Sudan via Egypt to Australia. But as soon as he landed in Australia, the key stopped working.[2]

There are two elements of Franklin's experience that he shares with virtually all our participants. First, his English-language learning journey started long before his arrival in Australia. Some of our participants had been educated through the medium of English, like Franklin. Others had studied English as a school subject, often over many years. Even those who had not had much opportunity to learn English were, like Franklin's father, keenly aware of its status and

Life in a New Language. Ingrid Piller, Donna Butorac, Emily Farrell, Loy Lising, Shiva Motaghi-Tabari, and Vera Williams Tetteh, Oxford University Press. © Oxford University Press 2024. DOI: 10.1093/oso/9780190084288.003.0002

power. Second, all participants experienced a mismatch between the English they brought and the English they encountered. For most, this came as a shock, as it did for Franklin, because their English had worked for them in their previous contexts. For others, the mismatch was unsurprising because they saw themselves as beginners. At one level, these mismatches related to the form of English—differences in pronunciation, words, or expressions. At another, more deeply felt level, the mismatches were in practice and value. In their previous lives, English worked in a multilingual context because they needed English to pass exams or to communicate in a multilingual marketplace. They had other languages for other things. In Australia, English became all-encompassing. Furthermore, in many of our participants' origin countries, even a little knowledge of English may be a marker of relatively high levels of education and social status. In Australia, that association between English and a good education was broken, and the participants' English ended up at the bottom of the linguistic hierarchy.

This chapter explores the transition from pre-migration English to post-migration English. While the deceptively simple label of "English" suggests some bounded object that the learner must acquire, this is not how participants experienced it. What they experienced were connections and disjoints on a language-learning journey, with arrival in Australia standing out as a major disruption.

Arrival Shocks

Lou spent his first night in Australia sleeping rough on the streets of Darwin. Years later, he was still livid about the pain, anger, and frustration he had felt as he struggled with exhaustion from the 20-hour flight from Shanghai via Singapore, the chill of a night in the dry season, hunger, and his heavy luggage. For the pampered only son of a well-to-do Chinese family, the experience came as a rude shock. After all, his family had invested heavily into bringing him to Australia for his postgraduate education. This was not supposed to happen. Lou and his six group mates were under the assumption that airport pick-up, transfer, and accommodation had been pre-arranged as part of the study package they had paid for. What grated on him most was that he could not assert his rights:

> Such a nightmare! None of the seven people could even go in and ask the receptionist, "Why the hell?" You know, we have to sleep on the street and none, NONE of us would even call the university to complain. None of us would do this. None of us could speak a single English word. Really pissed me off. (Lou)

The statement "none of us could speak a single English word" is not literally true. In fact, Lou had studied English as a school subject in Shanghai throughout his secondary education. In addition, he had taken private English-language lessons to prepare for the Test of English as a Foreign Language (TOEFL). The TOEFL score he achieved prior to arrival—and which was required for university admission—was in the "high-intermediate" range. This means that he had demonstrated that he could "understand the main ideas and important details of academic passages in English at the introductory university level [and] of conversations and lectures that take place in academic settings." He had also demonstrated his ability "to write in English well on general or familiar topics." The version of TOEFL that was in use in the 1990s, when Lou took it, was focused on listening, reading, writing, and grammar skills, but did not include a speaking component.[3]

The English that Lou arrived with was focused on written rather than spoken English. "My writing was good, and my reading was good," he told us. "But no speak English." His initial voicelessness manifested as physical exhaustion. He reported sleeping long hours during his first few months in Australia. He had trouble staying awake, even during the day. His university courses literally put him to sleep: "The teacher just basically entertained himself and was talking around. I didn't know where he was going. I didn't care. I just slept."

Such accounts of physical reactions to the new language are not uncommon. Azim's reaction was one of the most extreme and constituted a serious health crisis. Unlike Lou, Azim came to Australia with strong speaking skills in English. The talented son of an upper-middle-class family in Pakistan, Azim had attended an English-medium high school in Islamabad. Students in the school were forbidden to speak the national language, a fact Azim appreciated because it created ample English-language practice opportunities. Azim also served as school captain for 3 years, which offered further practice opportunities: "So I had to speak English all the time. I had to face teachers and I had to face students and make speeches. You know that kind of stuff, in English, all the time. I had to be a role model for students."

When Azim came to Australia as an 18-year-old to pursue a physics degree at one of Australia's leading universities, he went from being a model English speaker to finding himself a complete novice in the language: "The first day I didn't understand anything! [. . .] I was like so much homesick and shocked, and I couldn't talk for the first couple of weeks." The condition Azim describes is akin to selective mutism, a developmental disorder where children fail to speak in contexts that cause them severe anxiety, most often school settings.[4] Azim's mutism was accompanied by sudden uncontrollable crying fits and an inability to eat. Over a period of a few months, he lost 17 kilos (about 37 pounds) in weight. His situation became so bad that his host family was close to sending him back home. They sought medical help for him, and his condition improved after receiving counseling for about half a year. The counselor visited him two or three times a week, and went for walks with him, and their conversations gradually restored his ability to communicate in English. Even so, he continued to find Australian English bewildering after almost 3 years in the country: "Australian accent is entirely different. [. . .] Even academics they sort of crumble a sentence. They speak a lot more slang in it. And, they say things which, erm, I would not understand."

An initial period of non-understanding was reported by most of our participants. In some cases, this was not surprising when someone arrived with minimal English, like Goran, a refugee from the Yugoslav wars. English had not been offered as a foreign language in Goran's high school in Bosnia, and he had studied German and Russian instead. In 1997, when he was 20 years old and he and his family were offered resettlement in Australia, he received eight predeparture English-language lessons of about 2 hours each over a period of 4 weeks. His first real-life opportunity to try out the little he had learned in those eight lessons came at the airport in Singapore en route to Australia. Wanting to know when his plane would land in Sydney, he approached the inquiry desk. As the interaction unfolded, he started to see himself through the eyes of the receptionist: "And she was looking at me and she was thinking, 'What a dumb person.'"

The feeling of being perceived as "dumb," "stupid," "an idiot," or "tedious" was not restricted to people like Goran, who objectively knew very little English on arrival. Oldouz, from Iran, who had studied English for many years prior to coming to Australia, used the metaphor of deafness and muteness to illustrate her arrival experience: "*When you come here, no matter how much you know, still you are like deaf and mute.*" The experience of Elizabeth from Ghana, a multilingual country where English is the official language,[5] was similar: "*I understood English in Ghana because they spoke it slowly but in New Zealand it was very fast. So, I was quiet. I didn't talk.*" Another example comes from Nahid, a software developer from Iran. Her high level of English-language proficiency was one of the reasons she received a skilled independent visa to Australia. Even so, on arrival, she felt the language she had studied was completely different from the one she encountered. Her confidence was shattered when, on her first day, she went to buy a mobile phone. "*The salesman explained a lot and I just kept looking at him. I truly couldn't understand what he was saying.*"

Accounts of an initial "language shock" come up again and again in our data. Rouya, also from Iran, reported that whenever she and her family left the house in the early days after their arrival, they would come back home "*depressed,*" wondering, "*What are they saying? What are we hearing? What is that language? What did we study?*" Like Rouya, many participants explicitly put their shock down to the mismatch between their pre-migration English and the English they encountered, such as Verena from Austria. Reflecting on "the English you learn at school or university," she concluded that, "you have to go out there and really experience it." Like others, her initial experience was "really like this shock" because "I couldn't understand hardly anything."

English as a Diverse Language

Benjamin from Sudan blamed his language problems on Australian English:

> It's very hard to understand. The accent is quite different. The Australians is speaking for me very fast, where I could not get that. And I say why, these people are just speaking too fast. Compare with the other people, English speaker. I give you example, because Sudan have been colonized with the British. British English a bit better. I understand them. Now here, Australians speak fast. [makes a clicking sound and claps his hands]. Finish! (Benjamin)

Benjamin's clicking sound and hand clap indicate that Australian English did not sound like a language to him, but just like so much noise. Regardless of where they came from, many participants shared Benjamin's view that Australian English was the problem. Nicolas from Poland, for example, was disappointed when he discovered that people in Australia did not speak "Oxford-type of English" but "Aussie with some other cultural backgrounds." Speaking "Aussie" was generally evaluated negatively by participants. Danica from Russia, for instance, described Australian English as "horrible." When asked to justify her assessment, she laughingly said, "because nobody speaks Oxford English. That's pretty disappointing." Venus from Sierra Leone was equally scathing: "I speak English, not Aussie," she said in a tone that was almost spitting out "Aussie." Suda from Thailand attributed her communication difficulties in Australia to the fact that she had learned "American English" and therefore could not understand the "Australian accent." Rita from the Philippines explained that "we are speaking American English" and jokingly claimed that Australians could not understand her because her English is "clear." Paulina, also from the Philippines, praised the English of one of her work supervisors because "*he really knows how to speak English that we can understand back home. It is like* American English, *not* British English."

Although participants pined for British English or American English instead of the incomprehensible Australian English, they did, of course, in actual fact, not speak British or American English themselves. However, they had been taught English with these two reference varieties as models, and, maybe more importantly, they had been taught that these two varieties constitute the best forms of English. To understand how they had come to lionize these two varieties of English, we need to briefly consider the role of English as a global language.

English today is the most widely learned and used language globally. English is the de jure official language of 54 countries, from Antigua to Zimbabwe. It is the de facto official language of another 21 countries, from Australia to the United Arab Emirates. In another 31 non-sovereign territories, from American Samoa to the Virgin Islands, English also enjoys official status.[6] Even in countries where English has few societal functions, it is widely studied. English is taught in compulsory and supplementary education, from preschool to university, in almost all countries on earth.[7] English is the target of about 80% of all language learning that goes on globally. The supplementary English-language teaching industry alone was estimated to be worth 44 billion USD in 2021.[8] Around a third of the world's population are estimated to be able to speak English with some fluency, and the number of those who have learned at least some English is much larger. As a result, multilingual users who learned English later in life as an additional language significantly outnumber monolingual native speakers, by some estimates by a factor of four to one.[9]

Although English is used so widely and by so many people, not all forms of English are created equal. American and British English sit on top of a linguistic hierarchy, with three distinct types of English underneath them. One way to understand these different varieties and to account for their relationships with each other is through a model with three concentric circles.[10] In this model, the English in the British settler colonies of Australia, Canada, Ireland, New Zealand, and South Africa sits below the norm-giving varieties of American and British English, but above other varieties of English. Below this so-called inner circle of Center English varieties sits an "outer circle" of countries that were at some point British or US extraction colonies. In these countries, English today enjoys official status, sometimes alongside one or more other languages. These are postcolonial societies where imageries of English are contested.[11] Some may continue to view English as the language of the colonizers, while others have adopted it as an Indigenous language with local characteristics. English is widely used as a medium of instruction; proficiency in English is therefore a marker of formal education. Often the numbers of English speakers in these societies are relatively low, particularly if access to schooling is severely disrupted due to war, civil unrest, or corruption.[12] Of our participants, 52 of 130 hailed from outer-circle countries, namely Ghana, Kenya, Liberia, Pakistan, Philippines, Sierra Leone, Singapore, Sudan,[13] and Zimbabwe. Beyond the outer circle lies the "expanding circle" where English is learned as a foreign language. As in outer circle contexts, English in expanding circle contexts is tied to formal education but it is not usually the medium of instruction, and learners do not have much opportunity to practice English outside of their language lessons. Of our participants, 78 of 130 came from expanding-circle countries in Africa (Burundi,[14] Congo, Ethiopia), Asia (China, Indonesia, Iran, Japan, Taiwan, Thailand, Vietnam), Europe (Austria, Bulgaria, Czech Republic, Georgia, Germany, Italy, Poland, Portugal, Russia, Spain, Yugoslavia), and Latin America (Brazil, Chile, Colombia).

Although they did not know it by that name, the circles model of global English intuitively made sense to our participants as a model of national varieties of English. In the context of English as a global language, language learning becomes imagined as an encounter between previously learned target varieties, mostly American and British English, and a new target variety, Australian English. However, participants' accounts of communication problems—their inability to order apple juice, their impotence in dealing with negligent arrival services, their helplessness when confronted with a mobile phone plan—were not primarily due to differences between national varieties of English. In the migration process, national ways of seeing linguistic variation are overlaid by other selection processes, most notably immigration legislation. In Australian immigration legislation, a binary exists between "competent English," which is a requirement for most immigration visas, except humanitarian and family reunion, and an unnamed variety that is its opposite. The opposite is the marker of those who are excluded from Australia. The definition of "competent English" is as follows:

To prove you have competent English, provide evidence:

- that you are a citizen of and hold a valid passport issued by the United Kingdom,* the United States of America, Canada, New Zealand or the Republic of Ireland, with your application. *British National (Overseas) passports are not acceptable as evidence of competent English. or
- you have an [*sic*] obtained one of the following English language test results: [followed by list of admissible tests and required results].[15]

This definition, provided by the Australian Immigration Department, mixes identity criteria (being a citizen and passport holder) with criteria based on language test results. It establishes a binary between speakers of the Anglophone inner circle and everyone else. Our participants from expanding-circle countries, by and large, accepted that binary, at least at the time of arrival. Having their English tested was nothing new to them. It was associated with their progression through the education system, and their English had always been subjected to tests. We will discuss their experiences in the next section, "Bringing Tested English." For our participants from outer-circle countries, the situation was more complicated. Those who had high levels of English-language proficiency objected to the way their English was demoted to learner English; and those who had low levels of English-language proficiency found language testing and associated practices of formal language teaching an impractical and useless imposition. Their experiences are the focus of the section on "Bringing Street English."

Bringing Tested English

Many of our participants had to pass an English-language test to be admitted to Australia, as we explained in Chapter 1. This is true of most of those who entered as economic migrants, as well as those who arrived as international students. Among our participants is a cohort of 34 migrants from one single country of origin, Iran. Given the relative uniformity of their pre-migration language-learning experiences, they will be the focus of this section.

Since the Islamic Revolution of 1979, ever more Iranians have left their country.[16] Their preferred destinations have been Europe and North America, but the Iran-born population in Australia has also grown substantially, from 21,000 in 2000 to 78,000 in 2021.[17] Australia has treated asylum seekers from Iran exceedingly harshly and, by and large, has denied them entry, subjected them to mandatory offshore detention in Papua New Guinea or Nauru, and left them in legal limbo on a string of temporary protection visas. The journalist Behrouz Boochani is the best-known victim of this approach.[18] However, simultaneously with the exclusion of asylum seekers from Iran, Australia has welcomed large numbers of Iranians on skilled and business visas. Applicants in this stream receive points for their skills and qualifications, their age, their work experience, and their English proficiency.[19] These visa criteria result in a recognizable group with shared characteristics. They are tertiary-educated professionals with qualifications in accounting, engineering, information technology (IT), and the sciences. They arrived as couples in the years around 2010 when they were in their late 20s to early 40s. And they had demonstrated high levels of English-language proficiency before being admitted to Australia.

To be eligible for a skilled independent visa, they would have needed to provide evidence of "competent English," and to receive additional points on their application for English, they would have needed to demonstrate even higher levels of English, namely "proficient English" (10 points) or "superior English" (20 points).[20] The meanings of these terms are somewhat different depending on the test taken, as the Immigration Department accepts five different commercial English-language tests.[21] As a shortcut, it helps to know that "competent" is the same level required for admission to most university courses.[22] "Proficient" is equal to the level usually required for admission to university PhD research, and "superior" can be thought of as equal to the language proficiency of an educated native speaker.

These high levels of certified English-language proficiency did not save the participants in this cohort from the arrival shocks described above. Nahid, for instance, felt like the language she encountered in Australia was "*completely different*" from the one she had studied so diligently for so long, and which the Australian government had recognized as meeting their English-language skills criteria. To understand this mismatch, we need to trace the pre-migration language-learning trajectories of this cohort.

The foundations that allowed our participants to meet the stringent English-language proficiency requirements for admission to Australia on a skilled independent visa had been laid in childhood. In Iran, as in many countries of the expanding circle, English is a compulsory school subject starting in year 6 or year 7 and continuing until the end of high school. This amounts to about 500 hours of English-language instruction that each Iranian high school student would have received by the time they graduate.[23] Most university courses also include compulsory English study for the specific purposes of the degree. In these formal educational contexts, English is like any other school subject, with a test focus for academic advancement from one year group to the next. Memorizing vocabulary and grammar rules are at the core of the subject.

Participants were scathing about the kind of English they had experienced in Iranian schools and universities. They told us about the tedium of rote memorization, incompetent teachers, and meaningless textbooks. Diba complained that the outcome of all her years of English-language study in school was "*some grammar with some vocabulary.*" Cetareh said, "*the English at school is so weak,*" and Saman lamented, "*unfortunately, English is not taught well in our country.*" Their main gripe was that all their formal studies had not taught them to communicate.[24]

Although our Iranian participants seemed to believe that English-language teaching in Iran was particularly bad, their criticisms of "school English" echo through our data and internationally, as Alexa from Spain explained:

> The kind of exposure you get in high school is just like, grammar activities; you know ENDLESS! So you learn the- your present perfect, your past perfect, all that. You learn that really, really well. But you can't even say, "Hello, how are you?" You know, after three or four years. I know it sounds amazing, but I was talking to this- erm these Chinese students of mine, and they said, "Well, it's the same in China." You know, we know lots of grammar. But we come here and, we can't even put two sentences together. It's horrible. (Alexa)

Given the dismal reputation of school language learning, upwardly mobile parents in Iran, as elsewhere, may choose to support their children's English-language learning through extracurricular activities. Many participants came from families who valued the English language highly. Amin's father, for instance, started to teach his son English from the age of 7, well before English was introduced as a school subject. Amin told us that "*my family forced me to learn English. There were always English books and they forced me, my father taught me and then, later on, when my siblings grew up, they also started teaching me English.*" Other participants had attended supplementary schools, had received private tutoring, or had perused a great variety of self-study materials. Self-study also included avid consumption of English-language media, such as reading books, listening to music, and watching videos and TV.[25] For some, the presence of students who engaged in extracurricular English-language learning further increased their dissatisfaction with school English, as Qasem reflected: "*I wasn't a very clever student in English. Those students who had attended private English classes were much better than me.*"

Private English-language learning went into overdrive once participants started to actively pursue their migration projects. The prospect of living in Australia fueled their desire to develop their English-language skills. Participants went about it in the way they knew best and in the way immigration policies suggested was most effective: by studying for a test. Amin, a project manager with a physics degree, detailed his English-language preparation:

AMIN: *When we got serious about coming to Australia, I started my classes. I think I attended classes for about three consecutive years. I worked hard at home, too. I was always on the computer, and there were always my* IELTS *books spread around the house, and I was busy working.*

SHIVA: *Because you wanted a high score?*

AMIN: *Because I needed a high score, yes. Then, I attended another course in another institute for only two* skills, listening *and* reading*. Because my* speaking *and* writing *were very good. My* reading *was my weakest* skill, *and my* listening, *well, it was so-so. Then, I placed my last focus on those two* skills, *and I got my* IELTS *score and passed.*

SHIVA: *Can I ask what your score was?*

AMIN: *6, I wanted 6 and I got an* overall *6.5. However, in my previous tests, I had higher* overall *scores. But my* writing *was generally 7,* my listening *and* writing *were never below 6, but I kept getting 5.5 in my* reading.[26]

SHIVA: *Oh, so you did the test more than once?*

AMIN: *Yes, I did it five times.*[27]

Amin displays all the characteristics of a high-achieving academic learner. He identified his goal and systematically prepared himself. Working hard, targeting weaknesses, and studying to the test, English, for Amin, became an IELTS score, as is apparent from his many code-switches into English, when he speaks about "reading, writing, listening, speaking skills" as well as "overall" scores. Outside language-testing circles, such fluency in the skills targeted by IELTS is rare. The same is true for the casual mention of scores as if they were self-evident indicators of language proficiency that needed no further explanation. Like many of our participants, Amin had to become an expert in language testing to come to Australia. Participants' IELTS scores were one of the most important test results of their lives, and they had become part of their identities in the same way that many people never forget their high school graduation result.[28]

Once participants had achieved the required IELTS score and were granted their skilled independent visa, they felt as if the Australian government had certified that their English was "*good*" and "*at the right level*" to start their new lives in Australia. They were in for a rude shock, as network engineer Farah shares:

> *My* speaking *was 7. My* listening *was 7. My* reading *and* writing *were 6. And then the* overall *came to 6.5. Then we* applied *and we came here. But when we came here, I realized that I could not speak English at all. And I couldn't understand what they were saying at all, like at all. I basically couldn't say anything. Because when you study for* IELTS, *you memorize a set of sentences, you prepare a set of sentences to pass the exam. You are not actually able to speak.* (Farah)

Like Farah, most of our participants from expanding-circle countries felt that their tested English let them down around their communicative competence. It was mundane, everyday interactions that frustrated them most. Having learned English through formal education all their lives, they sought out English-language courses to remedy their communicative deficits. As new arrivals entering on a skilled or business visa, most of them were not eligible for government support, as we discussed in Chapter 1. This includes English-language training. Even for those willing to pay, there is a scarcity of suitable courses teaching communicative competence. Most English-language teaching in Australia is geared toward international students and IELTS preparation. Having already achieved high IELTS scores prior to arrival, there were no formal English-language education offerings that met their needs to improve everyday communication. Some of our participants who brought high levels of tested English were turned back from the language-teaching programs in which they sought to enroll because no courses at their level were on offer. Those who did enroll in English-language classes were deeply dissatisfied with programs that did not meet their specific needs. Behnaz, a civil engineer, provides an example. Behnaz was a secondary applicant on her husband's skilled independent visa. Secondary applicants may either demonstrate "competent English" through a recognized test result, or they may choose to prepay for 510 hours of English-language instruction in the AMEP. That is what Behnaz chose to do. The English course was a disappointment, and she let most of her entitlement lapse:

> *The aim of the* "English for Further Study" *course was to prepare for future university studies. Like how to do* research. *I know these things well. I don't want to waste my time on these things. I want to spend my time learning the everyday language. They filled the program with childish and ridiculous projects, and didn't teach us the things that we were aiming to learn so that we could enter society and speak English.* (Behnaz)

To speak English, Behnaz, like all our participants, would need to attend the school of life of everyday interactions, as we will explore in Chapter 4.

Bringing Street English

The experience of skilled migrants from Iran contrasts sharply with that of another cohort among our participants, namely humanitarian entrants from Anglophone Africa. These participants felt they were being funneled into English-language classes, even though they did not wish to attend them. Their reluctance to attend formal English-language training had two main reasons: they already brought high levels of oral communicative competence, and they were skeptical of the efficacy of language learning in the classroom. In this section, we explore the English brought by these participants and how it was mismatched in a different way from those who brought tested English. Their oral proficiencies were erased because they were not accompanied by much formal education and because they involved multilingual ways of speaking.[29]

The economic migrants from Iran had spent their youths progressing through formal education from one year level to the next, and from primary via secondary to tertiary education, acquiring recognized and certified skills, including English, along the way. In other words, they accumulated institutionally recognized capital that they could eventually transform into Australian citizenship.[30] The experiences of the humanitarian entrants from Africa were very different. Their educational trajectories were disrupted, often ending at primary school level. Their youth was spent on the move, often fleeing from one place of refuge to another. Their school was the school of life, where they also learned English along the way.

This is how Ahmed, a man from South Sudan whose life was disrupted by the Second Sudanese Civil War (1983–2005),[31] described his pre-migration English-language learning:

> Actually, I learned English back home when I was working. Because I used to move a lot. I learn English just in the street. Because I was in Uganda, I was in Kenya, and both of them, they talk English. They talk some languages, and English as well. So I learn Kiswahili and English. My language is Arabic, and then Kiswahili, and a little bit English. (Ahmed)

Ahmed is an engaging storyteller and his modest self-assessment ("a little bit English") stands in stark contrast to his fluency. In fact, disclaiming their English-language proficiency was not unusual for those who had little formal education. For many of our African participants, "English" was almost a synonym for formal education, as was the case for Amina, who responded to the question whether she had learned English with "not really because I'm not educated" in English, during an English-language research interview. Amina arrived in Australia in her late 40s from Guinea, a transit country where she had found refuge from the Sierra Leone Civil War (1991–2002).[32] Her home languages were Temne and Krio. Krio is an English-based creole language that has its origins in one of the more curious British colonial projects.[33] When British public opinion began to turn against the slave trade in the late 18th century, a cohort of the "Black Poor" of London were rounded up and shipped to a tract of land that was later to become the site of Freetown, the capital of Sierra Leone. These initial settlers were soon followed by a contingent of "Nova Scotians," emancipated slaves from the American South who had been promised their freedom in exchange for fighting on the side of the British in the American War of Independence. Next came a contingent of freed slaves from Jamaica. And these were followed by passengers on any European slave ship which the British took it upon themselves to intercept after the British Abolition Act of 1808. The idea was that these diverse groups of people would become "Black Englishmen" and help secure British interests in West Africa. To form this class of Black colonials, the British shielded the newcomers from the Indigenous people of the place, the Temne and Mende peoples, and invested significantly in their education. For example, the first—and for a long time the only—English-medium university in sub-Saharan Africa, Fourah Bay College, was established in Freetown in 1827.[34]

The colonial project behind the establishment of Freetown was disastrous in many ways, including the seeding of ethnic conflicts that continue to plague Sierra Leone and the wider region. Ultimately, it is the reason Amina and other refugees from Sierra Leone find themselves in Australia today.[35] Yet it was successful to the degree that it established English in Sierra Leone. It is an English that is heavily influenced by the other languages the new settlers brought, most prominently Yoruba, Hausa, Wolof, Portuguese, Jamaican Creole, Arabic, Fanti, French, and Fula, but also the languages of established people in the area, Temne and Mende. That English is today called "Krio." It is spoken by over 95% of Sierra Leone's population and serves as the lingua franca that links the country's multilingual population. Sierra Leone has at least 16 languages with sizable speaker groups, the largest being Mende and Temne, which together account for close to 60% of the population. All Indigenous language groups have substantial cross-border populations in neighboring countries. The official language of Sierra Leone and the medium of instruction in schools is not Krio, though, but "English proper," which only 10% of the population claim to be proficient in. This educated minority views Krio with disdain, "as a 'mixed' language lacking the authority and purity of either English or other indigenous languages."[36] For everyone else, Krio is, in fact, seen as a stepping stone that can be upgraded toward the recognized "English" should the opportunity for further education or migration arise.

The multilingual ecology of Sierra Leone provides the background to Amina's language-learning journey. Born into a Temne family, Temne was her first language, but she cannot remember a point in her life when she did not also speak Krio. After her marriage to a Temne man, they raised their three children in both Temne and Krio. The use of multiple languages came naturally to Amina, who had to leave school when she was 10 years old to help support her family. Working as a petty trader, ability in customers' and wholesalers' languages was a distinct asset, and so she also learned to speak Klao,[37] Kono, Madingo, and Susu. While she confidently claimed these six languages, she was bashful about English. She felt that someone like her, with only 4 years of primary school and limited literacy, was not entitled to claim English proficiency, even after 5 years in Australia and during a research interview conducted entirely in English.

Highly multilingual repertoires like Amina's are not exceptional in Africa. Learning multiple languages through everyday interaction is a normal process of social symbiosis, where language learning is a byproduct of going about one's life in a diverse world.[38] Another example of such a multilingual language-learning trajectory comes from Fatima. Born in the 1980s on the other side of the continent into an Oromo family in Ethiopia, Fatima learned to speak Oromo in the home. In school, Amharic was the medium of instruction, and Fatima started to learn how to read and write in Amharic. Sadly, her education was cut short when she was about 10 years old and civil unrest engulfed her area.[39] During their flight, her family became separated, and Fatima ended up in Kenya's Kakuma refugee camp as an orphan. She quickly picked up Kiswahili, the camp's lingua franca, while working as a kitchen hand to support herself. As a teenager, she started seeing a Dinka man from Sudan. Moving in with the Sudanese section of the camp, she soon learned Dinka, but spoke Oromo with her three children who were born over the next few years. During this time her husband became increasingly abusive, and Fatima had to seek protection in one of the women's shelters within the camp. Most of the women in the shelter were Sudanese and their common language was Arabic. When Fatima applied for resettlement in Australia as the head of her family, she managed the process, including the paperwork, in English. Even so, and although all her communications with Vera were in English, she considered herself "only" quinti-lingual in Oromo, Amharic, Kiswahili, Dinka, and Arabic, but insisted that she had "no English."

What the process of multilingual language learning and communication might have looked like at the interactional level can be gleaned from an account by Violet. Violet is originally from Sudan, but came to Australia from a refugee camp in Uganda. Her language is Acholi, a cross-border language spoken both in Sudan and Uganda. Additionally, she had learned Kiswahili, Arabic, and English. Unlike others, Violet had received some formal education in English in the camp and so was happy to claim it as one of her languages. Violet worked as a nurse's aide in the camp, and her job was to register patients who were seeking medical attention. She described her task as follows: "People speak to me and then I ask, 'What is your name?' And, 'What are you feeling? What is bad from you?' Then they will be telling me. Then I will start writing in English." When asked which languages she was using to speak to patients, Violet responded, "We were using English and other language. Acholi, and other language, like Arabic, Swahili, and Bari. Many, many of them."

In sum, humanitarian entrants from Africa arrive in Australia with rich multilingual repertoires. Learning new languages is unremarkable to them. Having experienced immense hardship, language learning had not been something they had the luxury to worry about and so they had just "got on with it." However, arrival in Australia changed that. Their ability to quickly learn a new language through everyday interactions and their multilingual repertories were erased. Their African languages were discounted, and so was the ease with which they had previously learned to communicate. Instead, only one language counted now—English. And the spotlight was not on what they could do in English, but rather what they could *not* do in English. As Venus from Sierra Leone observed, Australians "got the perception that every Africans don't know English." The same is true for their remarkable language-learning abilities. Learning in the street was not considered of any value in Australia, where formal language learning is the only recognized pathway to remedying their supposed deficit.

Amina's experience provides an example. The accomplished multilingual who had picked up seven languages trading on the streets of Sierra Leone and Guinea suddenly found that it was impossible for her to progress further with her English. With her limited school education, Amina's ambition was to learn how to read and write in English, and she believed her AMEP entitlement would enable her to achieve her dream. Due to her high oral proficiency, she was placed in the highest level of English learning available in the AMEP. This is a course where she might have encountered peers like Behnaz, with 15 years of formal education under her belt. For Amina, this created an insurmountable barrier:

> We were mingled with people who have degrees from other country, and they can understand more than us. You see, some of these Chinese, Indian, these people who come over, they have their own education. They have degrees. So they can understand faster, more than us [. . .]. The way I look at it, these people are degree holders. I'm just a beginner, I don't even want to sit with them. I said, "I don't think I'll go with these people." So I decided to stop. (Amina)

Participants like Amina, who had little formal education, accepted, to a degree, that their English was "not good" because they saw English as tied to formal education. They were also acutely aware of their limited literacy skills. For them to be able to develop their full potential and capitalize on their high levels of oral proficiency, they would have needed the opportunity to extend their literacy skills in an environment that met their specific needs and where they would not be compared to highly educated language learners from other countries.

The deficit perspective on African varieties of English and African ways of learning was even more troubling to high school graduates. Enjoying a high level of formal education and "good English" by the standards of their countries, they were still treated as illiterate non-speakers in Australia. Three high school graduates from West Africa—Lewis, Lucy, and Venus—stand out because they all wanted to start university studies but were directed to undertake English-language classes instead. All three rejected the idea. Venus said, "I'm not doing any English language, because I even did English in my country." Lucy reported, "They were learning these things that I've learnt in primary school. ABC and what. And I said, 'No, this is not for me.' So I had to leave the same day. And I didn't come back there anymore." Lewis also dropped out of his English-language classes:

> I felt my English was ready. When I came, I wanted to do study in medical science, but at the time I was told, I had to attend the [AMEP] English classes. And I was attending that for about three months. And all that they were teaching there, were not anything that I really needed, so why I was attending there? (Lewis)

Being erroneously enrolled in English-language classes cost all three of them the opportunity to align their formal education and launch them on a pathway to further education and employment at their level, as we will discuss in the next chapter.

3

"In My World, No One's Got a Job with an Australian Company"

Looking for Work in a New Language

"Without a Job You Are Nothing"

Michiko, a woman from Japan who had migrated to Australia after meeting and marrying an Australian man, believed that it was impossible for migrants to find jobs or establish meaningful careers. "In my world, no one's got a job with an Australian company," she told us. When she said, "in my world," she was referring to her circle of female friends in Perth, most of whom had, like herself, migrated from Japan or Korea. On the other side of the continent, her gloomy assessment was echoed by Franklin, a man from South Sudan, who had arrived in Australia on a humanitarian visa. Franklin argued that the lack of jobs in Regional City "made life very difficult for us." "Us" in this case referred to his social circle of people from various African countries.

Discussions about the difficulty of finding work reverberate through our data. Employment was central to participants' migration projects, and the experience of looking for work animated many of our conversations, irrespective of whether participants were employed or unemployed, whether they were part of the labor force or had left it, or whether they were satisfied with their employment situation or not. Although their countries of origin, reasons for migration, educational backgrounds, professional qualifications, and employment aspirations differed widely, most of our participants reported negative experiences in their search for work and felt a strong sense of disadvantage in the labor market.[1] Labor market statistics confirm that they were not exaggerating, with family reunion and humanitarian entrants struggling the most.[2] To examine participants' job search experiences, we first explore Franklin's trajectory in some detail to provide a holistic understanding of the key challenges in the context of one case. From there, we explore the main barriers to finding employment, namely linguistic proficiency, educational qualifications, and local experience.

Franklin was one of those participants who volunteered to join our research precisely because he wanted to tell the story of his 5-year search for work. He hoped that, through our research, this story would be heard "in government

Life in a New Language. Ingrid Piller, Donna Butorac, Emily Farrell, Loy Lising, Shiva Motaghi-Tabari, and Vera Williams Tetteh, Oxford University Press. © Oxford University Press 2024. DOI: 10.1093/oso/9780190084288.003.0003

offices." We therefore tell his story in some detail as it illustrates the interplay between a deficit view of language proficiency, non-recognition of skills, and absence of meaningful career guidance and pathways that channel some migrants into dead-end jobs, preventing them from fulfilling their career aspirations and fully contributing to the community.

Franklin arrived in Australia in 2003 as a refugee from Sudan. Hailing from Juba, the main urban center of South Sudan, he was relatively well educated by South Sudanese standards. As we heard in Chapter 2, he had attended an English-medium high school. After graduation, he went on to teacher training in a Catholic tertiary college in the relatively calm period between the First Sudanese Civil War (1955–1972) and the Second Sudanese Civil War (1983–2005). He obtained a teaching qualification as an English and catechism teacher, but his flight from Juba via Khartoum and Cairo as a young adult completely disrupted his career, and he spent most of his 20s and early 30s in refugee camps. When he was selected for resettlement in Australia—a country about which he "did not know anything"—he was rearing to go, rebuild his life, and make a career for himself. However, half a decade after his arrival, when Vera met him, he was still in employment limbo, and he was worried that his life was being wasted. "My age will be going for nothing," he lamented.

The first obstacle on his path to employment had emerged right on arrival, when he was erroneously directed to enroll in English-language study in the AMEP by his refugee resettlement case manager. As we showed in Chapter 2, many of our participants, particularly humanitarian entrants, are routinely directed to "learn English" as a precondition for entering vocational training or finding work. This advice is not necessarily based on a proficiency assessment but a blanket assumption of migrants' English-language deficit. That such an unassessed deficit assumption was at work in Franklin's case is apparent from the fact that, in addition to having been educated through the medium of English,[3] Franklin had also worked as an English teacher both in Sudan and Egypt. Furthermore, he had gained professional experience as an interpreter with the Australian embassy and a media team reporting for US networks in Cairo.

Failure to undertake an individual, holistic, and professional language-proficiency assessment relative to employment aspirations and as part of career counseling damaged Franklin's employment prospects right from the start. Upon the advice of his case manager, he dutifully enrolled in the AMEP despite his high level of English-language proficiency. Once there, it quickly became apparent that his English-language proficiency was way above anything offered in the AMEP. After a few classes, his teacher advised him to withdraw. Still, no assessment of his qualifications, skills, experiences, and aspirations was undertaken at this point, and he was told to switch from an AMEP English course "to do any other course." The course options were limited in the college where Franklin had been made to enroll because his English-language proficiency had been misjudged by his case manager. From the available options, Franklin selected a computer course. While the course provided him with a valuable generic skill, it did not offer a career pathway. Franklin aspired to recapture his teaching career, but how to bridge the gap between his Sudanese qualifications and an Australian pathway to a teaching career remained a mystery to him. The computer course in which he was enrolled certainly did little to demystify the sector for him, or even the Australian job market more generally. Therefore, on his own initiative he began to explore work options through his church networks. This way he found casual work as a teachers' aide with a Catholic education office and was able to gain local experience through volunteer roles. Unfortunately, he soon discovered that he was welcome to work in volunteer roles but was considered unqualified for paid roles, as his Sudanese post-secondary degree was not recognized in Australia. Given his financial obligations, this put him in an impossible situation: "For me, with my age and with my young family, I can't be just a volunteer."

Establishing himself as a teacher in Australia increasingly seemed like an impossible dream, but his volunteering roles had allowed him to see related careers in social work and community services. For these, too, he would have to put himself through university and gain an Australian bachelor's degree as a mature adult. This presented another roadblock on Franklin's career journey. In Australia, a Bachelor of Social Work is a degree that involves 4 years of full-time study. Yet, in his late 30s and with a growing family, Franklin could not rely solely on study support and welfare assistance to fulfill his role as his family's breadwinner. To achieve his conflicting educational and financial aims, Franklin embarked on an ambitious plan to work by day and study at night. He enrolled in an online university degree in social work and, simultaneously, took up a job as a meat packer in an abattoir. For that job, he had to leave home at half past five in the morning. He would then work a 10-hour shift and return home by five o'clock in the evening. Unsurprisingly, the labor left him exhausted, and after a day's work, he found that "your body does not even want to get up. So you will not think of going to class." Indeed, the juggling act soon proved too much. Franklin gave up his educational aspirations and settled for full-time work as a meat packer because he needed the money.

The abattoir job enabled him and his wife, a fellow refugee from Juba, to purchase their first car and basic furniture items like beds and a sofa. They also tried to set some money aside to be able to support their families back in Sudan, particularly as both of Franklin's parents were ailing and needed medical assistance. Sadly, the money he was able to send them to buy medicines was not enough: "They just simply died because there's not much money that I'm supposed to send during that time to rescue their life." Franklin had given up his career aspirations for a job whose sole attractions were that he had been able to get it and that it paid a wage. Since that wage did not even enable him to buy medicines for his parents, Franklin felt caught in a trap where he could neither provide for his family nor further his career. He summed up his situation thus: "I feel totally depressed. I feel totally like handcuffed."

To overcome his depression, Franklin eventually gave up his dead-end abattoir job and went back to university to complete his degree. Half a decade after their arrival in Australia, the family was back relying on welfare to get by, and with the completion of his degree imminent, Franklin was searching for work in social services. At that point, despite his English-language proficiency, his Australian degree, his experience, his assiduous networking, and his undoubted grit, the career he aspired to still seemed out of Franklin's reach. The only paid employment in his field he could get was a few hours of casual work as a community liaison officer. "How can I survive on a once-a-week job?" he asked. In Regional City, he considered his employment prospects slim and concluded, "here, there is nothing, nothing." Therefore, he was getting ready to move on and to uproot his family yet again in the hope that he would be able to find stable full-time employment in his field in a larger city such as Sydney.

Franklin's story demonstrates several points that recur throughout our data. First, English-language proficiency does intersect with finding work, unsurprisingly. However, it does so not in the form of low English-language proficiency on the part of the migrant, but in the form of a deficit assumption on the part of Australian society, in this case represented by Franklin's refugee resettlement coordinator. Second, in addition to his English proficiency, Franklin's prior skills were also rendered invisible. His Sudanese teaching qualification was completely discounted, and he was demoted to the status of a high school leaver without further qualifications. Third, he received no obvious guidance on how to bridge the gap between his existing qualifications and the qualifications needed to fulfill his career aspirations. This absence of targeted career advice left him floundering and reliant on his own devices. Despite Franklin's considerable personal initiative, as a newcomer to the country he did not have the financial and social resources to bridge the gap on his own. In the absence of transition support, he was essentially forced, for financial reasons, to undertake a low-skilled meat-worker job without any career prospects. While bringing in a wage, such dead-end jobs can become a permanent obstacle to (re)gaining qualifications and embarking on a desired career.

In the following, we will explore these three aspects in greater detail. Throughout this chapter we stress that, as Franklin's story demonstrates, finding employment is an essential component of successful settlement. Work is much more than a means to make a living.[4] A decent wage is a central component of meaningful work, of course, as Franklin explained: "We are living in this materialistic world, everything is money." However, beyond meeting his material needs and being able to provide for his family, Franklin considered work essential in order to live a meaningful life, to have dignity and a place in the community. Thinking back to his life in Africa, he reminisced: "When I walk around the street, it's known that this is Franklin going. The community, the communion, and the socialization of the people, of the street. But here, it's just I, I, I." He believed that once he had decent work, he would be able to recapture his sense of himself as a member of the community who is more than an individual and who is making a meaningful contribution because "a job is the backbone of life, without a job, of course, you are nothing."

Franklin was not the only participant who saw meaningful work and successful settlement as intrinsically linked. In another example, Danica, a family reunion migrant from Russia, lamented that she did not belong anywhere—neither her native Russia, where she had "missed too much" during her years of absence, nor in Australia, where she was working various jobs but had not been able to re-establish herself as an arts teacher. "If I make a career here, like I had in Russia, of course, I will belong here," she said, "because a career isn't only about the money. It is appreciation. If you do something and it is appreciated by the community, the society, or someone other than your husband. Having a place in society is the most important." Although most of our participants desperately desired to be someone, to be appreciated by the community, and to find a place in society through work, the careers they aspired to eluded many of them. In the following we will explore the three main barriers to achieving their aspirations: English-language proficiency, non-recognition of qualifications, and limited social capital.

Creating the Migrant English-Language Deficit

When asked to rate her English-language proficiency, Mercy stated "can't speak"—in English and as part of a research interview that was conducted entirely in English. Originally from South Sudan, Mercy had spent almost two decades in Egypt before being resettled in Australia on a humanitarian visa. Despite her low levels of education—she had completed only 4 years of primary school—she had supported herself and her family during her time in Egypt by working in childcare and cleaning. Her employment aspirations in Australia were similarly modest. All she wanted was a job to support herself so that she would not have to rely on welfare. However, in 6 years in Australia, all her attempts to find a job had proven futile. Despite her extensive experience as a cleaner, she had been repeatedly rejected for cleaning positions and had been told that her English was not good enough to undertake such work. This is how she related her experience:

> No jobs, no anything. I go to other place. I want to do the cleaner. They say no. Your English is not. Instead to do some. If you come here, we, what will we do about you? And I say, no, just the cleaner. Because in Egypt, it's easy for us. We work in their homes. We clean the Egyptian places, and we get the money in there. This is why we live in Egypt for long time. We stay like the Egyptian. No, not something hard for us there. Because we working in job, the cleaner. I can do it. This is, it's not, it's not difficult for me to do it. And they say no. (Mercy)

As this extended narrative demonstrates, Mercy is perfectly capable of telling a complex story in English, despite her humble self-assessment as a non-speaker of English. The story provides necessary background about her prior work experience as a cleaner and mounts an argument why her English-language proficiency should be considered sufficient to undertake the work. Ethnographic research into the language skills needed for cleaning work confirms that Mercy is right: the communication requirements involved in cleaning work are very low, and cleaners are, in fact, not usually expected to speak as part of their work.[5]

As is obvious, Mercy has the English-language proficiency to explain that excluding her from a cleaning job because of her English-language proficiency does not make sense. This is probably a higher level of English-language proficiency than is required to actually perform the work of a cleaner. However, her English-language proficiency still serves as the pretext to reject her job applications. All she can do is accept the finality of her exclusion based on an abstract level of English-language proficiency that seems relatively independent of her linguistic ability and the communicative requirements of the job she aspired to: "And they say no."

At the other end of the proficiency spectrum, Eva found herself in exactly the same position of having to accept an English-proficiency assessment that seemed unreasonable and unfair. Eva had arrived in Australia from Chile in 1985 on a humanitarian visa when she was in her early 30s. Like most members of her family, Eva is highly educated. Back home, she had undertaken a university degree majoring in English and French, with a view to becoming a language teacher. This was a 5-year degree, but she had only completed 4 years when universities in Chile were closed after Pinochet's coup in 1973. By the time the universities reopened, she had two young children and so she never sat for her graduation exams. However, there can be no doubt that she had a high level of English-language proficiency when she arrived in Australia. Furthermore, before participating in our research she had lived in the country for almost 20 years and had plenty of opportunities to improve her English. The only linguistic difference between Eva and a native speaker of English was probably her Spanish-inflected accent.

In Chile, Eva's husband, a mechanical engineer, had been the sole breadwinner, but because he initially struggled to find work after migration, Eva needed to work outside the home, too. Since coming to Australia, she had held a series of jobs in school libraries, aged care, and public service. Simultaneously, she undertook several tertiary certificate courses to establish a career that would be more than a series of jobs. She first completed a vocational degree in diversional therapy, a role that involves running leisure programs for the elderly, but soon discovered that working in aged care did not suit her. She then completed a Spanish-language teaching certificate but found that job opportunities in Spanish-language teaching in Australia were extremely limited. Eventually, Eva decided to undertake a TESOL degree, which she had hoped would enable her to work as an English-language teacher in Sydney's booming ELICOS industry.[6] Having completed all her required units, she needed to find a practicum placement in order to graduate. Students needed to arrange a practicum place themselves by applying to schools. Although a practicum is not a paid position, Eva was unable to find a placement despite her persistent efforts. While she was never explicitly told the reason for the repeated rejections, she became convinced that the problem was her accent and her "funny surname." As evidence, she told the story of a school principal whom she imitated as having said to her on the phone, "I'm so sorry, but we are so busy this year. It's not possible. Maybe next year, alright?" That conversation had taken place on a Monday morning and on the Wednesday afternoon, Eva discovered that a fellow student, who had called the same school that very morning, had been accepted for a practicum place straightaway. The difference between her and the student who got accepted was that the latter was "Australian." Eva, who is a naturalized citizen, is technically "Australian," too, but, like most participants, she reserved the label "Australian" for native-born Anglo-Australians, as we will further discuss in Chapters 6 and 7.

After that experience, Eva decided to give up on a TESOL career, reasoning that if she could not even get a practicum placement, employment in the industry too would remain beyond her grasp:

> I left like a hundred messages. EVERY PLACE! I cannot believe it, every place I have rung! They say, they're totally busy, or they are going to call me back. But they never call me back! It's the same when you apply for a job. They're discriminating. (Eva)

As Mercy's and Eva's experiences show, English-language proficiency is deeply entangled with job search experiences. However, the association is not as straightforward as that assumed in the human resources and labor policy literature, where level of English is linked to employment outcomes.[7] Both women clearly have the level of English-language proficiency that is adequate for the roles they seek. Instead, the barrier is created by the ideological association of migrants with an English-language deficit. Both women believed that prospective employers saw them as a potential problem and therefore shied away from giving them a chance.

That English-language proficiency is related to employment outcomes in Australia is, in and of itself, not particularly surprising. As a 2017 Australian parliamentary inquiry states, "It is self-evident that capacity to speak English impacts profoundly on a person's capacity to obtain work."[8] The commonsense notion that English-language proficiency and finding employment go hand in hand is further normalized through the AMEP and other government-sponsored language programs, whose efficacy is regularly measured in terms of employment outcomes.[9] However, this global undifferentiated language-employment nexus hides as much as it explains. First, the commonsense notion that there is a relationship between English-language proficiency and employment outcomes obscures what it actually means to have "good English" or "limited English." As we will discuss throughout this book, everyday assessments of language proficiency are not a straightforward matter that is independent of the identity of the speaker, the hearer, the interaction, and the purpose of the assessment.[10] The point we stress here is that the association between migrants and an English-language deficit has become entrenched to such a degree that the poor employment outcomes of migrants from non-English-speaking backgrounds are now a self-fulfilling prophecy. Migrants are denied access to jobs because their English-language proficiency is assumed to be too low, regardless of their actual proficiency or the communicative requirements of a specific position.[11]

Internalizing the English-Language Deficit

That they were assumed to be linguistically deficient was experienced as highly oppressive by participants. Like all systems of oppression, the discourse of the linguistic deficit may also be internalized by individuals as feelings of inferiority.[12] In this section, we continue the focus on the role of English-language proficiency in the job search by illuminating experiences of loss of linguistic confidence. Some of our participants had internalized the idea that their English-language proficiency was too low to work in Australia to such a degree that they left the labor market. Such decisions were highly gendered, and linguistic insecurity often was inextricably entangled with women's withdrawal into the private sphere, as the example of Michiko demonstrates.[13] As noted at the beginning of this chapter, Michiko stated that in her circle of migrant women from various Asian countries, "no one's got a job with an Australian company." She herself was no exception. Michiko had graduated from college in Japan with a degree in Japanese art and culture, and before committing to the adult world of work and marriage had chosen to undertake a period of extended travel. Her travels initially took her to the United States, where she first developed the desire to study English to a higher level than that afforded by her high school studies back in Japan.[14] Over the next 10 years, she pursued a pattern of returning to Japan periodically to work part-time and save some money to finance her extended travels. In 1998, she spent a year in the United Kingdom, mostly studying in an English-language school. After that year, she was quite confident in her English, and after returning to Japan for another work stint set off on a backpacking trip around Australia. A few weeks into her trip, she met and fell in love with an Australian man who would later become her husband. For the next couple of years, they traveled the world together, supporting themselves through casual work as they went along. They communicated exclusively in English, as Michiko's partner does not speak any other language. In 2006, they decided that it was time to settle down and moved to Perth.

At that time, Michiko felt confident in her English, as she had been immersed in the language for a decade. To move beyond her pattern of casual work and to establish a career, Michiko enrolled in a 1-year childcare certificate course. On completion of that course and despite her long-established trajectory of finding casual work quickly and easily, she hesitated to apply for work in childcare. This was partly because she had discovered during her work placements that lifting toddlers onto the change table challenged the limits of her physical strength. More importantly, she had lost confidence in her English and believed that it was not good enough to work in an "Australian" setting. An experience that had severely undermined her belief in her ability to find work was the story of the friend who had been unable to find a job, presumably because of her English-language proficiency:

MICHIKO: Cos my friend tried to get job and, you know, your English is not enough to do=

DONNA: =Did they tell her that?

MICHIKO: No, they didn't. But you know that's their thought. [. . .] Yeah, my friends told me. Cos my English not enough, they can't get a job, so that's- I thought, oh, it could be my English too, it's not enough to get a job.

Although Michiko admits that neither she nor her friends have been explicitly told that their English is not good enough for employment, they have internalized the idea of migrants' English-language deficit to such a degree that they do not need to be told explicitly. With her confidence in her English-language proficiency so diminished, Michiko decided to better prepare herself by enrolling in an English-language class before seeking work. Over the course of a year, she completed a Certificate IV in Spoken and Written English. This certificate is widely considered as equivalent to an IELTS score of 6.0, which is the English-language proficiency level required for entry into most university courses.[15] In other words, on top of her decade-long immersion in spoken English, Michiko now also had a formal English-language qualification demonstrating proficiency at a level suitable for university entry.

Perversely, English-language training had made Michiko less confident in her English-language ability than before. She was now able to pinpoint the weaknesses in her English and identified these as her lack of formal grammatical knowledge and writing skills: "I realized I think I need grammar to find a job, or communicate with native people, and more writing. Actually, writing is my weak point." This assessment overlooks two vital linguistic facts: first, grammar is implicit in language usage, and formal grammatical training does not necessarily improve someone's ability to communicate. Few first-language speakers receive explicit grammatical instruction, yet are usually thought to be able to communicate well. In principle, the relationship between explicit grammatical knowledge and communicative ability is no different in second-language speakers.[16] Second, the writing requirements of childcare work are relatively low. Most of the writing involved in childcare work is formulaic and routine, relating to record keeping and "paperwork" to meet auditing requirements.[17]

In the end, Michiko's deep insecurity about whether her English-language proficiency would be acceptable in an Australian workplace kept her from even applying for jobs. When we last met Michiko, she was unsure where her employment trajectory was headed, considering yet another career change, maybe to librarian or dental hygienist. At the same time, she was happy in her role as a full-time homemaker, and starting a family and becoming a stay-at-home mother was another option she was considering. It might be argued that Michiko's insecurities about her English-language proficiency were of her own making, and that she did not try hard enough to find a job because she anticipated rejection. We certainly encountered cases in which a participant's linguistic insecurity was so strong that it even kept them from taking up options that were offered to them, as was the case with Jessie. Jessie was a PhD student from Taiwan, who intended to return to Taiwan after graduation to seek academic employment there because she did not believe she would be considered for a university teaching position in Australia. At the same time, she very much desired Australian teaching experience, although she had recently turned down a casual university teaching offer:

INGRID: But if you were able to find a job here? Would you? I mean, would you like to live in Australia, if you had the same job opportunities?

JESSIE: If I got a job here, I would like to work for like, couple of years and to, to see what's the difference. Teach in Taiwan and teach in Australia. Yeah. I- I want to experience it. Probably, they are very different. You never know. [Ingrid reminds her of a casual teaching opportunity that had recently been offered to Jessie and which she had turned down] But I was, I was not- I was not sure about my ability. Really, I'm not sure about my English ability. The- my main concern's like- okay, my English is not good enough. So that's why. I really, yeah that's- that really- that, that's the main reason. Yeah because, I- I know I've got a problem with my English and- so that's why I'm not really confident.

Jessie's rationalization, with its contradictory statements, its many hesitations, hedges, false starts, and repetitions, is indicative of her deep linguistic insecurity. At the same time, Jessie's claim that her "English is not good enough" and that she has "a problem with [her] English" is delivered in perfect English. When that conversation took place, she was also writing a PhD thesis in English—a linguistic accomplishment that is beyond most native speakers of English. Like Michiko's linguistic insecurity, Jessie's is ultimately informed by an abstract ideal that is both unrealistic and disconnected from the communicative requirements of her job aspirations.[18]

Such cases of deep-seated self-limiting linguistic insecurity demonstrate that the internalization of the belief in migrants' linguistic deficit functions to transform the linguistic barrier to employment from a social fact to an individual responsibility. In the process, choices such as Michiko's to concentrate on gendered domestic roles, or Jessie's to leave Australia for better employment prospects elsewhere, come to be seen as individual choices. That the discourse of migrants' English-language deficit produces these choices becomes obscured. Nonetheless, the English-language deficit is made in Australia, as we will further demonstrate in the next section, where we focus on the devaluation of another key component of migrants' symbolic capital, their professional qualifications.

Human Capital Deficit Made in Australia

Despite the many barriers our participants reported to gaining access to the kind of work they wanted, those who needed to work found jobs.[19] Commentators like to point to the virtually identical unemployment rates after 5–10 years in the country as evidence of the success of the Australian migration program.[20] Yet, such sanguine assessments overlook the fact that 5–10 years of labor market adjustment are a long time for an individual in the prime of their working life, as we saw in Franklin's case. Furthermore, such early struggles may be deeply traumatizing and may set migrants on a path toward underemployment, another form of disadvantage that is hidden in the employment rate.

Underemployment takes two forms: someone is considered underemployed if they work fewer hours than they would like to, or if they are engaged in work for which they are overqualified. In Franklin's case, both forms of underemployment were present: he worked for one day a week in a community service role but would have liked to work full-time, and he worked as a meat packer despite having teaching qualifications and undertaking university education. Numerous studies have found that migrants are disproportionately affected by both forms of underemployment, and that migration often entails a downward career trajectory.[21] A 2019 survey of 1,700 skilled migrants to South Australia, for instance, found that 53% had not been able to secure work that adequately utilized their skills and abilities.[22] In contrast to the unemployment rate, migrants' underemployment rate does not converge to that of the native-born with time in the country, except for migrants from English-speaking backgrounds.[23] The occupational attainment gap does narrow over time for migrants from non-English-speaking backgrounds hailing from Europe. However, severe overqualification remains a permanent career feature for racialized migrants from Africa and Asia.[24]

How underemployment comes about can be seen clearly in the story of Vesna, an experienced midwife, for whom migration to Australia resulted in a downward career trajectory to phlebotomist. When Vesna arrived in Australia in 2008 at the age of 56 to be with her British husband, a long-term Australian resident, she had been practicing as a midwife for over 30 years, not only in her native Bulgaria, but also in Libya and the United Arab Emirates (UAE). In Abu Dhabi, where she practiced as a midwife in a British hospital for a decade, she had met her husband, and when his work contract in the oil industry there ended, they decided to settle in Australia. In the lead-up to the move, Vesna looked forward to another decade working as a midwife before reaching retirement age. It did not occur to her that she would never practice midwifery again. Indeed, there was no reason for her to be anything but optimistic about her new life in Australia. After high school, she had completed a 4-year midwifery degree in Bulgaria in the 1970s and had an uninterrupted record of practice since graduation. Not only did she have solid qualifications and experience, but she had kept an eye on job ads in the lead-up to the move to Australia and had seen many job openings in her field.[25]

She did not consider her English-language proficiency to be a barrier, either. After all, she had experience working in hospitals where the medium of communication was not her native language. In her late 20s, she had taken up a 4-year contract as part of a Bulgarian medical team to Libya, where she had had to learn to function in Arabic. A decade later, when the Bulgarian economy collapsed after the end of the Cold War, she sought work abroad and found a job in a British hospital in Abu Dhabi, where the medium of communication was English. While she described her English as very limited at the time, this had not daunted her. She told herself that she knew Arabic and that would be a base: "I can start with this Arabic where I know, and I will learn slowly English." And indeed, she found that the hospital supported her to learn their routines and she was soon working comfortably through the medium of English. All these professional and linguistic skills and experiences provided Vesna with the confidence that she would go on to deliver babies after her move to Australia: "I could never think I can have a problem to work here in the hospital, because this is my place. I work thirty-something years."

Sadly, this is not how it turned out. Upon arrival, Vesna applied to have her midwifery qualifications assessed for Australian equivalence by the Overseas Qualifications Unit (OQU) in Western Australia (WA).[26] With few exceptions, such as for people holding qualifications from some British post-secondary institutions, this is a process that must be undertaken by any person who has gained an educational qualification outside Australia and who wishes to use this qualification for further study, or to secure employment in a relevant field of work in Australia. In the process, many migrants experience a demotion. Although the process differs across states and territories, certifying bodies, and professions, non-recognition of overseas qualifications, or recognition at a lower level, is the most likely outcome. In fact, it has been argued that the equivalence assessment process constitutes the most serious form of discrimination imposed on non-British migrants in Australia.[27]

Vesna certainly felt discriminated against and treated unjustly when her 4-year Bulgarian midwifery qualification, together with her 30 years of work experience, was rejected for registration with the WA Nursing Federation, the professional body that oversees midwifery in WA. On top of that, she was told she would need to complete an entire nursing degree before being eligible, as all hospital midwives in WA must be registered nurses. Unsurprisingly, Vesna found this decision difficult to understand. Against the background of Australia's midwife shortage, she contrasted her rejection in Australia with her positive reception in the UAE. "Everywhere the medicine is the same," she said scornfully.

Describing her disappointment, Vesna kept repeating that she "felt really upset, really upset" about the decision. She was left with no other option but to give up on midwifery. Undertaking a full 4-year nursing degree did not constitute a viable option for her, considering her age and her English-language proficiency. She pointed out that studying at university would be difficult for her: "I can talk, I can read, but my English is not on the level where I can write a big essay; my English is not academic level." Vesna is right to point out that the English-language proficiency that is required for academic training is often quite different, and usually higher, than that required for professional practice.[28] However, given that Vesna had worked as a midwife through the medium of English for 10 years, it seems nonsensical to impose academic English-language proficiency requirements to achieve a degree in the field on her.

Vesna was advised by OQU that childcare might constitute an alternative employment option, an idea she dismissed straightway because it would have topped her demotion with her removal from the medical field entirely. To continue working in a hospital, she undertook a short course as a pharmacy assistant, which got her accepted into a phlebotomy course. On completion of this course, she soon found work in a hospital-based blood-collection unit, and, 2 years after arriving in Australia, she was finally back at work. In the employment statistics, she had become a number evidencing Australia's success in integrating migrants into the labor market. This "success story" has come at the price of an enormous skills wastage. Vesna would never work as a midwife again, and her skills and experience had been lost both to her personally and to Australian society and its healthcare system, where midwives continue to be in high demand. When Donna last spoke to Vesna, she was happy to be back in a familiar work environment, but still irked by the fact that the low-status and low-paid role of phlebotomist engaged only a fraction of her capabilities.

Non-recognition of overseas qualifications can also result from the fact that certain professions do not even exist in Australia, as is the case with specialist early childhood education.[29] Danica had a Russian university degree as an arts teacher with a focus on early childhood education. Such a role does not exist in Australia, as Danica was shocked to discover. She found Australian attitudes toward teaching and early childhood education "heart-breaking" and "deeply depressing." Although she had been trained in the "extremely important" profession of early arts teaching, she never got the chance to contribute her skills to enhance child development in Australia's "ordinary childcare." Danica's exclusion from the labor market meant that there was no pathway to transfer her valuable skills and knowledge into Australian society. For her personally, it also meant a career setback from which she did not quite know how to recover. After more than 6 years in Australia, she was still working odd jobs and considering going back to university to study special education.

These experiences of downward occupational mobility constitute a key facet of migrant disadvantage in the labor market. Just like Franklin, Vesna's and Danica's problem was not so much finding work, but finding work that was consistent with their skills and experiences, and that they found meaningful. Other examples of stark downward occupational mobility among our participants included Tina from China, whose 7-year law degree (bachelor and master) was not recognized in Australia, and who ended up taking a short course and then working as a paralegal. Similarly, the psychology degree of Samuel from Congo was not recognized, and he retrained to work as a nurse. The engineering degree of Katja from Poland was not recognized, and she retrained as a beautician. The list could go on. It was not only the tertiary-educated who found that their previous qualifications were not recognized. Nina from Sierra Leone had trained and worked as an auto mechanic. When her qualifications were not recognized, she initially thought she could easily do the vocational certification course. However, she discovered that she was the only woman on the course and that female auto mechanics are exceedingly rare in Australia. The sexist and racist harassment she experienced in the vocational college made her drop out. Like many of our participants who ran out of options, she eventually pursued qualifications in aged care.

These participants are only the proverbial tip of the iceberg because many more gave up on re-establishing their careers. Those who needed to work relied on a series of casual and part-time jobs or moved from one fixed-term contract to another. Yet others were back in education, hoping to re-establish their careers once they had received Australian degrees. Women, in particular, often chose to give up on their careers, or put them on hold for the time being to concentrate on caregiving roles, as full-time homemakers and mothers. A few opted to leave Australia and return to their home countries, as in Jessie's case.

One participant even opted for onward migration to a third country to fulfill her career aspirations. Kumiko was a spousal entrant from Japan who rejected the idea of becoming a full-time housewife because she considered having a "hard-core job" and being "independent with a full-time job" essential to living a fulfilled life. With an internationally recognized Microsoft certification as an IT engineer under her belt, she set herself an ultimatum of a 2-year job search in Australia. When she was unable to secure employment at her level during that period, she accepted a role with a Swiss multinational company based in Singapore, where she could be "a fantastic bilingual" instead of someone with an English deficit.[30]

These experiences serve to further question the prevailing notion that migrant disadvantage in the labor market results from a deficit in their human capital. Vesna and others had the right kind of human capital. Yet, in Australia, this human capital was systematically devalued: her qualification was not deemed equivalent to an Australian qualification, her work experience was discounted, and her language proficiency was judged against an unrealistic academic standard independent of the communicative requirements of the work. Educational qualifications, professional experience, and language proficiency are widely understood as forms of human capital. The poor labor market outcomes of migrants are then explained as resulting from their deficit in human capital. However, the value of human capital depends on institutional legitimation.[31] As we have shown here, institutional legitimation may be withdrawn in the process of migration. This withdrawal of the institutional recognition of existing human capital brings the widely deplored migrant deficit in human capital into existence. In other words, migrants' human capital deficit may not be something they bring with them to Australia, but something that is made in Australia. This means that the central problem of migrants' labor market disadvantage is an exchange problem: How can their existing forms of human capital be translated into Australian careers more effectively?

The Value of Social Networks

In contrast to the participants discussed so far, Timothy was entirely satisfied with the way his Australian career had turned out to date. We now explore this contrastive case to understand the role of social networks in labor market outcomes. Timothy is a man from South Sudan, who cherished his work for a car parts manufacturer. To understand why Timothy took such pride in his job, we first need to explain the role of work in the local slaughterhouse for Africans in Regional City. Africans in Regional City believed that they were being funneled into abattoir work by being excluded from other employment opportunities.[32] That meat work was the only full-time option available even to tertiary-educated Franklin certainly lends credence to that conviction. As we showed above, Franklin felt a meat-packing job was a waste of his talent and human resources, as it clearly was, and he quit to concentrate on his studies. Despite his disdain for meat work, Franklin was convinced that the abattoir was the only employer in town—a conviction that was shared by every African to whom Vera spoke in that regional hub in rural NSW. However, this conviction is not factually true. In reality, the largest industry by employment in the town is healthcare and social services, followed by retail services, education and training, and public administration and safety.[33] What is true is that the abattoir seemed to provide the only employment that was readily accessible to Africans, irrespective of their qualifications.

Like Franklin, many in this group were clearly overqualified for meat work or, if they were not yet, aspired to an education that would eventually set them on a path to a professional career. This was the case for Eric, who had been a first-year law student in his native Sierra Leone when his family was forced to flee the Sierra Leone Civil War (1991–2002). After more than 10 years as a refugee in Guinea, he was eventually resettled in Australia in his 30s, when his older sister sponsored him. Although a single man, he had obligations and responsibilities toward extended family still in Guinea. The only job he had been able to find that enabled him to meet those obligations and responsibilities was in the local meat works. The fact that his work there constituted an obstacle to his personal desire to pursue an education and to improve himself tore at him:

> I want to pick up a full-time course, I want to take a full-time course. I don't want anything to obstruct me. Even though of late I've heard that they want to start a double shift, morning as well as night shift, if that materializes, it will be my savior. Not only me but all the guys who want to pursue their education. (Eric)

Indeed, pursuing an education was what most tried to do on the side. Venus, also from Sierra Leone, who had worked as an administrative assistant before coming to Australia, explained, "We are just there [=in the meat factory] to make money, that's all. I'm going to TAFE at night."[34] Like Venus, most needed the money, and only those who were relatively free of financial obligations and willing to live an extremely frugal lifestyle could "choose" not to work in the abattoir. One of these was Peter, a Dinka man in his 30s, whose education had been interrupted by the many years he spent fleeing from the war in Sudan. He justified living on a small study subsidy instead of signing up for a meat job by saying, "because you can get a job any time, but education, you can't get."

Franklin, Eric, Venus, and Peter all felt forced into meat work for financial reasons. They imagined further education—vocational training or university study—as an avenue away from work in the slaughterhouse. However, further education and study were not the pathway taken by the only participant in Regional City who was in full-time employment outside the abattoir. In contrast to participants with far higher levels of formal education, professional experience, and English-language proficiency, Timothy, an outgoing young man in his late 20s, in fact, seemed like an ideal candidate for meat work. With only 4 years of primary school, limited English, and no aspirations for further education or a professional career, this healthy, able-bodied man is the ideal laborer. As the breadwinner for a young family, he applied to and was hired by the abattoir almost immediately upon arrival in Australia. Almost immediately, too, he started to scheme how to leave his brand-new "3D job" (*d*irty, *d*angerous, and *d*ifficult).[35] Like many Bari people, who revere cattle, he considered working in a slaughterhouse "the worst job possible."[36] However, his reasons for seeking a way out were not merely, or even predominantly, cultural. Rather, they were similar to those of the other Africans: he found the job exploitative; he considered it a dead end without opportunities to improve his English, and to find a viable pathway into Australian society; and he was fully alive to the racism implicit in the fact that meat work was the only employment option readily open to Africans.

So how did Timothy manage to escape from the abattoir and land his factory dream job? A conversation about racism provided Timothy with a ticket out of the slaughterhouse. As he recounts it, one of his White Australian neighbors accosted him one day and asked why Africans did not work and relied on welfare. That Africans are "dole bludgers" and "welfare cheats" is a racist stereotype familiar in Australia and other Western countries.[37] Timothy recognized the racism inherent in the question, but instead of hunkering down, he set about educating his neighbor and appealed to his sense of a fair go.[38] He told his neighbor how Africans never received a call back for an interview, no matter how many applications they put in, and contrasted this with the practice of the abattoir: "If you apply with them, they call you immediately. Why?" Timothy's neighbor, a foreman with a car parts manufacturer, took him at his word. A few days after the conversation, he showed up at Timothy's door with an application form and recommended him to his factory, where they have been colleagues since. In other words, it was a chance encounter that provided Timothy with the right contact that enabled him to fulfill his employment aspiration.

As we have shown throughout this chapter, migrants' linguistic and human capital deficit is a discursive construction that is as much a product of Australian society as it is something that is inherent to individual migrants. However, there is something that most newcomers truly lack: the social capital that opens doors. As is often the case for new migrants, the primary social networks of most of our participants were with other migrants, often from the same national and/or ethnic background.[39] Social networks with other migrants are valuable, too, of course. Much-needed advice and useful contacts may be passed on that are helpful in finding work. However, unlike Timothy's non-migrant foreman neighbor, other migrants are less likely to be in gatekeeping positions themselves. Furthermore, having to rely only on fellow migrants means that gaps in cultural capital, or even misinformation that may limit access to better jobs, may also be shared.[40] Several participants told us of stories that circulated in their communities and served to hold them back. Irrespective of truth value, we already encountered one such limiting story in Michiko's case, who believed there was no point applying for jobs because she thought that Asian women would not be hired by Australian companies anyway. Daisy, a trained secretary from Kenya who had arrived in Australia on a tourist visa and needed to find a job to be allowed to stay on, shared a similar story. She was told by other Africans that there are no Africans working in offices in Australia and that she should seek work in aged care instead. However, in contrast to Michiko, Daisy rejected the advice that was circulating in her social network:

> And when I came here, I was being told- I used to check on the local newspaper a lot. I could see a lot of jobs I can do, because I'm a secretary by profession.

> And I remember my friend telling me, don't waste your time, you cannot get a job in an office. This country is racist. They can never give an African an office job. I didn't know much about the people, but I never judged people because of other people. I just said this is the job I'm gonna do. But if worse comes to worst, I can still do the nursing job. (Daisy)

Daisy was indeed successful and eventually found administrative work in the public service. She was uneasy about some members of her community, who she believed had been trying to mislead her. However, we should not be too hasty to fault migrant communities. Knowledge about pathways to work and the ability to facilitate such pathways is clearly unequally distributed. New and emerging communities, such as those from African countries, will have less social capital than long-established communities. Furthermore, as we have shown in this chapter, such pathways do not necessarily even exist. The disconnects between migrants' pre- and post-migration employment trajectories are in many cases impossible to bridge by the individual job seeker on their own. Where high-value social networks are accessible, finding decent work and re-establishing a career may not be so difficult, as Timothy's example has shown. The establishment of new social networks is inextricably tied to language, as we will discuss in the next chapter.

4
"Our Life Is Becoming Colorful Again"
Finding a Voice in a New Language

Facing the Growing Pains

Five years after his ghastly early days in Darwin, where we left him in Chapter 2, Lou bore little resemblance to his younger self. He was now outgoing, charming, exuberant, and full of confidence. After graduating from his Master of Business Development (MBD) program, he moved from Darwin to Sydney, obtained permanent residency, and embarked on a career. Things were going well, too, in his personal life. He had fallen in love with an Anglo-Australian man, they had recently moved in together, and enjoyed their openly gay lifestyle in a city widely known for being gay-friendly.[1] He now spoke fluent English, with a pronounced Australian accent, and his speech was peppered with slang expressions and swear words—linguistic features highly prized in Australian English.[2] When Ingrid first met him, her research focus was on adult language learners who were passing for a native speaker, and she noted excitedly in her research diary that he was "indistinguishable from a native speaker."[3]

How had this remarkable transformation come about?

For Lou, the humiliation he had felt on that first day in Australia when he was sleeping rough on the streets of Darwin provided strong motivation:

> I want to learn English. I want to express myself. And I want to let you guys know, "I'm from China alright." But doesn't necessarily mean, all Chinese people are really like the people you see on TV. "I'm from Shanghai!" Even better than Sydney. So you better be careful! [spoken laughingly] I have to learn English. So all these- like these impulses. Everything, every day. I was just- I was so keen to learn, you know, how to swear. (Lou)

The 1.5 years of his university studies had provided him with few opportunities to act on that motivation.[4] He found the course content boring but easy to pass. University life was largely restricted to attending lectures and provided little opportunity for interaction. His social circle consisted almost entirely of other Chinese students. He also took a casual job as a receptionist in a small hotel

Life in a New Language. Ingrid Piller, Donna Butorac, Emily Farrell, Loy Lising, Shiva Motaghi-Tabari, and Vera Williams Tetteh, Oxford University Press. © Oxford University Press 2024. DOI: 10.1093/oso/9780190084288.003.0004

where he worked the night shift. This customer-facing role provided Lou with his first real opportunity to interact in English:

> I had to be awake for twelve hours. Everyday six p.m. until six a.m. So every, every, night, I'll be coming in. [. . .] Aboriginals were very nice to me. They are- they were my major clients, so I had to speak in- speak English to them. Of course we had overseas erm tourists coming in at 4 o'clock in the morning. Some people from Netherland, some people from Paris. Erm some people from rural country. Speak really ocker.[5] "G'day mate." That kind of thing. So at that time I improved my English a little bit. Not very strongly. (Lou)

After graduating, Lou did not want to return to China, where homosexuality was only decriminalized in 1997 and negative attitudes toward same-sex relationships persist.[6] Nor did he want to stay in Darwin, which he considered a backwater. So he decided to move to Australia's largest city, Sydney, "like an idiot." He did not know anyone there, which made his move both "very brave" but also "very blind." His "blindness" meant that he had to proceed by trial and error when it came to meeting the necessities of life, such as finding accommodation and a job. The first room he rented turned out to be a disaster:

> I lived in Redfern.[7] The first stop. The reason being is no one told me Redfern was a very dangerous place. Cause I didn't know anyone. No one. So I just looked. "Oh its cheap. Sixty bucks. Oh good." I just moved in. But you know the people who I lived with? They were- one of them was drug dealer, the other one was a prostitute. The other two, unemployed. I was like an alien came- coming to this country. Like a little naïve, like innocent. So was very stressful. (Lou)

His job search also turned out to be full of pitfalls. Despite his MBD degree, he discovered that, without local experience, "you can't get a decent job."[8] So he first accepted a role as a bar attendant in a restaurant where "the people were very nasty" and he was subjected to bullying and racist abuse. His next job was as a packaging worker in a warehouse without any opportunity to meet new people and interact with anyone, as the job involved "just standing there nine hours continuously." In his third job, he "got very lucky" because the receptionist role in a major centrally located hotel provided "a good chance for me to practice English." However, after being harassed by a "lying and cheating" co-worker, he was back at square one again and he responded to a newspaper ad for a sales representative. The ad mentioned Top Telco, one of Australia's main telecommunications providers, and he assumed that would be the employer, not realizing that he was dealing with a subcontractor. The other thing he did not realize was that the position was commission-based, and he would only get paid for actual sales. His job was to door-knock in residential neighborhoods and try to persuade residents to switch their phone line from one provider to another. In his first week, he scored four successes, well short of the required 20 minimum to get paid. Lou recalled how lost he felt: "First of all, I didn't understand a single word these sales reps talking about. [. . .] I didn't know until later. I don't know- didn't know anything about Australia. Honestly, I was like isolated. Totally irrelevant to this country."

Without any support, Lou was at his wit's end and considered returning to China. He confided in his team leader, a Greek man:

> I said to him, I said, "Uh sorry. I- I really can't do it." "I miss my mum." [in a whining childish voice] "I don't need this- this things anymore. I'm sorry. I can't. I don't need it. I want to go home." And he was very patient. He said erm, "Uh I know. I started as a sales rep as well. I know every- all the feeling you have and- just don't take personally this- all this shits from people, from customers, right? Who refuse you. Who rude sometimes. They slam door on your face, everything. Just- just ignore them. Because they're not important in your life. Don't take it personally. Think about money. When you reach one goal, one customer, you're much closer to your- you know twenty sales target." So he basically comfort me, and he showed me how he did it. He took me to some streets and knocked the door. He basically gave live presentation, how to sell things. Then erm I thought, I have no choice, I have to talk. I just followed him. Second week I did twenty-five. That was a miracle! I was very lucky. It was lucky. (Lou)

Once Lou had mastered the art of door-knocking, he sought out a similar role in a call-center, not only because it was less physically taxing, but also because he wanted to practice his telephone skills. On the strength of these experiences and his bilingual skills in Chinese, he was soon after hired as a customer service officer by a mortgage broker, where he finally felt he was building his career. The role was no longer in sales but was focused on existing customers who needed help with managing their repayments, interest, and mortgage variations. From there, in a major career move, he started to work as an investment broker for one of Australia's major banks. Lou took each of these roles not only as work, but also as learning opportunities to improve himself and his English. These learning opportunities had come in the form of interactions with customers, co-workers, and supervisors. For instance, he dramatized for us what he had learned during his door-knocking job:

> The sales representative job really helped me, right? You knock the door, people are like, "I was in the middle of dinner. Why did you knock on the door?" [grumpy voice] "Uh, sorry sir!" [exaggerated apologetic tone; audience

> laughter] So you have to be bold! "So sorry sir. I'm from Top Telco, and my name is Lou, and I'm really happy to give you some good news about Top Telco!" [more audience laughter] Go, go, go! You just spiel on, every day. Like I said, it's growing pains. You have to open your heart to other people. Don't think it's a guilt. It's nothing wrong. Just speak some other language. If today you can't speak well, maybe tomorrow you can speak better. But today, just learn. (Lou)

This is just one example of Lou's amazing ability to retell and dramatize interactions and to then draw a lesson from each interaction he had experienced. He re-enacted interactions with all kinds of different people he had met in Australia: "Some were very nasty, some were very nice. Some were very pushy, and some were very tedious. Some are very stupid, some are very stubborn. Some were very funny." Over the years, he had gained an exceptional street-savviness. In addition to his own interactional experiences, he also consciously modeled his speech on that of others. This included not only real-life models like his Greek supervisor who had given him a demo in door-knocking, but also interactions in the media. Lou avidly watched TV and movies, always on the lookout for model conversations. He was particularly invested in two Australian soap operas, *Neighbours* and *Home and Away*.[9] He told us how he would discuss scenes and characters from these shows with his partner, and how they would dissect them linguistically and psychologically, so that he could "learn how to get around, not piss people off, but how to get around and ease them. But at the same time protect yourself. That's everything to do with your English skill." Over the course of 5 years, Lou's initial "blindness" had given way to "such natural and magical beautiful sense of living." He saw his personal and linguistic growth as inextricably linked, and almost reveled in the growing pains that had effected this transformation: "If you wanna learn English, you have to be ready to face all the challenges. To face all the pain, and to face all frustration. Otherwise, you can never grow. Just like the growing pains, same thing."

The language of pain, struggle, hardship, and suffering echoes throughout our data in descriptions of English-language learning in Australia. "*Every day is a struggle for me*," as Bernardo, an IT technician from the Philippines said. However, the problem is not purely linguistic. Language-learning difficulties are inextricably intertwined with the challenges of building a new life, settling in a new place, forging careers, sustaining family, making friends, and chasing dreams. When a small linguistic error—such as mistaking a dodgy enterprise that is a borderline scam operation for a secure job at Top Telco—can have big consequences, migrants' well-being hinges on their linguistic dexterity. Each interaction is a language-practice opportunity and a language test with material and emotional repercussions. The inescapable remedy to the initial language shocks we explored in Chapter 2 is more interactions. In this chapter, we explore how naturalistic language learning through interaction unfolded for our participants. Their interactions both shaped and were shaped by their settlement trajectories. To communicate, adult migrants must find interlocutors, they must establish common ground, they must deal with misunderstandings, and they must manage negative feelings of anxiety and shame.

Making Friends and Finding Common Ground

Naturalistic language learning through immersion is often imagined as the high road to adult language learning. Being surrounded by the target language is widely believed to mimic child language learning most closely and to result in almost effortless language learning as the new language is soaked up through interaction. Research does not corroborate this rosy view, and language-learning experiences in naturalistic settings and the quality and frequency of interactions in the target language have been found to vary enormously.[10] Prior to migration, many of our participants had shared the belief that their English would improve quickly and dramatically once they would be—as they imagined it—surrounded by supportive and chatty native speakers. As a teenager in Tokyo, Yumiko, for instance, had developed a crush on the actor Tom Cruise, when she watched the film *Top Gun*.[11] Her dream was to go abroad and interact in English with people "who looked like him." Yumiko was not the only participant who imagined interactions with celebrities and other attractive, engaging, and cool interlocutors in whose company they would quickly become fluent.[12] Bijan from Iran, for example, had dreamed of a busy "social life" where he would go to parties often, "*take holiday trips with Australians, and things like these*."

The anticipated interactional pleasures and accompanying positive self-identity with their associated language-learning benefits were rare for participants. Part of the problem was that the imagined interlocutors were not easy to come by. This may sound like stating the obvious when it comes to meeting attractive celebrities, delightful partygoers, or appealing fellow tourists. However, before we blame participants for being naïve, we must consider who our most sustained, engaging, and supportive interlocutors are, and how and when we met them.

The people all of us communicate with the most are either family members or friends.[13] Who these are is determined relatively early in life. To begin with, members of the birth family, such as parents and siblings, are a given and hardly change over the life-course.[14] Selection of romantic partners for the formation of a new family is a major opportunity to extend one's social circle. Partner selection mostly takes place in late adolescence and early adulthood. In terms of interactional opportunities in migration, this creates a clear difference between participants who migrated with spouses and those who married into an Australian family. Those who arrived as a family unit generally maintained the origin language as their home language, as we show in Chapter 5. Their social circles were also usually less diverse and more likely to be restricted to people from the same ethnic and/or national background. This had consequences for their interactional opportunities, as Katja and Nicolas, a couple from Poland, observed, when they compared their own English-language learning to that of some of their friends who were married to Australians. Those married to Australians had picked up the language much faster, they believed, because they had many more language-practice opportunities.

Friendship circles are more open, and membership in those circles is more varied than family, but selection mechanisms differ across the life span. Childhood and adolescent friendships usually arise from joint educational experiences and may last a lifetime. For adults, it becomes harder to form new friendships, and any new friends tend to be sourced from among co-workers. Such friendships do not always endure after the end of the joint work relationship. Even later in life, neighbors and voluntary groups become the main sources of new friends. These patterns create obvious difficulties for adult migrants, as childhood and adolescent friendships have been formed in the old country, are established in the first language, and have usually been left behind. Jaime from Chile, who arrived in Australia shortly after he had completed high school, illustrated this pattern when he lamented: "When you come to a different country, you lose all your friends. You lose all your life. Like I think when we are fifteen, sixteen, you start making friends. And friends for life. That's what I missed."

The main source for new friendships in adulthood is through work. Yet, for migrants, opportunities to make new friends at work may be limited due to the employment difficulties we described in Chapter 3. Migrants' opportunities to make new friends at work may be further curtailed by patterns of homophily, the preference to make friends with people who are like oneself. Homophily has been found to be particularly pronounced in mid-life.[15] This means that established residents simply may not be particularly interested in forming relationships with newcomers, as Verena from Austria observed when she mused about her small social circle in Australia. Although she was actively looking both for a partner and for friends, she felt that Australians of a similar age to her, in their 30s, simply were not open to meeting new people or exploring new activities other than sports. An avid traveler with broad cultural interests in theater, opera, and books, she could not find an interlocutor to go beyond "the basic, you know, chit chat, small talk."

In some cases, this resulted in patterns of the near-complete absence of interlocutors with whom participants could speak English. Suda, a PhD student from Thailand, for instance, reckoned that she had had more opportunities to practice English back home in Bangkok than in Sydney. In Bangkok, she had spoken English at university as her department had instituted an "English Only" policy for members to create an artificial immersion environment. She had also had regular opportunities to speak English in her job as a tourist guide. In Sydney, all that changed. At university, the main opportunity to interact in English was her monthly meeting with her PhD supervisor. Interactions with fellow students were rare. Outside university, she worked two jobs to earn some money. One was delivering newspapers in the small hours of the morning. This was lonely work and, other than receiving brief instructions from her employer, was conducted in silence.[16] That employer was the only "Australian" contact in her life whom she could think of, and she had trouble understanding her accent: "She says 'piper, piper' instead of paper that I'm familiar with. Something like that. I don't know." Her other job was as a delivery driver for a Thai restaurant, where all her co-workers and her boss were Thai, and where her customer interactions were minimal. Suda also shared a flat with three other Thai women. The disappointing result of all these arrangements was that she lived in Sydney but had "no chance to practice English."

Suda, who projected an outgoing, loud, and gregarious personality in our meetings, was not the only participant who was pained by a lack of interlocutors. Some of the most isolated individuals among our participants were, in fact, PhD students.[17] For instance, when Ingrid asked Wang, an Economics PhD student from China, to draw a network diagram to identify all his main contacts and the language he used with them, he refused. He said the exercise was pointless because "I only live with my dog. Office, room, read papers. I seldom speak with others. No opportunities." Knowing that Wang shared a house with another participant, Gesang, a fellow PhD student from Indonesia, Ingrid pressed on to ask him about his relationship with Gesang:

> I live with him. Yeah. We live in a townhouse. We have our own bedroom. But we share the living room and kitchen. Sometimes we talk with each other. But not so much. Only the living matters. . . . I- erm I like chatting with Gesang about the political environment, the history of Indonesia. And the history of China. Yeah. And that's useful. But- but not very often. (Wang)

Wang's explanation suggests two other issues that restricted participants' interactional opportunities. Although he patently interacted with Gesang in English, Wang discounted him as a legitimate interlocutor. He also discounted the "living matters" they spoke about as legitimate conversation topics. Wang is no exception. At least initially, many participants considered native English-speaking White Australians as desirable interlocutors while discounting migrants like themselves. Cyrus, for instance, explicitly identified "Chinese" and "Asian" people as undesirable English-language interlocutors:

> *After all a part of language learning is imitation. People who come here do not wish to learn the grammar. They imitate. Now if they imitate the right people, well, their language will improve. However, if they are in a* community, *for instance they are with* Chinese *people, or with* Asians, *or they are in a* community *in which they are involved with the language with people other than* native *speakers, their language will develop like theirs.* (Cyrus)

The language ideologies of Wang and Cyrus—that some ways of speaking are better than others and some speakers are better than others—led them to discount or even forgo valuable language-practice opportunities with people whom they did not consider legitimate English speakers and, hence, undesirable interlocutors.[18] Coupled with their inability to find native-speaker interlocutors, these language ideologies could produce a sense of failure and shame. Suda, for instance, whom we saw above painting a picture of living in an almost exclusively Thai-language world in Sydney, also told us about a lively friendship group with whom she spoke in English on their regular nights out. Still, she only mentioned these friends after repeated probing and in a way as if she were confessing to a shameful secret: "I make friends with Asians. The whole time! [spoken embarrassed-laughingly] I- I didn't mean to, but it just happens. Hong Kong, people from Hong Kong. . . . Jenny is from New Zealand, but she's like Chinese national [regretful laugh]."

Participants desired to interact with Anglo-Australians, yet also felt intimidated by them. Qasem, for instance, told us how conflicted he felt about interacting with other parents in his daughter's primary school:

> *They have been together for years, from way back. So they have their own* community. *Entering the* community *is not easy. When I go there* [=school grounds where parents hang out around drop off and pick up times], *sometimes I cannot find anyone to talk to* [except other Iranians]. *Sometimes you don't feel so good about it. When you go and see how everyone is being together. And then you go there. And you have to go there, and wait until our daughter comes out, and then pick her up, and bring her back home. Well, you won't like it, you know. You would like to be with them, to talk, to laugh, and to chat.* (Qasem)

Qasem did not blame the other parents for excluding him. In fact, he believed that "*they do their best to include us.*" The problem, he felt, was a lack of common ground:

> *We don't know what they think. We can't know, like, if I now ask about that thing, if I now say that word, if I now behave that way, how would they judge me? It is so difficult until the ice is broken, you know? It takes time, and it's not good. I mean you don't have good feelings. You would like to talk, and laugh with everyone, when you go somewhere.* (Qasem)

Qasem was not alone in perceiving himself as a deficient interlocutor. Diba confessed, "*I feel like I am so* boring" to fellow parents in her daughter's school. While English-language proficiency was a part of the deficiency participants attributed to themselves, the issue ran deeper and related to knowing not only how to say something, but also what to say. Elham summed up the problem: "*Sometimes I think, like, what am I supposed to do and say*?" Another participant from Iran, Daryoush, also lamented his "*inability to* socialize" because he did not know how to "*initiate the conversation*." Some attributed that inability to a lack of historical knowledge:

> *Still, I don't have the* skills *for daily communication. And that is related to so many things. To historical* backgrounds. *For instance, within the past fifty years what has happened in this country? How do I* refer *something to the past?* (Amin)

The loss of past and future is, in fact, a common trope in migrant autobiographies. The migrant loses access to their previous history as stories become untellable in a different environment without gaining a connection to the stories of their new environment. Former topics and identities become meaningless, and topics and identity options valued in the new environment may be neither understood nor appealing.[19]

Intercultural communication problems arose not only if participants did not know what to say, but also if they knew what they were expected to say but did not wish to comply. Maria from Brazil, for instance, recounted how she had offended an English teacher in her AMEP class. The topic of the lesson had been "real life responding sympathetically," and the teacher had asked students to role-play what they would say to "a friend who is in tears at the end of a sad film." Maria had responded, "Well, for me, I will say, 'Come on. Pull yourself together.'" The teacher was horrified and asked her to come up with a more sympathetic response. Maria stood her ground and said that she did not wish to "pretend or faking." To Maria, the tears were caused by film effects such as the soundtrack, and thus not a cause for sympathy but for vicarious embarrassment. She considered the tears of the hypothetical moviegoer to be "pathetic" in comparison to the real suffering she had seen in her life.

Dealing with Misunderstandings and Managing Emotions

Participants' struggles with making friends and finding common ground in conversation caused them frustration, nervousness, anxiety, and even depression. These negative emotional states sometimes made it more difficult for them to achieve their interactional goals. Even after a quarter century in Australia, Jaime, for instance, confided: "When I meet someone new, I become really nervous and, you know, just erm become deaf. Because they're talking to you, and you go, 'What was that?'" Agatha from Georgia also described long-term negative effects of the initial language shock she had experienced:

> Australian English, it was completely, like alien to me. And I developed a kind of phobia for- for quite a long time. Probably for a couple of years, if not more. I was scared to go out by myself. I couldn't. Cause I was just completely scared. I would never answer the telephone. Because it was just so embarrassing, you know, that I couldn't understand. [...] because I developed this phobia, eventually it affected my speech as well. I became so concerned, with my English, that even my speaking English, became almost like- you know, stumbling. I couldn't speak properly. I would again start losing words, and erm you know, even my pronunciation would become- my accent would become stronger. (Agatha)

Agatha had worked as a literary translator back home and had translated books from English, French, and Georgian into Russian. When her teenage daughter decided to migrate to Australia in 1990, after the fall of the Soviet Union, Agatha joined her for what she thought would be a short visit. The visit turned into a permanent move when she fell in love with an Australian man. To her dismay, she discovered that employment opportunities for literary translators are minuscule in Australia and nonexistent for those working into Russian. This means that migration transformed Agatha in two ways. First, she was transformed from a sophisticated multilingual who was "all about languages" in an environment where languages were valued as indicators of education and high culture into a deficient speaker of English in a monolingual environment where English is widely regarded as the only language that matters.[20] Second, she was transformed from a working woman who earned her own income into a housewife. Within her reduced sphere of influence, she acted confidently, as was evident from her surprised reaction when asked how she had communicated with her husband during her years of English phobia: "Oh. At home it was not a problem. It's only with the strangers that I had problem."

Language anxiety is usually taken to be a psychological problem, where poor language-learning outcomes are both the cause and result of negative emotions. As a psychological problem, suggested solutions are typically focused on the individual, too, and include specific teaching strategies and behavioral modifications.[21] Agatha did not see her phobia as something that could be solved by language teachers or therapists. What she needed was to get back to work and find a profession where her passion for languages would be valued. By the time we met her, she had long since taken the bull by the horns, having undertaken a postgraduate degree in linguistics and reinventing herself as an English-language teacher. With the reinvention of her public self, her phobia of interacting in English had disappeared, too.

Agatha's phobia had included answering the phone. Speaking on the phone was, in fact, many participants' greatest interactional fear. Lena from Russia provides another example:

> Before, I could not come to the phone. Because I knew if I speak with a person, just face to face, I can understand some emotion or something. If I speak on the phone, I understand only a quarter of their talking. Yes, I am sweating when I- [laughs] ... now I can take a phone and answer, so it's ok. (Lena)

Many reported avoidance strategies, such as not answering the phone or getting another household member to make unavoidable calls. Unavoidable calls included interactions with banks, insurance companies, and some government agencies. With these, a popular avoidance strategy was to attend in person rather than speak on the phone, even if it was much more time-consuming and inconvenient. Face-to-face encounters made it easier to negotiate meaning as paralinguistic cues and material props could be used to support linguistic skills in the pursuit of interactional goals.[22] Paulina, for instance, developed a routine that allowed her to minimize interactional problems when she was sending remittances back to the Philippines:

> *I just say,* "Can I withdraw the, saving, for my savings in . . . my ATM card." *That's all I say. Then the teller will ask who I'm sending the money to. And that's when I simply hand her the details. I just hand it over to her.* (Paulina)

Attending in person and being well prepared does not necessarily guarantee a successful outcome, though. Difficulties can arise when an interaction takes an unexpected turn, as happened to Maria when she was overcharged on a video rental. To complain, Maria needed the receipt as a prop so that she could point to the amount that was due, show the change she had received, and argue her case with reference to this evidence. However, the cashier was distracted and had not given her a receipt. In the heat of the moment, Maria could not remember the word for "receipt" and so came up with "sheet" as an alternative word. If you do not distinguish between long and short vowels, as is common for some second-language speakers, "sheet" can sound like "shit," so what she said to the cashier was "You don't give me a shit." Instead of the desired refund, this further complicated the situation. Maria felt "so angry inside."

Interactions with Centrelink, Australia's welfare office and the central agency for dispensing social security payments, could be particularly fraught. The paperwork was perceived as confusing and intimidating by some participants. Nina from Sierra Leone, for instance, referred to written communications she received from Centrelink as "threat letters." These stressed her out so much that she opted to give up her studies prior to graduation and to take a factory job solely so that she would no longer have to deal with the Centrelink communication: "So I decided even like leaving school, and just continuing to work. So like I won't get any threat letters. Because you come for peace, you don't need any other thing. So I looked for a factory job." That Nina was not alone in her perception can be gleaned from the fact that, after a wave of suicides by welfare recipients, a Royal Commission was set up in 2022 to investigate the use of automated communication by Centrelink and the deliberate withholding of information from clients. The report found that Centrelink communications in the 2010s might have reinforced stigma and shame for individual clients. It recommended, inter alia, to "facilitate[e] easy and efficient engagement with options of online, in person and telephone communication which is sensitive to the particular circumstances of the customer cohort."[23] In 2008, when the Royal Commission was still well into the future, Serena from Sudan blamed herself for her struggles to communicate with Centrelink:

> I'm trying, I'm trying my best. But it was hard for me because everywhere. I have to go to Centrelink, and I have to fill form. And sometimes I just take the form without filling, and we just go and talk there. But sometimes I don't understand the letter, they- you know, they send to me. And I have to go back. So sometimes you just talk, and sometimes they don't understand what you're saying. So they have to say, "What? I don't understanding. I don't get you." So you have to explain it more, more . . . and sometimes I get really ashamed by myself. "Why I don't know this?" (Serena)

Like Serena, many participants blamed themselves for any communication problems, even if the other person made no attempt to "*stop for you*," as Goudarz put it. His vision of fair communication was that interlocutors "*ensure that you reach them. Then you continue alongside each other.*" Unfortunately, that happened rarely, and mostly, "*they are running, and you have to run after them.*" The point Goudarz makes so eloquently is that interlocutors must share the communicative burden to ensure success. When misunderstandings occur in communication, it is rarely only the fault of one person. Conversation proceeds like a dance, where speakers need to work to make themselves understood; listeners need to work to understand what is said; and these roles are continuously passed back and forth. However, we know from intercultural communication research that this shared dance often breaks down in communication between speakers who are believed to have different levels of legitimacy.[24] In such cases, more powerful speakers often opt out of sharing the communicative burden in interactions. Instead, they place the responsibility for ensuring communicative success exclusively on the shoulders of less powerful speakers, who are then faced with a double handicap: despite having fewer linguistic resources at their disposal, they must shoulder more of the communicative burden with uncooperative interlocutors. As both parties believe this insidious pattern to be legitimate, migrant speakers also have to deal with the emotional fallout of misunderstandings in the form of embarrassment and shame.[25]

Shame at their failure to understand kept some participants from seeking clarification. Maria, for instance, told us, "Sometime when I didn't understand, I keep quiet. I not say, 'I don't understand.' I don't know why I do that, but I feel embarrassing." Shame could be triggered by even the most innocuous misunderstandings. Elizabeth from Ghana, for instance, told us of a small misunderstanding where she had taken the phrase "Hang on!" to mean "Hang up!" As a result, she abruptly put down the receiver and ended a telephone conversation with a volunteer English tutor in mid-sentence.[26] When the misunderstanding was clarified during a call-back, Elizabeth's immediate reaction was to feel "*tedious, frustrated, and ashamed.*"

Gaining Recognition

Sometime after the "hang on/hang up" misunderstanding that had caused Elizabeth so much grief, she confided her desperation at "*not speaking English*" and "*not understanding*" to her tutor, Margaret. Margaret's response marked a turning point in Elizabeth's language-learning trajectory:

> *She said you are a beautiful girl, and very brave. There is nothing wrong if you don't understand English. It's not your language. You speak another language. And you came here by yourself, to this country. Look at me! I don't even have a passport. I have never been out of my country. I don't know a word in your language. Don't be ashamed! One day you will speak it, it is not your language.* (Elizabeth)

The response acknowledges Elizabeth's struggles as a newcomer and a language learner and recognizes the courage it takes to embark on such a journey. It provided Elizabeth with an alternative way of seeing herself and her English:

> *So I said to myself, yes! It is not my language! It is someone else's language. So what does it matter if I don't speak it well? It doesn't matter at all. I shouldn't feel ashamed. I will try to speak it. This is different here. The white people don't laugh at you when you make mistakes. It is not like Ghana where they laugh at your English.* (Elizabeth)

Margaret provided Elizabeth with two important resources. First, she offered language-practice opportunities. This included her regular phone calls to check in for a chat. Additionally, Margaret took Elizabeth to go shopping and "*to go places*." This provided further language-practice opportunities and allowed Elizabeth to gain confidence in public spaces, something many participants initially struggled with, as we have seen throughout this chapter. Second, Margaret validated Elizabeth as a legitimate speaker of English whose language was neither remarkable nor cause for shame. In short, Margaret helped Elizabeth to restore her confidence and provided her with a way into her new society.[27]

Like Elizabeth, many of our participants had a turning-point narrative about their language learning.[28] These were stories of a memorable event that had provided them with an opportunity to interact in English as equals and that had boosted their confidence. The protagonists in these validation stories were family members, housemates, church members, language teachers, fellow migrants, colleagues, and strangers. A validating encounter early after arrival could change participants' language-learning trajectories, as it did for Nahid, who regained her confidence in her English on her third day in Australia:

> *I met an older Australian couple in the park. They were locals. They realized I was upset. They asked me how long I'd been here. I said three days. Then they started talking to me, but they spoke slowly, at least I think they did. They said, "No, your English is very good. You have no problem at all. Although you've only been here for three days, you are speaking with us, and we understand you. Why have you lost your confidence?" This was a very good encounter.* (Nahid)

Farah, a network engineer from Iran, similarly described how she felt a sense of empowerment early in her settlement when she attended an industry conference, where she had the opportunity to interact with professional leaders in her field. This changed her perception of Australian IT professionals from intimidating figures to approachable colleagues. The realization invigorated her job search.

> *Attending the conference raised my self-confidence a lot. Because the people that were there, they were all like* CIO *or* CEO. *Or they were like, senior Australian people. Very charismatic. So when I spoke to them about their jobs, and what their company was about, what services they provided, it gave me a lot of confidence to be able to do that. That these are the people! And when I went for the* interview, *I was not shaking in my boots anymore.* (Farah)

Some participants experienced a sense of recognition and validation through relatively fleeting encounters, such as Nahid and Farah. For others, this was a longer process, and resulted from the experience of escaping a dangerous situation not only unharmed, but with greater linguistic skills. This was the experience of Alexa, who accidentally moved into a drug house in Melbourne: "I moved into a house where everyone was doing hard drugs. Everyone. So speed, heroin, just full on. You know selling them, consuming them." The housemates had even lied to her when they leased her a room because there actually was no vacant room in the house. Alexa had to sleep in the garage. Despite these difficult circumstances, Alexa learned a lot from her co-tenants: "I actually made friends with two of the guys, and I had these really weird experiences in that house. I felt miserable but a lot of the time I actually also had fun with that element of the unexpected." Leaving that situation proved difficult, and Alexa proudly told us how she managed the challenge:

> The day before I moved out, Steve, who was the sort of- he ran the whole show. Said to me, "It's not because of the drug situation, is it?" And I said, "Oh no. No!" [laughs] "Nothing to do with that." [spoken laughingly] And he's like, "It's not because Johnny's catatonic? And he was in hospital for a whole year? And he's schizophrenic. And he doesn't talk to anyone but you. Is it?" [deep threatening male voice] "No! No! No, Steve! Nothing to do with that!" [. . .] So I moved out of there, and then it all started rolling. [. . .] It wasn't just that my English had improved but [. . .] I felt quite confident with things and then, things started happening. I met someone else and that really helped because I met many people. So then I was suddenly surrounded by Australians and I thought that was really good. (Alexa)

Along with turning-point interactions, time in Australia was a major factor that provided participants with a sense that their English had become normal and natural. After 15 years in the country, Julio, for example, explained:

> The first year was really, really bad. Like trying to- when you speak, like for me, when I speak English, the sounds of your own voice are different. And so you don't sound natural. [. . .] I think the first two years. I would say the first two

> years were the more- were the more difficult. And after that it just became sort of- part of myself. I would say the first two years, really difficult. And then, this is about the second year, and from there on, it's just, you know, you don't have to think that much in English. It comes more naturally. (Julio)

Some participants could not identify a particular turning point in their English-language interactions. Marlene, for instance, told us how her English had improved imperceptibly. She sometimes went away from a conversation surprised and thinking to herself, "Ooh-ooh, I used that new word." Such little triumphs gave her confidence and she felt she was no longer "really nervous when we're sitting with a new group of young people our age." Previously, on such occasions she had felt that "everyone looks at you and thinks, 'Ooh, the foreigner's saying something.'"

Over time, participants also came to realize that Australia is diverse, and that Anglo-Australians are not the only legitimate interlocutors. For some, the realization that there are many ways of speaking English in Australia provided an important boost to their confidence. For Anna, this realization came in the AMEP, where she was surrounded by other new arrivals and English-language learners:

> Because if you don't have a- . . . that basic confident, you know, you will just- you will feel isolated. But when you start to meet people, you know, and talk with them, and having new friends, you know. It's different, you know, and especially here [=AMEP], you can find, erm so many people. Similar like you are, you know, but they are just from another country, you know. And you just feel like, "Oh, there is people like me!" They don't know English so well, you know, and they can live here. (Anna)

Jaime liked to reflect on the linguistic and cultural characteristics of each of his many workplaces. At one job, "the culture was Yugoslav," at another "Turkey," at yet another "Greeks and Italian." As a result, Jaime realized that perfecting his English was not a priority. What was a priority was "to accommodate the other guys. The way you speak. You have to transform your image." In Jaime's estimation, no one at work would understand him "when you talk to them properly." His advice was to "get used to the slang of the place. Put the swear word at the end of the sentence." Realizing that "there's a lot of people, they don't speak very good English, and they've been here forty years," assured him that he, too, fit right in.

We started this chapter with the story of Lou, who metaphorically described his linguistic and personal journey of interacting in English as one from blindness to vision. He was not the only one to use this metaphor. Lena from Russia also noticed how her life was "becoming colorful again." Initially, everything seemed painted with a broad brush, as she could only grasp the topic of an interaction. Over time, as she regained her ability to understand and express more and more details and nuances, the canvas of her new life started to fill in with the details. The details of Australian life that participants learned to see over time were not always beautiful, as we will show in Chapter 6. However, with time, all participants found or forged a space—sometimes large, sometimes small—for themselves from which they could speak.

5

"This Is All for Our Children, for Their Future"

Doing Family in a New Language

Families on the Move

From the day they were born until the day she left Manila for Tiny Town, Ellen had never spent a night away from her children. Tiny Town is a small settlement in rural Queensland with a population of about 2,000. Tiny Town is also home to the slaughterhouse of one of Australia's largest beef exporters, Big Beef. Big Beef recruits virtually all its butchers from the Philippines on temporary skilled visas. One of them was Ellen's husband, Fernando, who in 2006 was hired by a Big Beef recruiter straight out of a wet market in Manila. The family jumped at the chance to increase their income more than tenfold. However, securing the family's future also meant ripping it apart because bringing their two children, aged 3 and 7 at the time, was not an option. It was not an option for a combination of visa and financial reasons. Big Beef was sponsoring Fernando's visa and covering all his costs, but not those of dependent visa holders.[1] While bringing the children was not an option, Ellen, like the wives of all newly recruited butchers, was offered a job as a meat packer, which made her eligible for a secondary temporary skilled visa. Initially, she declined because she could not face the prospect of leaving her children behind. But her husband kept entreating her:

> All husbands, of course willing us wives to come here. So to those who willing, they're assigned to the company too. [. . .] So my husband ask me, "Ma, I want you to be here." [. . .] It's hard because homesick, yeah. But for me, "What about my kids?" Yeah. I'm really- before- before- for the first time, I don't like to be- to leave my kids. (Ellen)

Within 2 years, Ellen gave in. In addition to her husband's pleas, there were economic considerations. If she joined her husband, their costs in Australia would only increase marginally, as they could share a room. At the same time, their income would almost double yet again, raising it to about 20 times what was possible for them in the Philippines. Sacrificing her presence in her children's lives

Life in a New Language. Ingrid Piller, Donna Butorac, Emily Farrell, Loy Lising, Shiva Motaghi-Tabari, and Vera Williams Tetteh, Oxford University Press. © Oxford University Press 2024. DOI: 10.1093/oso/9780190084288.003.0005

meant that Ellen would be able to provide financially for them in a way that was otherwise unimaginable.

Ellen left her children in the care of her older sister. In exchange, she and Fernando agreed to put their niece through nursing college. This way, their sacrifice would not only benefit their own children but also their extended family. Ellen missed her children every day. Her separation from her children was not the only sacrifice she made for them. After only a year on the Big Beef conveyor belt, her heartache was compounded by the physical ache of constant exhaustion and chronic shoulder pain. "When we reach home [from the shift], after eating, then lie down, sleep. It's very hard. It's very hard to earn money, but this is all for our children, for their future."

All the butchers' wives we spoke to in Tiny Town explained their work in Australia, far from where their hearts were, as a sacrifice they made for their children and families.[2] Rosa, who also longed to be with her two children, aged 10 and 12, had this to say:

> It's hard to leave my children but then- before I decided to go here, I- we talk about it. My husband talk about it, and then erm- we try to find a family member that could erm resp- be responsible to take care of my children. And then I- I talk to my brother, and he said, "Take the opportunity because it's good. It's a great opportunity to work in Australia." So I grab it. And beside it, this is for my children more, and my- for my family. So that I could help them. (Rosa)

The Tiny Town butchers' wives were not alone in considering their families in their migration decisions. Most parents among our participants were, at least in part, motivated to migrate for the sake of their children. Some wanted to secure a better economic future for their children, as was the case for the temporary skilled migrants. Some wanted safety and security for their children, as was the case for the humanitarian entrants. Others wanted their children to grow up outside the narrow strictures placed on young people, particularly women, by the Islamic Republic of Iran. Yet others wanted more relaxed childhoods and less rigid adult-child relationships, as was the case for some participants who might best be described as lifestyle migrants.

The family is the basic social unit in almost all cultures and societies. Family is the focus of most individuals' daily lives. Family members live together, they seek each other's company and advice, they share resources, and they undertake common tasks and responsibilities, including childrearing. Although family is central in almost all cultures, what family means and how one's life as a family member should be lived are subject to myriad variations. Who is considered a member of a family? Which family members should live together? What obligations do family members have toward each other? How do families accumulate and share resources? How do they allocate and undertake tasks? Answers to these questions differ widely, not only from one society to the next but also within societies. There are innumerable ways to create and sustain family relationships, to define family boundaries, and to perform family roles and responsibilities.[3]

The meaning and performance of family not only differ across cultures, but also are subject to change across the life span. Migration is a major catalyst for family change. This is most obvious when it comes to the relationship between migrant family members and those who stay behind. In the absence of one party, relationships between parents and children, between partners, or between siblings inevitably change. Some family relationships may fade away. Others may be transformed into relationships that are primarily economic, for instance through remittance sending and receiving. Aspects of the relationship that depend on physical co-presence—working together, lending a hand, giving care, touching, sharing a meal, sitting together—become impossible and may be replaced with letters, phone calls, and social media communications.[4]

While family separation may be the starkest form of family change resulting from migration, it is far from the only one. Family members who migrate together also redefine their relationships. Family boundaries are redrawn. New ways of procuring and sharing resources develop. New ways of allocating family tasks and responsibilities emerge. And new family concerns may appear that are specific to the migration context. Among the latter, the questions of choosing a family language and rearing children bilingually stand out. Our participants experienced their migration not only as individuals but also as family members. This chapter explores how life in a new language is lived by families.

Changing Families

Abenet and Amot, a couple from Ethiopia, frequently argued over housework. Of course, couples arguing over housework is nothing unusual. In Australia, it is common knowledge that "lazy men [are] lumping women with household chores."[5] However, Abenet's and Amot's case is different because their problem was not that he was doing too little. On the contrary: it bothered Amot that Abenet participated in housework. She felt the kitchen was no place for an African man.

Abenet and Amot were in their late teens when they were married, back home in Gambela state, in the southwest of Ethiopia. They had what to Western eyes might seem like a traditional marriage: Amot kept house and Abenet was the breadwinner. Two children were born in quick succession. Yet, by the norms of their society, their marriage was unconventional. To show why, we first need to provide some background on Gambela and the Anuak people.[6]

Both Abenet and Amot are Anuak people. The Anuak are an ethnic group whose traditional lands are in southwestern Ethiopia and across the border in Sudan. In the Ethiopian region of Gambela State, a territory about the size of Belgium, Anuak constituted the majority until the 1980s. Since then, they have become a persecuted minority in their own land. This is because Gambela is one of the most water-rich parts of Ethiopia. It is also blessed—or cursed—with oil and minerals, and still contains vast tracts of uncultivated land. To get to the wealth of Gambela, the Ethiopian central state has systematically displaced the Anuak and has orchestrated substantial population transfers from other parts of the country. The war in neighboring South Sudan further fueled the crisis.

Born in 1970, Abenet, like his father before him, is a natural leader. Smart and talented, he was sent to attend high school, which was unusual for children from his village. High school was a 10-hour journey away from his family, and his father gave him a plot of land close to the school to farm. While excelling academically and as school captain, he also learned to live off the fruits of his own labor. For his university entrance exam, he received the highest score in the country and was offered a scholarship to continue his studies in the United Kingdom. However, by then he had gotten involved in opposition politics, and the government denied him the opportunity. He became a high school teacher and head of the education department in his state, and was elected a member of the Gambela parliament. Throughout this time, he was repeatedly imprisoned for his political activities. When the election that saw him become a member of parliament was annulled, he feared that the resulting detention might be his last. Unexpectedly released after a mock execution in 2002, he did not wait to be rearrested, but left the country and fled to Kenya. Probably none too soon, as the 2003 Gambela Massacre saw many Anuak killed and fueled a mass exodus to neighboring countries.

Back home, life was hard, but Abenet was also successful, and a man of his status in his community would normally take more than one wife. Although the Anuak were one of the first groups in the region to convert to Christianity, polygamy continues to be common, Abenet told us. It is a status symbol to be able to afford the dowry for multiple wives. Abenet's and Amot's relationship was unusual not only for its monogamy, but also because they resisted the pressure to have more children. In a society where having many children is highly valued, "there was great opposition" and they were constantly asked, "Why you only have one or two children?" Abenet explained that the reason they chose not to have more than two children was "because my life was very serious." He did not want to overburden Amot, either, as she suffered through his many absences from the family due to his work, political commitments, and stints in prison.

Abenet's role in the family changed in Kenya, when he went from being an absentee father to a stay-at-home dad. He felt this necessitated an adjustment of his responsibilities:

> This is one of my struggles with my wife. I cook because- I didn't start here. They [=my wife and children] know, I started right when we are in Africa. When I was in Kenya, I was the one preparing breakfast for the kids. Because they go to school, and I have to do that, because I got assistance from someone. Amnesty International was sending money for my kids to go to school. So what will be my contribution? I don't have money, I'm not making money. Therefore I had to cook. Their breakfast is my duty. When we came here, I am just continuing. But I have a lot of tension with my wife. Sometimes you know she says that. "What are you doing in the kitchen? This is not your place." (Abenet)

In Australia, Abenet, with his unbridled drive and ambition, was back at work. Despite not having his Ethiopian qualifications recognized, he had quickly obtained an undergraduate degree in social work.[7] Soon, he was not only working full-time as a youth worker but was also enrolled in a postgraduate degree. His job was to support African youths to complete their schooling. This involved the provision of homework supervision, liaising with schools and other relevant institutions, and providing career counseling. Abenet took it upon himself to extend the role to educate the parents of the young people in his care about the importance of education. For him, this involved empowering women and opposing damaging traditions. For instance, he campaigned against dowries, which he believed to be harmful to the career prospects of young people from East African backgrounds. Abenet lived what he preached and strove for gender equality in his own household, too:

> Even though I am working and getting money, we have to share the role and being a part of- well, I'm doing community work. And I have to be changed from traditional way of life to the modern way, modern thinking. So we cook together, and I enjoy that. [. . .] My advice to most African men is that we have to share the work. Otherwise there is no way out. The reason for all of this- you know family breakdown and whatever it is, because of a lot of expectation. And mothers, the whole day you know cooking, taking the children to childcare. Everything. But I started in Africa and developed here. [. . .] But there is a lot of struggle. My wife is not happy to see me in the kitchen. But I told her that this is the way, this is the new way of life. We have to go through this channel, no way out. This is the right channel, sharing responsibility. (Abenet)

Abenet was one of the participants who was most eloquent about the way in which migration had transformed roles and relationships in his family. But everyone experienced changes in their domestic roles and responsibilities. Women who had been in the labor force before migration became housewives in Australia. Young adults who had lived with their parents had to learn how to manage their own affairs. Children had to become guides for their parents and take on roles as language brokers and experts on Australian society.

These transformations were experienced differently by different family members, and tensions were inevitable. A major source of tension in families resulted from the fact that reproductive labor—housework and childrearing—increased significantly with migration. This is because migration usually reduces family size, and work that had been shared with multiple people back home now fell on the shoulders of just one or two adults. Shirley, a mother of four young children and the wife of Franklin, whom we met in Chapter 3, reflected on the increased workload she experienced in Australia:

SHIRLEY: Very, very busy. From sunrise to sunset, just busy. Like cleaning, cooking, washing them [=three of her four children were preschool age], doing washing and everything. [. . .] For me, like here, now with my online study, the frustration is because I'm doing it by myself, no one helping. [. . .] Sometimes my assignments and my studies, I can't start because sometime I get tired, and I just want to go to bed, yeah. Which is not good because I need to do a lot of work, do a lot of studies and a lot of assignments, writing and what- reading, yeah. But I can't do that because I'm exhausted, and tired, and just I want to go to bed. And tomorrow I wake up, the same thing. Sometimes I study little bit and it's not enough, it's not enough.

VERA: Does Franklin help?

SHIRLEY: Yeah, he helps a lot. He helps a lot. He helps with everything in the house. Cleaning, everything with the kids. He's very helpful husband, yeah. [. . .] This is the problem here. Because back home if you want to study and house keep, someone will come and stay with you. And you will do your things, you go to school, or you go to uni, or go to institute, or somewhere. Your mum is there, your sisters are there. Your sisters-in-law, they are there. But here no one, only you. See the point? [laughter] Very difficult.

As extended families shrank to nuclear families, individuals struggled to cope with their increased household duties. As a result of the greater load of reproductive work that needed to be shouldered by individuals, women, paradoxically, often found themselves in more traditional gender roles post-migration. No longer able to draw on the support of extended family or paid household help, straddling paid and reproductive work became much more difficult in Australia.[8]

Some duties that had not even existed prior to migration further increased their load. One such new duty related to bilingual parenting: whether and how to raise children bilingually was added to all the other parenting quandaries that participants faced.

Making Language Choices

It is often assumed that the children of immigrants become bilingual easily and effortlessly. This is incorrect. A large US study, for instance, found that only around 20% of the children of immigrants achieve high levels of bilingual proficiency in English and their parents' language.[9] Another 20% end up with low levels of proficiency in both languages, and master neither English nor their parents' language well. The majority of around 60% were found to be English dominant, with low or no proficiency in the heritage language. Migrant parents thus face a range of questions: Can they assume that their children's English will develop in school and within the wider society, or should they boost their children's English by using the language at home in the family, too? Or must they assume that English will take over anyway and that they should shore up the heritage language as much as possible? Is the heritage language even worth maintaining into the next generation in the new country? What is the best way to support both languages to the highest possible level? Who is responsible for children's language development? And is it acceptable to use children as practice partners to improve one's own English?[10] The following extended excerpt shows how a Spanish-speaking couple, Sofia from Colombia and Julio from Chile, grappled with these questions when it came to raising their 3-year-old daughter Valentina, who had been born in Australia:

SOFIA: We sort of made the decision that, erm . . . she should learn her English first and then- [. . .] Just from what I could see, when I went to uni, and I did all my classes. Like that I could see that children that spoke the parents' language at home were having a lot of difficulty at school. [. . .]

JULIO: I didn't know that, for the records. [. . .] See, it took her [=Sofia] a while to convince me that, getting her [=Valentina] English first was the- the- the best thing to do that=

SOFIA: =I mean=

JULIO: =that Spanish would- should be erm the second language. Because otherwise they lose it, and then it's very hard for them to get into it, and this and that=

SOFIA: =of course everybody has different=

JULIO: =yeah=

SOFIA: =you know different opinions about that. [. . .] I did special education, and erm I used to teach a few little kindergarteners. And what I found is, that they went to school, and they couldn't even say, "I want to go to the toilet." Or, "I want my mum." Or, "I want a drink." Because they had no English whatsoever. So, they were always behind, you know, the other children.

JULIO: Well. Because it's like, we've got Sofia's little brother. He's not little anymore. His mother used to talk to him in English. Obviously her English is not that good. So she would use- she would do this to practice as well. And then the kid, he would go, and you talk to him in Spanish or whatever, and he wouldn't understand. So that- he's lost completely the other, the other language=

SOFIA: =but he hasn't lost- he understands.

JULIO: I know. Anyway. No. I always thought that they- you know eventually they wanna learn English. Eventually they will try at school, friends, this and that. This is an English-speaking country, they wanna learn English. So why don't you do your most to teach them Spanish? Or whatever the other language is. That was my ideal and- erm but then she [=Sofia] said, "Oh there were books. And studies. And this and that." And well, I had to give in.

This conversation comes from a research interview where Ingrid, a research assistant, and the couple's little daughter were also present. We had already covered Julio's and Sofia's language-learning trajectories, educational and occupational backgrounds, and intercultural experiences. Until the point when we started to ask about their bilingual parenting, the conversation had been pleasant and harmonious. The tone changed once it came to language policy in their family.[11] Julio and Sofia started to contradict each other, interrupt each other, and the atmosphere grew tense when Julio stated, quite formally, "I didn't know that, for records." In the interest of conciseness, we have edited out some indicators of conversational trouble such as false starts, awkward laughter, and participants wresting the word from each other. We have also edited out attempts by Ingrid and the research assistant to try to change the topic, as we grew increasingly alarmed that we might have a quarrel on our hands. The problem behind this tense exchange was a disagreement about language. Earlier, Julio and Sofia had told us that they had exclusively spoken Spanish to each other when they first met. Over time, this had changed to something like a 40:60 ratio in favor of English. The birth of Valentina had been a major turning point and the decision was made to prioritize English in the family. According to Sofia this was a joint decision, according to Julio it was Sofia's decision. From the excerpt, it is obvious that language choice continued to be a sore point for the couple, even 3 years after Valentina's birth.

In their reasoning, each partner drew on their own experiences. Sofia referred to her university studies in special education and to encounters she had had with young children who started school without English. She also drew on her own arrival memories: one of the youngest arrivals among our participants, she had only been 14 years old when her family moved from Colombia to Australia. She recalled how she was "a little bit afraid" of her classmates and "very afraid" of saying anything in school. These experiences provided the rationale for prioritizing English in the family so that Valentina would be spared such difficulties. By contrast, Julio cited Sofia's younger brother as an example of an adult child of immigrant parents who had lost the heritage language. For him, doing right by his daughter involved providing her with a strong foundation in Spanish so that she could be bilingual as an adult.

Sofia and Julio both wanted to secure the advantages of bilingualism for Valentina. Their disagreement was over how best to achieve that goal. The same is true for other parent participants, too. They all wished to foster English for their children's academic success and for the family's integration into Australian society. At the same time, many also desired to cultivate the heritage language for strong family bonds, enduring connections with the origin country, and other benefits of bilingualism.[12] While most participants wanted their children to grow up bilingually, how to achieve that goal was unclear and raised tensions not only between partners, but also between children and parents.

Whether explicitly or implicitly, migrant parents make decisions about language use in the family.[13] Their decisions are influenced by their prior experiences and their beliefs. However, language-choice decisions are not set in stone and may change over time, as children grow older. Furthermore, policies and practices do not always align. In the remainder of this chapter, we explore the realities of bilingual parenting among our participants from Iran. These form a distinct cohort of parents because one of the research recruitment criteria for this group had been that they should have at least one child.[14] At the time of the research, these children were between 8 and 12 years old and attended primary school. By then, they had been in Australia between 1 and 7 years. On arrival, they had spoken little or no English.

Supporting English and Academic Development

There is a widespread belief that, in contrast to their parents, child migrants learn the new language quickly and easily. The reality is more complicated. It is true that young learners have an advantage when it comes to oral fluency and accent. Migrant children may sound indistinguishable from their native-born peers within months of arrival in the new environment. By contrast, adult arrivals rarely ever end up sounding like their native-born peers. However, the ease with which younger learners achieve oral fluency and the target accent usually masks that they are still learning the context-reduced and cognitively demanding language that is necessary to succeed in school. Research from a variety of immigration contexts shows that it takes new-arrival students about 5 to 7 years to catch up to their native-born peers. Some students catch up faster, and some never catch up.[15]

Initially, participants were not concerned about their children's English and assumed that children would learn quickly through immersion. Before migration, some had sent their children for some private tutoring to ease the transition but, by and large, they were happy to leave their children's English-language development until arrival in Australia. They expected that going to school and making new friends would take care of their children's English-language learning more or less automatically.

On arrival, school-aged children were immediately enrolled in school. Some schools placed newcomers initially in ESL programs. In Australia, ESL programs typically involve the removal of the child from their usual class group for a limited time or the provision of individual tutoring support.[16] Given their strong faith in children's natural language acquisition, participants resented it if their children were placed in ESL classes. Instead of supporting their children's English-language learning, they believed that ESL programs actually reduced their opportunities to practice English. For instance, Golara's children Gavin and Gilda were placed in pull-out ESL programs during their first year in Australia, and the mother was livid:

> *At a* time *when the teacher is teaching something in the classroom, they send the child to* ESL. *The children go there to learn the language, but they miss the class lessons. It was so hard. It was so annoying and so wrong. Like no one there was mindful of what they were doing to the children. Like, there was no coordination at all between the class programs and the* ESL *program.* ESL *was about one and a half hours, something like that. When the teacher was doing something with the other students in the class, like checking their homework, giving them tips and points, and then our children were in* ESL *classes.* (Golara)

Conversely, not being placed in an ESL program or being placed there for only a short while was a point of pride. Ladan, for instance, proudly reported that she had taken her daughter Lida, who was 4 years old on arrival, to the park every day for over half a year so that she could play with other children and learn English this way. The result of her efforts was that the child did not have to attend ESL classes at all.

ESL classes can carry remedial stigma and may inscribe a deficit identity in students.[17] This was one of the reasons parents were almost unanimously opposed to ESL classes for their children. The other reason was their faith in natural language learning. However, that faith was shaken once they realized that their children's integration into the new school environment was not as smooth as they had expected. Just like the adults we discussed in Chapter 2, children experienced initial language shock. Farah, whose daughter Fariba was 5 years old on arrival, later discovered that Fariba had not uttered a single word in school during her first term. Nahid, whose daughter Negin was also 5 on arrival, lamented that Negin "*was really tormented because she couldn't communicate.*" Oldouz reported that her 6-year-old daughter Orkideh "*was really stressed [. . .] was extremely hard for her. It was so dreadful.*" Goudarz said about his two children, who were 7 and 9 on arrival: "*It was an extremely hard time for the kids. I could see it in their eyes, from their moods and behaviors. How much pressure was on them. There was so much pressure on them.*"

The children's initial language challenges were part and parcel of fitting into their new school and environment. English mediated their learning and friendships. Amin's son Aria, who was 7 on arrival, reported to his dad that the world around him had become "blah blah blah." The children's initial language shocks had lasting effects on their academic and social development. Nahid's daughter Negin, for instance, has been placed in the lowest mathematics group within her year group ever since coming to Australia, much to the chagrin of her parents, who both hold degrees in engineering. In addition to negative academic consequences, parents observed disturbing personality changes in their children. Fariba's transformation was one of the most extreme:

FARZAD: *Here at school she was really under pressure. Sometimes the teachers even took her- brought a Persian student, they were like, "Ask her if she can speak at all." To check if she has speech problems. She suffered a lot in this process=*

FARAH: *=it was very hard for her.*

FARZAD: *Well, this caused her now to become very* shy *and isolated. Or at least to be stereotyped like that. But she doesn't have such traits. After all she is normal, you know? Because she wasn't like that in Persian. But here, she was perceived like that. The impression arose that this kid has a low level of intelligence.*

Farah and Farzad did everything they could to support their daughter and help her regain her former sense of self. Although Farzad was a stay-at-home dad while he was waiting for his Iranian qualifications as a medical doctor to be re-accredited, the couple decided to invest in after-school care and vacation care for Fariba. They attempted to maximize her exposure to English in every way they could. This included making the painful decision to change the home language from Persian to English.

Supporting the Heritage Language and Family Connections

In contrast to families whose children were born in Australia, participants who migrated with children had an established family language. In the case of the Iranian families, their habitual language with each other was Persian. Even so, many had been advised by other Iranian immigrants or by their child's teachers to switch to English. Qasem even claimed, "*When we first came, everybody told us to speak English at home.*" Despite the advice to switch to English for the sake of gaining practice opportunities for their children and for themselves, participants were hesitant. Partly, their resistance to making English their family language related to their own deficiencies in English.[18] They were worried that their children would pick up their accents, their mistakes, and their "*incorrect*" English, as Iman told us:

> *I saw many of our friends who started speaking English when they first came, so that their child would learn English. I don't know, maybe if our English was very good, we would have done the same. But we always thought that it's better that she* [=their daughter Ideh] *wouldn't learn anything incorrect from us. It would be better that she'd learn from someone whose first language is English rather than us telling her something inaccurate.* (Iman)

Besides not wanting to model inauthentic English for their children, there was a second reason parents resisted the advice to switch to English in the home: they feared for their children's Persian. This fear may seem misplaced. After all, it is commonly assumed that children who grow up in homes where a language other than English is spoken will automatically become bilingual. Unfortunately, that assumption is incorrect. A recent meta-study of language outcomes of children who had been raised bilingually in different countries in Asia, Europe, and North America found that a quarter of all children ended up unable to speak their heritage language.[19] In fact, it is not uncommon for children learning a new language to lose the old one.[20] The realization that their children's English-language learning might threaten their Persian sometimes took a while to sink in, as in Homa's case, whose daughter Hasti was 3 on arrival. In Australia, Homa initially became a stay-at-home mom and Hasti's exposure to English did not start in earnest until she started school. Even so, after a few years in school, Homa noticed that Hasti had lost active command of Persian:

> *Because she already knew Persian. Therefore I thought that, "Well she already knows it." [. . .] I didn't think that she would forget. [. . .] I am also speaking Persian to her. But after one or two years, I realized that when I asked her a question in Persian, she would not reply in Persian. She could understand, but she would answer in English.*

Like Homa, many participants noticed after a while in Australia that just speaking Persian at home was not enough for their children to maintain the language, let alone develop it. Some parents started to pretend they did not understand their children if they spoke English. Others kept reminding their children to speak in Persian. Yet others ignored children's utterances in English, and one participant, Parvin, even resorted to responding to any utterance in English with Turkish, a language her children did not know at all. However creative, none of these strategies really worked. The charade of not understanding English was impossible to keep up for long. Constantly reminding children that they should speak Persian instead of English proved tedious and frustrating. And not attending to utterances in English only worked episodically. It often had unintended consequences, such as children interpreting a non-response as permission.[21]

Many parents claimed that they had set firm language rules in the home. Jamileh, for example, had instituted a "*no English at home*" rule, and Mina stated, "*Since we've come here, I made a rule that we must speak Persian at home.*" However, such language rules could quickly turn into wedge issues, particularly if children discovered that parental views on "the rule" were not necessarily aligned.[22] Behnaz, for example, blamed her husband Bijan for undermining Persian in their home by speaking English to their daughter Bita. Bita, in fact, spoke Persian well and even conducted a formal research interview in Persian with Shiva when she was 11 years old and had been in Australia for 4 years. This was different for Negin, who had arrived in Australia aged 5, and 3 years later could no longer speak Persian. Negin's mother, Nahid, blamed her husband for this situation. While she had made every effort to resist the creep of English, her husband had given up, she felt, and was speaking English all the time.

The main reason why parents wanted to maintain their children's Persian was related to family. In the first instance, they wanted the children to be able to maintain close connections with extended family back in Iran. Oldouz, for example, explained that her daughter Orkideh's "*grandfather and grandmother, her own father, they are all Iranians. They don't know that much English. If she cannot make connections with them, it would be like nothing.*" Participants saw Persian not only as the key means to maintain bonds with absent family, but also as enabling a specific bond within their nuclear family. Persian was the language of their heart, and they wanted to be able to share it fully with their children.

Madjid explained that "*it is easier for me and her mother to express to Melody what we think, what we feel in Persian.*" Ehsan argued that Persian enabled him and his wife to have an authentic relationship with their daughter: "*We feel that we've learnt English artificially. We've always been concerned about how we could do ourselves justice if we had to express our emotions in English.*" The emotional bonds parents had built with their children in Persian became increasingly frayed as English became the children's dominant language.

Transforming Parent-Child Relationships

As we explained above, children's oral proficiency and everyday language can quickly become indistinguishable from that of their native-born peers. While children developed fluency, parents continued to struggle with everyday language. Their formal and academic English may well have been far ahead of that of their children, but their oral displays were lacking. This discrepancy began to undermine parent-child relationships as children began to feel linguistically superior to their parents, as Homa told us about 10-year-old Hasti:

> *She herself thinks that she knows more than me. For instance, I am teaching her. Well, her grammar is not very good yet. Like, I explain that for instance, "Here you need to write it like this." Then she says, "No. Your English is not good. I know English better." But- well, she goes to school and her teacher corrects her homework. And then she realizes that I was right. [. . .] she herself says, "My English is better." And because she speaks better and her pronunciation is better, she thinks that her English is better.* (Homa)

Children interpreted their parents' English as indicators of other shortcomings, such as an inability to provide credible homework assistance, as in this example. As a result, parents felt they needed to prove their English to maintain face and authority. Homa, for instance, went on, "*I constantly tell her the spellings of words. Then I say, 'See, my English is better than yours.'* [Laughs] *'See how I know the spelling of all these words? I say it off by heart, but you don't.' Then she's like, 'Oh well, my speaking is better than yours.'*" Homa's competition with her daughter over whose English is better suggests a sensitive issue in the relationship. They are not alone. Other children, too, felt embarrassment and shame at the way their parents spoke English, as 9-year-old Bita and 12-year-old Donya confided to Shiva:

DONYA: Mum's English is kheili (*very*) embarrassing.
BITA: Her pronunciation is ye kam (*a little*) different.

SHIVA: Is that important? Do you mind?
DONYA: YES! Yes, I do.

Anita's 9-year-old son Aria was even more dramatic: "*Then with* [my Australian friend] *my mum comes and says,* 'Hello darling!' [in an exaggerated high-pitched voice with lengthened vowels]. *And I am like, 'Oh my God. I want to kill myself!'*"

Learning a language is not only about learning its sounds, grammar, and words. It also involves acquiring the ideologies and dispositions associated with the language.[23] As we discussed in Chapter 2, one such language ideology relates to the hierarchical ordering of different forms of English. In Australia, native-sounding English is more highly valued than forms of English that carry traces of migration histories. Shedding those traces thus was not only about learning English, but also about escaping stigma. While the children were quickly able to align their oral English with the preferred variety, this was not possible for their parents. Just as parents could not escape their ways of speaking, neither could the children escape their parents. They had to suffer what they perceived to be their parents' linguistic inferiority vicariously.[24]

Even if children were not as explicit in their criticism as Aria, Bita, Donya, and Hasti, parents noticed that their children sometimes seemed to disavow them in public. They would try to stay away from them in the presence of their friends, would try to keep conversations short, or use other avoidance strategies. Some parents accepted their children's embarrassment and complied with their wishes by minimizing speaking English in public when their children were present. Others tried to reason with their children. Jamileh, for instance, pointed to the superiority of her multilingualism. Jamileh is a member of Iran's Azeri-speaking minority and had grown up bilingually with Persian and Azeri, a language also known as (Azerbaijani) Turkish.[25] When her daughter Jeyran asked her to keep a low profile in her school, Jamileh told her, "*Jeyran, look, I know Persian. I know Turkish. I also know enough English to live here. If you are comparing me to an Australian mum, just remember that she only knows English.*"

Rational explanations do not necessarily mitigate feelings of shame and embarrassment. It is unpleasant for any parent to be told, or even to sense, that their children find them embarrassing.[26] Already feeling insecure about their English, being overtaken in their English development by their school-aged children was confronting for parents. It resulted in conflicting emotions. Parents began to fear for their face and authority as parents, as Majid shared in an awkward exchange marked by uncomfortable laughter and self-interruptions:

MAJID: *Her understanding only goes so far, and so the matter may become a bit* complicated [laughs]. *Because she may start to think that we do not know*

many other things either. If that happened, it would be problematic. The positions would be displaced and- a bit like- yeah.
SHIVA: *You mean the* authority *that parents have?*
MAJID: *Yeah, they might lose it.*

While managing their own need to maintain parental authority, participants also wanted to raise their children's self-esteem and confidence.[27] They understood that their children were struggling, too, as we explained above. One strategy to manage these tensions was to ask children for help with their English. Given the scarcity of English-language interlocutors we discussed in Chapter 4, children can be an invaluable resource to practice English and to learn about aspects of Australian society that were otherwise inaccessible to adult participants. Additionally, seeking linguistic input from children could also serve as a strategy to maintain harmonious family relationships.

AMIN: *Aria often says something like, "You've used this word incorrectly." Well, I don't get offended. After all this is a two-way relationship. [. . .] Sometimes I even ask him, I say, "Aria, I haven't heard this word before. Do you know what it means?" He either knows it or doesn't. If he does, well, he will say it. If he doesn't, then we'll look it up in the* dictionary, *and we'll see what the meaning is. [. . .] This in itself is a good relationship for learning English. Then I tell him, I say, "because your English-"I constantly boost his confidence. "Because your English is very good, you should teach me and your mum."*

Outside the language classroom, correcting others' linguistic errors always constitutes a face threat. In effect, any correction reframes the relationship between the person who is corrected and the person who does the correcting into a student-teacher relationship. Even teachers are rarely oblivious to the face threat emanating from a correction and frequently mitigate it by smiling and other strategies.[28] Where the role reversal brought about by negative feedback is drastic because it comes from child to parent, offense might easily be taken, as Amir acknowledges. However, by not getting offended and by recasting the occasion as an opportunity to boost his son's confidence, Amir reframes the relationship yet again as an opportunity to present himself as a model father whose prime concern is his son's self-esteem, by "*even*" seeking out his son's corrections. While unsolicited corrections may indicate a potential role reversal in the parent-child relationship, voluntarily seeking out corrections may be a safe arrangement.[29]

The transformations in parent-child relationships that become apparent in dealing with the children's shame at their parents' English and with their linguistic corrections are one manifestation of destabilized family relationships in the migration context. Parent-child relationships are being renegotiated as linguistic expertise overlays parental expertise, and consequently, changes in the structure of migrant families are inevitable. We started this chapter with the observation that wanting the best for their children was an important factor behind parents' migration projects. Yet, migration also unsettled what it means to do right by one's children. The conflicting emotions related to language choices that we have explored in this chapter inevitably turned to parental guilt. Parental guilt is, of course, not restricted to migrant parents.[30] Yet, migrant parents face more radical family transformations than most. Some of these transformations may be welcome, others less so. Within them, language and family connections are deeply intertwined and may provide completely unanticipated sources of parental guilt, as Goudarz lyrically explains:

> *Sometimes I really really blame myself, and I think I have done injustice to my kids. [. . .] We say they will learn the language. The child who is let's say in Year 2 would be 8 or 9 years old. Within these 8, 9 years, the child has learnt Persian. The Persian that mum and dad have taught them beautifully, with love and affection. You know, uncles, aunts, beautifully with love and affection. Then for this child, you want to get their English to the same level. And they are just only now beginning to learn maths,* science, *and science, and this and that. This is difficult for the child. And I think this will go on forever. I mean not forever, but until the end of their childhood.* (Goudarz)

The temptation for parents to blame themselves for their children's failures and take credit for their achievements is inevitably high, particularly when it comes to heritage language maintenance.[31] Yet, the family transformations we have discussed here do not take place in a vacuum. They are deeply shaped by the exclusions and inclusions that migrant families experience in their new society, as we will discuss in the next chapters.

6

"Sometimes the White People Get Angry"

Facing Discrimination in a New Language

Encountering Difference in Australia

Anna from Yugoslavia and Kumiko from Japan both came to Australia for love. Born in the 1970s, they settled in Perth at about the same time in late 2007 and early 2008. Neither of them had ever imagined making Australia home until they met Australian men whom they eventually married. The similarity of key aspects of their stories allows us to explore racial differences in the experiences of white-looking Anna and Asian-looking Kumiko. We will therefore tell their stories in parallel in the introduction to this chapter.

Anna had been born into a Slovak family in Yugoslavia and grew up bilingually with Slovakian and Serbo-Croatian.[1] Her part of the country, Vojvodina in the north of Serbia, was relatively unaffected by the Yugoslav wars in the 1990s, and while she recalls some animosity toward Slovaks, she mostly remembers a "normal" childhood. After graduating from high school, Anna pursued a college degree in electrical engineering and worked as an electrician until the day she left for Australia. Anna's romance started during a party at a friend's house back in Serbia. One of the attendees was Marko, a visitor from Australia. Born into a Croatian family in Perth, Marko spoke Serbo-Croatian, and the two of them got chatting. Their acquaintance turned into something more over the course of Marko's next holiday in Serbia a year later. On a third trip there, he proposed. Anna accepted and the two of them returned to Perth together to live there. She had never been to Australia before, and her marriage migration upended her life "like thunder."

Kumiko hailed from a small city outside Tokyo. She, too, remembers a conventional Japanese childhood. At university, she studied ancient history with the aim of becoming an archaeologist "like Indiana Jones." However, after graduation, she never worked in the field, but became an "office lady" at a travel company. Not enjoying the position much, she left after 3 years to travel and see the world. Her trip took her to Australia on a work and travel visa with the goal of improving her English. During one of her jobs, she met an Australian colleague, Michael, who spoke Japanese. Michael had initially learned Japanese in school and then perfected it through work as an English teacher in Japan. In fact,

Life in a New Language. Ingrid Piller, Donna Butorac, Emily Farrell, Loy Lising, Shiva Motaghi-Tabari, and Vera Williams Tetteh, Oxford University Press. © Oxford University Press 2024. DOI: 10.1093/oso/9780190084288.003.0006

Michael was back in Perth for only a short time and planned to return to Japan soon. He had recently suffered a snowboarding accident and was back in his childhood home to recuperate in the care of his parents. As their romance began to blossom over the next few months, they moved back to Japan together once Kumiko's visa was up. Over the next 6 years, Kumiko and Michael first lived in metropolitan Tokyo as a dual-career couple. Kumiko worked in IT after having pursued additional qualifications in the field, and Michael was teaching English. After a while they decided to move to a small city in Hokkaido in northern Japan, where Michael had been offered a head teacher position and where the skiing was good. While this was a great career move for Michael, Kumiko was unable to find work there. Being a stay-at-home housewife left her feeling unfulfilled and restless. At the time, they also wanted to start a family but could not conceive. Eventually, they felt it was time to move back to Perth in the hope that Kumiko would have better job prospects there and to pursue IVF (in vitro fertilization) treatment.

Both Anna and Kumiko initially conducted their relationships in a language other than English. Anna and Marko started their romance in Serbo-Croatian, and Kumiko and Michael in Japanese. For Marko, Serbo-Croatian was his heritage language, as his parents had migrated from Yugoslavia in the 1960s. They had spoken mostly Serbo-Croatian to each other and their children, while the children responded in English but maintained a degree of fluency in the language. For Michael, Japanese was a language he had learned in school, but his background included a heritage language that he had never learned. Like Marko, Michael is a second-generation Australian. His ethnically Chinese parents migrated from Malaysia in the 1970s and Michael was born and raised in a small mining town in Western Australia.[2] In contrast to Marko's parents, Michael's parents had chosen to speak English at home and Michael therefore never learned his parents' Chinese language.

Over time in Australia, both couples used English more and more. For Anna, this was a relatively smooth transition, as there was always the Serbo-Croatian of the extended family to fall back on. For Kumiko, the transition was less comfortable because when she spoke English with Michael, "I feel like I'm talking to someone strange. Someone I don't know." More importantly, Anna could see the rewards of assimilation, but Kumiko could not. On the contrary, she observed examples where her husband and his family were treated as outsiders, despite their English. For instance, Michael was addressed as a tourist when he went to buy a public transport pass. Despite speaking English with a native Australian accent, the agent assumed he was a temporary visitor from overseas and advised him, "When you go home, you can give the card to somebody else, and somebody can use it." Apparently, the agent, a white-looking woman, was under the assumption that an Asian-looking person can only ever be temporarily in

Australia. Sometimes, that assumption is made explicit and becomes a racist insult, as happened to a friend of Kumiko's mother-in-law:

> My mother-in-law's friend- she is also Chinese-Australian, one day she was walking along the river, and someone came from other direction. So she said, "Hi." The person said . . . what was it? . . . "Go back to your country!" But this IS her country. (Kumiko)

When Anna and Kumiko first came to Australia, they both accepted their own Otherness to a degree. They saw themselves as newcomers who, as yet, only had a tenuous claim on their new country. They were from somewhere else, as other people could hear whenever they opened their mouths. However, for Asian-looking Kumiko, but not for white-looking Anna, the experience of audible difference went hand in hand with visible difference. Although her Asian-looking husband and in-laws had erased their linguistic difference, they were still treated as outsiders every so often. These differential bases of their Otherness set the two women on different paths toward inclusion.

After 2 years in Australia, neither Anna nor Kumiko was in paid employment and both had become mothers. For Anna, this was a good situation. She had not looked for work and enjoyed her role as full-time wife and mother. She had begun to feel at home in Australia, "maybe because my husband is Australian, you know. I feel like a part of him." For Kumiko, things were more complicated. Despite having sent many job applications, she could not secure even a single interview, let alone find a job. Given her competitive IT qualifications and a strong tech job market, she came to believe that this was the result of a combination of English-language chauvinism and anti-Japanese racism.[3] Her family life was complicated, too. Feeling increasingly alienated and wanting to secure employment, Kumiko made the decision to leave Michael and their young daughter behind and accept a job offer in Singapore, as we discussed in Chapter 3.

In telling Anna's and Kumiko's stories in parallel, we do not wish to reduce their different experiences to race. That would undoubtedly be simplistic, as they are very different people, with different families, different careers, different personalities, different circumstances, and different stories. Telling their stories in parallel has enabled us to orient to the topic of this chapter, participants' experiences of Othering, exclusion, discrimination, and racism.

Being Made to Feel Out of Place

Even if immigration is central to Australian nation-building, as we showed in Chapter 1, newcomers do not immediately become Australians. Technically, migrants become Australians when they acquire citizenship, and their new status is underwritten by the Australian state.[4] To become a naturalized Australian citizen, permanent residents must demonstrate a "long-term commitment" to Australia and must meet five requirements, related to length of residence, good character, knowledge of Australia, language, and "close and continuing links to Australia." In terms of length of residence, an applicant must have resided in Australia for a minimum of 4 years on a valid visa, including at least 12 months as permanent resident. The minimum residence requirement used to be 2 years but was doubled to 4 years in 2007. Evidence to demonstrate close and continuing links includes having close family members who are Australian citizens, having a job in Australia, or owning property in Australia.[5] However, securing formal citizenship status did not necessarily make participants feel included in the Australian nation. Most did not even feel they were on a trajectory toward becoming Australian at some point in the future. Eva from Chile who, at the time of the research, had lived in Australia for 18 years and had been a citizen for 16 years, articulated this disconnect between her "paper identity" and the way she was made to feel:

> Because here we are the foreigners. No matter what the papers say. I mean you are a foreigner, and- and you feel it most of the time. Okay? So unfortunately, I- in the silly things, people make you feel it. (Eva)

The "silly things" that made Eva feel out of place in Australia "most of the time" are often referred to as "micro-aggressions."[6] Micro-aggressions are everyday interactional put-downs that keep social hierarchies in place. They serve to highlight an identity aspect of the target that is negatively valued and stigmatized, usually their race, gender, poverty, or sexuality. Micro-aggressions can be categorized into micro-assaults, micro-insults, and micro-invalidations. Participants reported examples of all of these. Micro-assaults are the most vicious and obvious form of denigration and include the use of racial slurs and other derogatory terms. The exclusionary intent of micro-assaults is undisputable. They are deliberate aggressions that are intended to hurt, oppress, or humiliate the target. Tina from China, for instance, was once called "stupid Chinese pig" by passengers of another car while she was filling up her car at a petrol station. Another time, she was riding her bike and passengers of a passing car wound down their window and shouted something at her which she did not quite catch—or did not wish to repeat—and which was "something like that [=stupid Chinese pig]." From her own experiences and those of others in her social circle, Tina had concluded that it was "normal" for Asian-looking people to be the target of racist insults in Australia:

> You know, one of my friends told me- one time- one night, he was- erm walking with his dog. And, you know, some of the Australian just- erm shouted- shouted at him, and say some- something bad, to him. And I asked, "How do you feel?" And he said, "Oh normal. Because I have a lot of experience." Because he- he came to Australia since he was in high school. (Tina)

The racist intent of such micro-assaults is undeniable, and Tina was resigned to racist abuse as a fact of life in Australia. With micro-assaults, at least the intent is clear. This is different with micro-insults and micro-invalidations, whose racist intent is not necessarily transparent. With the latter, the underlying biases are not made explicit and there is usually plausible deniability of racist intent. Micro-insults are aggressions that are rude, convey insensitivity, and demean an aspect of the target's identity. For instance, Dagmar from Austria reported an experience in a pub where she was clinking glasses with a new acquaintance. As they did so, the other person's attention was distracted, and Dagmar playfully pointed out that people who toasted each other should always look into each other's eyes. The startling response she received was, "If you don't like it, you can just go home!" Even participants who had never been told to "Just go home!" to their face might have come across the slogan in public spaces. For example, the slogans "Go back to where you came from!" and "We grew here, you flew here!" rose to national prominence in media coverage of the 2005 race riots at a Sydney beach, Cronulla, between predominantly White and Muslim men.[7] The same denial of migrant legitimacy can also be found on bumper stickers that proclaim "Australia—love it or leave it!" Even federal and state election ballot papers have at times included the slogan "Love Australia or Leave" as the name of a far-right anti-immigration party."[8]

Micro-invalidations are even less obvious than micro-insults. These are communications that exclude people, ignore them, or negate their needs, thoughts, and perceptions. For instance, Michiko from Japan observed that "Chinese" and "Australian" customers sometimes received different service in shops.[9] Only a few days before one interview, she had observed that "a Chinese girl" in a department store asked to try on a shirt she liked in a different color. The "lady shop assistant" responded, "No. There is another shop, David Jones [=name of major Australian department store chain]. You can go and look there." Shortly afterward, "an Australian person" asked the same sales assistant for a garment in a different size. This time, the sales assistant did not dismiss the customer but helped to source a different size by calling another store branch. This was, in fact, not the only instance of selective incivility that Michiko observed.[10] One of her passions was to attend flea markets as a seller. Her takings were usually slim, but she did it for the language practice opportunities and the intercultural insights, as she noted in her diary: "I found something important and interesting for me, although only could earn 70 cents that day." On "that day," the sellers operating their tables on either side of her were both migrants like herself: "One was unknown nationality, hard to talk with him but I heard what he said to customers" and the "other one was from Holland and he is 80 years old." One of the things she discovered was another instance of selective incivility, similar to her observation in the department store: "Unknown nationality seller gave cheaper price to Australian or Caucasian customers than dark skin and Asian customers. It was not only few dollars difference, it was more than 20 dollars gap between them." While the unknown nationality guy did not talk much and seemed to ignore Michiko, her other neighbor, the seller from Holland, could not stop talking to her. "He kept coming to talk to me even he had customers." However, his talkativeness was not comfortable for Michiko, either. On the one hand, she appreciated the practice opportunity and she "felt I was accepted from him." On the other hand, the content of the conversation was disturbing for her, and she noted her confusion in her diary:

> He said to me that he hates Chinese, African and Arabic people. I was very confused and upset from his opinion. I am studying with those people and I know those people's background more than him. Therefore I like to talk to them very much. [...]
>
> I do not understand why he treat differently between Migrants and Australian even though he is a Migrant. Why he could accept me although he can not accept Chinese? What's making so much difference between Japan and China? [...] I have never felt so much welcome from elder people except my husband's family and people who I met in England. Maybe I should've ask him about reasons why he hates those people. As you know I am a very polite person, how can I ask this question moreover I know he will upset if I ask. To be honest I was uncomfortable to listening about his strong discrimination opinions. On the other hand I couldn't stop listening as well. (Michiko)

Michiko's confusion is not an unusual reaction to micro-insults and micro-invalidations, as many psychological studies have found.[11] Targeted individuals "may find it easier to deal with micro-assaults because the intent of the aggressor is clear and obvious. By contrast, micro-insults and micro-invalidations involve considerable guesswork because of their ambiguous and invisible nature."[12] Therefore, they are sometimes described as the new face of racism, as "Racism 3.0."[13] The exclusion involved is neither stark, nor rare, nor deviant. Often, it is not even intentional. It may even masquerade as a compliment. Sally from Zimbabwe, for instance, was complimented by a neighbor on the fact that she had a driver's license. "Then she said, 'Aw [sound like cooing to a baby], aren't you a clever girl! Aw, very clever.'" Given that 95% of middle-aged Australians hold a driver's license,[14] the exaggerated compliment, with its infantilizing cooing, diminutive address form ("girl"), and exaggerated repetition ("clever [. . .] very clever"), obviously includes the unspoken proviso "for someone like you." Whether the implicit assumption that one should only expect childlike reduced competence and capability of a person like Sally refers to her status as a migrant to Australia, as an African person, or as a Black woman, remains open. All these identities are hailed as out of place by the invalidating compliment.[15]

Insults and invalidations powerfully undermine target individuals' sense of belonging, in two ways: first, by sending the implicit message that the target is out of place, and second, by invalidating their judgment. What can make them so insidious is the plausible deniability of racist intent, as is the case with the question "Where are you from?," which most of our participants reported to have been asked at one time or another. Paulo, an Australian citizen from Portugal who worked in a customer-facing role, was often asked this question. He dramatized the denial of racist intent when he called it out:

PAULO: Like they say, "Oh! You have an accent!" . . . Or, you know, "Where are you from?" And I say, "Why do you ask?" And they say, "Oh because you have an accent." And I say, "Does that bother you?"
EMILY: [laughs]
PAULO: "Oh! No no no no no!" They make very apologies, they become very apologetic, and- "It's just for erm- I mean it's just out of interest." And it's not out of interest. Because I know, you know, how the brain works. And it- they're trying to categorize and insert me, in the appropriate slot in the list.

However well-intentioned the question "Where are you from?" may be, its implicit message is always that the recipient is out of place in Australia.[16] While Paulo reported wrong-footing those who asked him about his origins, Alexa, an Australian citizen from Spain, felt humiliated each time she was asked the question. Her dearest wish was "for my European accent to disappear completely" so that the question would never be asked again: "Cause after so many years, you still get people saying, "Oh where are you from?" And it's like, "Ohhh!" [sad deflated sound].

Between Language and Race

While hurt by the regular Othering she experienced, Alexa could imagine a future without her accent. She assumed that, if her accent were to change, her national belonging would no longer be subject to scrutiny. For Daisy from Kenya, it was a different story. When she went for a job interview for a role as receptionist, the company director told her, "Daisy, you are very good. But I won't give you this job because I'll lose customers. Because they won't understand what you are saying because of your accent." Daisy speaks, in fact, fluent English with a clear and easy-to-understand pronunciation that differs from a standard British accent primarily in how she pronounces some vowels.[17] Similar to other highly educated participants from an outer-circle country, whom we discussed in Chapter 2, Daisy had been educated through the medium of English. Her first language is Kikuyu, but English had become her main language already back home in Kenya. In terms of her English, the director had little reason to worry. It is likely that his concern was not with the way Daisy sounded but with the way she looked. Was he afraid that a Black receptionist would drive customers away?

Our examples demonstrate that participants experienced Othering along the two axes of race and language. Sometimes, they were made to feel out of place because of the way they sounded, and sometimes because of the way they looked. Most of the time, these two dimensions could not be clearly distinguished but were intertwined in a process of racialization of visible and audible identity markers. The process of racialization is best understood with regard to skin color. Race is not a biological or objective category, but one that emerges in a process of racialization, where people are socialized into noticing skin color as a meaningful identity signal (in contrast to, say, earlobe shape). Because race is not biological but discursive, non-phenotypical identity markers may also be subject to the process of racialization.[18] The emergence of the Muslim hijab as a racial marker provides an example.[19] In the case of skin color and the hijab, racial markers are embodied and perceived visually. Additionally, audible signals—ways of speaking—may also be turned into markers of difference. Visible and audible identity markers form identity bundles where, for example, Daisy's skin color and accent combine to mark her racially.[20] Because visible and audible identity markers combine to form recognizable identity bundles, language becomes a proxy for race. This opens the door for racist discrimination to operate in perfectly legal ways, Australian anti-discrimination legislation notwithstanding. While it is unlawful to exclude Daisy from a receptionist job—or any other employment for which she is qualified—based on her "race, color, descent or national or ethnic origin," it is perfectly legal to exclude her based on her accent—or any other aspect of her language that anyone chooses to single out.[21]

There are numerous recognizable raciolinguistic identity bundles in Australia, but they are all constituted by their difference from the normative Australian raciolinguistic identity, which is imagined as White and English-speaking.[22] When our participants spoke of an "Australian" person, without any further qualification, they always referred to a native-born, White, English-speaking person. Saman from Iran, for instance, reflected on Australian multiculturalism by saying, "*Here* [=Sydney] Aussie *kids learn from a young age that there are also people whose eyes are not blue. Who have an* accent *and who speak differently. Who use some words wrong and translate incorrectly.*" Saman's point was to favorably compare multicultural Sydney with a regional town in NSW where he had previously lived, and which he felt lacked diversity. Yet, in either location he set up the normative identity as that of the "Aussie *kid*" who is blue-eyed and speaks unaccented and correct English.

Within these hierarchies of language and race, white-looking migrants occupy the least stereotyped space. In a way, their raciolinguistic identity bundle can be said to comprise conflicting signals. As long as they do not speak, they can pass for normative Australians.[23] Some of our participants did so, such as Milena from the Czech Republic. Blond and blue-eyed, Milena certainly looks the part. She had come to Australia straight out of high school when she was in her late teens. She was initially working as an au pair and her duty was to look after three little sisters. She fondly recalled how they taught her English:

> This was, I think the breakthrough for me in English, with three little girls, who were four, five, and six. And I had to do homework with them. And that was really interesting because- . . . I have, I've known just basic English that I've got from [a self-study] book. And now I was learn- RElearning it with their accents. And- and you know, their knowledge. So we're kind of feeding each other, and they were excellent in helping me. You know, pronounce things, and say things right. Because I've told them that erm I want them to- you know fix my English if they can. And they found that really exciting, and you know, that they can tell someone that they are saying something wrong! So, yeah, I think that helped me a lot, and I was with them a year. . . . and within that year I met my husband, and from then on, it- that was really fast. (Milena)

When Ingrid first met Milena in 2000, she spoke English fluently and with a relatively broad Australian accent. Ingrid only discovered that she was a migrant when Milena volunteered that information. This is something that happens a lot, Milena explained:

MILENA: Most of the people that I'd- now that I- if I say that I wasn't born here, they say they wouldn't tell- they couldn't tell. A slight accent.

INGRID: Is that something you are interested in? In terms of- you know, just trying to pass? . . . Often people are very proud=

MILENA: =yeah, yeah. At the beginning I was. I mean I felt really great if, you know two three years after I started speaking English, they were telling me that I sound like an Aussie.

People hear not only with their ears but also with their eyes. There is psycholinguistic evidence that in cases where our senses conflict, our sense of vision takes over.[24] In the context of the White-English identity complex, this can mean that English speakers who are racialized as Asian or Black may be perceived as less proficient and more accented than they really are. Conversely, White English speakers may be perceived as more proficient and less accented than they are, allowing them to pass. Where Asian or Black speakers are highly proficient, this perceptual discrepancy may account for compliments for how well they speak English.[25] In the contrasting case, low-proficiency White speakers may be judged particularly negatively.[26]

There may be another way in which the race-language bundles described here work to the benefit of White participants. It is likely that, as a group, they experience fewer micro-aggressions.[27] White participants not only reported fewer micro-aggressions, but also had more positive and inclusive experiences that validated them and affirmed their identities. Agatha from Georgia, for instance, is, in terms of conventional notions of female beauty, exceptionally good looking. Slim and petite, she was stylishly dressed, wearing high heels and elegant makeup whenever we met her. When asked what she liked most about Australia, she enthused: "Everyone smiles here. People are very friendly. I- I find Australians extremely friendly. And genuinely friendly. Not just you know- it's not just a polite smile, which doesn't have anything behind it."

Different experiences of differently racialized participants also surfaced in some of our group discussions. For instance, during one group discussion with Donna and two White women, three Asian women—Michiko and Kumiko from Japan, and Maria, an ethnically Chinese woman from Brazil—were riffing on the topic of how poorly Asians are treated in Australia:

MICHIKO: When I was traveling six years ago, around Australia. When I went into the shop to buy some groceries, I can't remember what, maybe tea or something. I went there, looking for tea section, and that old lady said, "We don't want any Asians in this shop."

MARIA: Yes, I- . . . I look the same. Because when I asking some information about the address . . . erm not the old lady, very young, said: "I don't talk with Korean person." [laughter] But I'm not Korean.

DONNA: "I'm not Korean. Talk to me!" [animated humorous voice; lots of laughter] I don't talk to Korean people? [disbelieving echo voice]

MARIA: Yeah.

MICHIKO: Yeah.

KUMIKO: Yeah, some people so mean to Asian people.

From there, the conversation turned to customer service and Michiko related her observation that an Asian customer and a White customer were treated differently in a department store, which we presented above. She then shared another story where she went to buy a car with her White Australian husband and the sales agent completely ignored her, talking only to her husband. At that point, Lena from Russia challenged the speakers and their assumption that race was the key factor in their experiences, suggesting alternative explanations for the selective incivility Michiko had observed. Lena was unwilling to concede that what Michiko had experienced was racism. She invalidated Michiko by saying, "It's you. More imagination of yours." Lena based her denial of racism on Australia's diverse population, where "half of the population comes from somewhere."

Even so, only a week later, Lena observed an instance of selective incivility herself. A keen tennis player, she noticed that she was always popular but that another club member, a woman from Malaysia, had difficulty securing partners for her matches. Lena confided to Donna:

> Do you remember this conversation when Asian girls said, it's- they're invisible? And I was thinking, "Yes." Because everybody was playing White people. [small laugh] White. . . . Everybody. . . . Yes. And I was thinking- I just was thinking yesterday, "Oh, it's nice to be beautiful White woman."

The confluence of these linguistic and racial identity dimensions set our participants on different trajectories of belonging where participants from Europe could imagine themselves—or at least their children—on a trajectory toward full inclusion that was not necessarily available to our participants from Africa and Asia. For the latter, even their Australia-born children could not necessarily escape discrimination, as Daniel from Sudan summed up: "African girls and boys speak English but do not get positions."

Coping in White-English Spaces

Shortly before Jaime turned 18, his family had to flee the Pinochet dictatorship in Chile.[28] They arrived in Sydney in November 1976 and were housed in a migrant hostel, along with other new arrivals from South America, Timor, and Germany. On a Friday evening just before Christmas of the same year, a group of teenagers from the hostel, including Jaime, went out to have some fun and experience Sydney's nightlife. The night was cut short by a racist attack. It all happened very fast. People yelled at them, but Jaime, who had arrived with "zero English," had no idea what was going on until, "straight away," they were "bashed by a large group of Australians."

Jaime escaped physically unscathed because "I was very fast and I run." Even so, the attack changed the course of his life. Already a shy and introverted kid, he became excessively anxious. He would never again go out to a pub, a club, or to dance. Instead, if they wanted to have a good time, he and his friends would buy drinks in a bottle shop and then "go to someone's place and go from one place to another."

Going out was not the only thing Jaime stopped doing. Although he had finished high school back in Chile, his high school certificate had not been recognized and he was made to redo sixth form, the final year of high school. He rarely attended. In addition to his anxiety, he also felt apathetic because he had already studied the content but could not follow the language. Instead of placement in a regular high school, what he needed was an intensive English-language course, he thought. Eventually, he missed school too often and ended up not graduating. This dashed his hopes to go to university and study philosophy, which he had dreamed of doing. Instead, his life became a string of jobs, divorces, custody battles, and financial struggles. He believed this is all because he wasted 1977: "My first year was the laziest year I've ever had in my life. And I regret that. Because I could have done something with my life." Social introversion, lethargy, and overall depression are recognized symptoms of post-traumatic stress.[29] Yet Jaime blames himself and his "laziness."

Physical violence is the most extreme version of challenging someone's right to a space. Jaime was the only one among our participants who shared an experience of racist assault with us. Yet aggression does not need to be frequent or even violent to engender fear or, at the very least, make everyday life uncomfortable. Jaime coped by avoiding public spaces. Yet avoiding public spaces that are dangerous for migrants is only feasible to a degree. It may be possible to perpetually avoid certain leisure activities, such as going out, as Jaime did. However, it is not possible for racialized people to avoid "Australian spaces" in education and employment. The Othered must navigate such White-English spaces, even if they are not safe for them.[30] So, how did our participants cope with White-English spaces?

Once Jaime's "lazy" high school year was over and finding a job became unavoidable, he attempted to reduce his audibility and visibility by changing his name to its English version: "I used to say my name 'Jaime'[31] . . . so I'd call myself James. And then from James it went to Jim, you know. So in the factory they call me Jim. James when I go out. Jaime at home." Anglicizing one's name is a long-standing migrant assimilation strategy and continues to this day, particularly among international students. In an early recognition of the bundling of language and race, the American linguist H. L. Mencken famously observed in 1919 that European immigrants were likely to give up their distinctive names in America for "protective coloration."[32]

A related strategy to reduce audible and visible difference is to not speak the heritage language with people from the same linguistic background. Among our participants, this strategy was mostly pursued by migrants from the Philippines who tended to be employed in workplaces with other people from the same country, such as the Big Beef abattoir in Tiny Town. Although Filipino workers constituted the numerical majority there, they experienced the atmosphere as hostile when they spoke Tagalog with each other. For instance, Donaldo, one of the butchers there, told Loy: "*When we first arrived, I felt they looked down on us like we were dogs. At work we get sworn at. It's like they make fun of us. We get yelled at,* 'Come back in Philippines.'" Another butcher, Torre, had the same feeling: "*I could sense that they were angry with us because we are foreigners.*" When they speak Tagalog with each other in the presence of non-Filipinos, they can feel the hostility ratchet up, as Roberto explained: "*When we speak Tagalog, sometimes the White people get annoyed. And then they say,* 'Talk English!' *They say that. They say that.*"

Work in the abattoir is organized on a conveyor belt system and there is hardly any occasion to speak during the shift. The only chance to chat is during break times. One would think that how workers communicate during break times with their mates is no one's business. However, non-Filipino overhearers regularly made it their business to tell them to speak in English. Instead of calling the overhearers out for meddling, Donaldo told us that the Filipinos would say: "Ah sorry sorry." Then they would make an effort to switch to English. Roberto, too, felt that Australians have a right to get angry when a language other than English is spoken in their presence: "*Because Australians are also thinking about what we might be saying, so they get mad at us.*" Some Filipinos took this sense of guilt and shame further. To avoid confrontations, they self-policed and campaigned among fellow Filipinos for the use of English. One of these was Ellen, whose strict "English only" policy, even in private with her husband, was motivated by her desire to avoid embarrassment.

Avoidance strategies were not the only way in which participants coped with racism. Some participants challenged their otherization and racialization, either explicitly to the face of the perpetrator or, more often, silently in their heads or off the record, after the fact, with their friends. Direct challenges were rare and include examples such as Paulo calling out the exclusionary assumptions behind the question "Where are you from?" Abenet from Ethiopia, whom we already met in Chapter 5, told us of an experience with street racism where he had called out the perpetrator and was then left in peace:

> There was a time when we went for shopping, and this White lady- she was intoxicated. She said, "What are you doing here? Go back to your home!" I told her that, "Are you crazy? The one that comes first, goes first." Because

> I know that this is the land of Aboriginals. And I told her that the one who came first, should go first. I came yesterday. And she didn't say anything. She went. (Abenet)

The most successful challenge to discrimination was mounted by Tania from Spain, who had been denied promotion in her workplace because "they said that my accent is going to hinder communication." In response, Tania threatened to sue the retail chain for which she worked under equal opportunity and anti-discrimination legislation. Not only was she given the promotion and a pay raise, but the supervisor who had made the initial decision was demoted and transferred out to another store.

Others would have liked to defend themselves against discrimination but felt that their English was not good enough, like Tina from China. Due to the limitations of her English, Tina believed that she "can't argue with them." Another reason why she chose to step back was that she herself accepted her inferior claim to space in Australia: "It's not my country, so I don't want to argue with them." Eric from Sierra Leone, another abattoir worker, also suggested that English-language proficiency played a role in being able to cope with racism:

> We work with people who are extremely racist. And yeah. They don't even wanna listen to you, because you are an African. But they realize, that if you understand them well, if you're a bit eloquent perhaps, they can consider Africans. Some racist supervisors look low upon Africans, especially some of those who come here, they don't make an effort to go to TAFE, to develop on their language, they bully them most of the time. Because they don't know how to defend themselves. They don't know how to put their case across, you know, even if they get angry. They just take advantage of that. It's hard. But I thank God I'm able to at least express myself a bit. (Eric)

Still others chose to remain silent because they found themselves confronted with so much ignorance about Africa that they believed it was pointless to argue. Serena and Timothy, a couple from Sudan, felt Australians "ask you stupid questions." Timothy, for instance, had been asked whether there were tomatoes in Africa, and Serena whether there was food. She concluded, "I don't know what they think in their mind." Her coping strategy was to ignore these questions, "Because what are you going to say?"[33]

Remaining silent comes at a psychological cost, even for bystanders. Cossette, a human resources manager from the Philippines, grappled with the fact that she observed other Filipinos in her workplace being mistreated while she herself was relatively safe:[34]

> I noticed also with these Australians, that they have- they have this very- you know, very- erm . . . They hate Filipinos. [. . .] So I don't say- I don't say anything. I don't normally also defend these guys. I just keep quiet and- what else can I? They have- anyway, their minds are closed. They won't- they won't listen to you. We are, erm second-class- or third-class citizens in Australia. This is not our country. So you just have to bear what they say. (Cossette)

Participants struggled with their non-responses and silences, and chewed over what they could have said. Years after she had been insulted by her neighbor with a compliment about her ability to drive, Sally still wondered what a good comeback might have been. Potential responses to past micro-aggressions still exercised participants' minds in what could be described as extreme cases of staircase wit. The term "staircase wit" was coined by the French philosopher Diderot, who upon being insulted during a dinner party found himself confused, perplexed, and incapable of exercising his usual sharp tongue and wit. By the time he thought of a good comeback to the insult—on his way home, at the bottom of a staircase—the moment had passed, and it was forever too late for him to come out of the encounter less agitated and settle the score.

Whether you choose to withdraw in the face of Othering, exclusion, discrimination, and racism, or try to make yourself small, or fight back, or replay the micro-aggressions and alternative responses in your head, being a target is exhausting. It distracts, and wastes time and energy, as Toni Morrison explains so well:

> The function, the very serious function of racism is distraction. It keeps you from doing your work. It keeps you explaining, over and over again, your reason for being. Somebody says you have no language and you spend twenty years proving that you do. Somebody says your head isn't shaped properly so you have scientists working on the fact that it is. Somebody says you have no art, so you dredge that up. Somebody says you have no kingdoms, so you dredge that up. None of this is necessary. There will always be one more thing.[35]

Abenet had come to the same conclusion. He wanted to ignore racism because he regarded it as "noise":

> Sometimes people are talking about discrimination in Australia. Say discrimination of Whites and all those things. I used to tell them that, "Please, this is not discrimination." Even we were discriminated when we were- you know home. The reason why we are here is simply because we were discriminated from our home. Therefore we are here to plan for our future. The best thing is to stick on what you are doing. Even though there are a lot of noise from right and left and

> whatever. If that, do something good for yourself and your community. [. . .] You will be discriminated against. But the most important thing is, know that you are someone. To do something good in your life. Don't be discouraged with so many noise, this noise. Take them as a positive thing to strive forward, that is the most important thing.

Like Abenet, most participants who experienced Othering, exclusion, discrimination, and racism refused to be defined by it. Even Jaime, whose life in Australia had been deeply shaped by the racism he experienced, decided in his 30s that he could not let it rule his life. He took up karate, reclaimed "Jaime" as his fighter name, got himself an earring, and took pride in the fact that his teenage daughter now thought he was gay. In the next chapter we will explore the identity projects that participants pursued to assert their belonging in Australia.

7
"I Have Many Faces"
Self-Making in a New Language

Home Is Where the Heart Is

"I'm Australian. I like Australia. It's my home. My children are here, so that's my country. [. . .] My most life was here. I belong here." These are the words of Jutta, recorded a few weeks before her 57th birthday. At that point, Jutta had lived in Australia for 34 years, having arrived in 1970 at the age of 23. In our data, Jutta's bold claim to Australian identity—"I'm Australian"—stands out. No one else produced such an unqualified statement without "ifs" or "buts." Most never even applied the designation "Australian," no matter how qualified, to themselves, but viewed it as the identity of native-born people, as we saw in Chapter 6. In this chapter, we explore what claims to identity and belonging our participants made. How do migrants construct a new sense of self and being at home?

For Jutta, her migration was not a salient part of her identity. The move to Australia had happened a long time ago, as she points out, and even back then it had not meant much. At age 23, as a young woman from a small village in Austria, she had found herself in West Berlin, then a heavily militarized enclave in the time of the Cold War.[1] A few years earlier, she had followed a German man to the city, and they now had a 5-year-old child and a new baby. Friends were floating the idea of starting a new life in Canada. Although Jutta "wasn't so keen on it," her husband jumped at the idea but did not fancy Canada. And that was how the couple, their two young children, and some friends ended up on a migrant ship bound for Australia. Their first stop was the Bonegilla Migrant Reception and Training Centre, a large arrival center for new migrants, mostly from continental Europe, that operated between 1947 and 1971.[2] From there, they made their way to the sugarcane plantations of Northern Queensland, where work was plentiful. The next few years saw several moves, a series of jobs, the birth of a third child, and divorce. By the time we met her, that transient lifestyle was long in the past, and Jutta had been living in the same house in Sydney for 15 years with her second husband and had been working for the same employer for just as long. She led a busy life structured by her shift work assembling food trays for an airline caterer. Her free time was devoted to her family, which included not only her three adult children but also her second husband's Croatian clan,

Life in a New Language. Ingrid Piller, Donna Butorac, Emily Farrell, Loy Lising, Shiva Motaghi-Tabari, and Vera Williams Tetteh, Oxford University Press. © Oxford University Press 2024. DOI: 10.1093/oso/9780190084288.003.0007

a group of 300 people who had all come from the same island in the Adriatic Sea in the 1950s and had settled in the same Sydney suburb.

One of our recorded conversations with Jutta, involving Emily, Ingrid, and Emily's grandmother, who was a neighbor of Jutta's and had originally introduced us, might best be described as a gossiping session. There is small talk, such as an extended comparison of the traffic in Sydney and rural Queensland. There is banter, such as an absurd back-and-forth about how to avoid being eaten by a crocodile. And there is a lot of talk about absent third parties and members of our families.[3] The most prominent among these were Jutta's mother-in-law, who had recently passed away, and her youngest daughter, who was undergoing treatment for a recurring cancer that had first been diagnosed 4 years earlier. The content of the conversation is informal and "intimate in style, personal and domestic in topic and setting."[4] For instance, Jutta spoke at great length about the food the mourners brought and consumed throughout the week-long funeral ceremony, the clothes they wore, and the work involved in hosting such a gathering. She told us about the daily habits of the elderly mother-in-law before her passing, matters involved in the disposal of her personal possessions, and the dietary preferences of the cat she had left behind. Through these and similarly quotidian topics, Jutta presents herself as a dutiful daughter-in-law, a hardworking wife, a worried mother, a doting grandmother, a caring neighbor, and a community-minded person. While she did not have much interest in more abstract explorations of identity and belonging, introducing the people and even pets in her social world in exquisite detail was her way of telling us what home meant to her. The very narrowness of Jutta's perspective on identity and belonging, as located in her workplace, her family, and her neighbors, where she was safely ensconced, enabled her grand and unproblematic identity claim to Australian-ness.

While Jutta's claim to Australian-ness is unique in our data, the idiosyncratic meanings she attributes to home are not. Home, for all participants, is a subjective emotional space where they forge new networks and attachments or maintain old ones. It is a complicated, ambivalent, conflicted, and shifting space that may relate to both their pre- and post-migration worlds, to neither, or to somewhere in between.[5] It may be related to feeling (un)comfortable, to (not) be in the same place as loved ones, to (not) be able to express or pursue one's true self, or to (not) live in communion with other people. Participants constructed identity and established belonging on many dimensions, related to family, work, gender, ethnicity, nation, language, religion, sport, service, or voluntary association.

Home is where people feel emotionally connected. For our participants, this was rarely a singular or uncontested space. Jutta was one of the few who located their home exclusively in Australia. Shirley, who had been forced "to run away from my country" due to the Sudanese Civil War, by contrast, was one of the few who located her home exclusively outside Australia:

> When you leave your country, you go to some other country, it's not like your home. Home is home, you know? It's not. I will say I'm happy, but I'm still not happy. Because this is not my country, you know? I'm still saying that it's not my country, even though I have Australian citizen. I'm Australian citizen, but I'm still- I feel, "No, I'm Sudanese." I'm still Sudanese, because I know where I'm come from. (Shirley)

For most participants, home was even more complicated. It could be multiple or lost entirely. An example of multiple belongings comes from Laura. For a party in her honor during a return visit to Italy, she asked for a cake in the shape of a love heart. The icing on one half of the heart was made to look like the Italian flag and the other half like the Australian flag. A passionate semiotician, Laura explained that the cake itself not only expressed her dual identities, but also symbolized multiplicity on a meta level. According to Laura, Italians do not usually decorate cakes with flags, so the idea was evidence that her "Australian part," where she is "a dag," had taken over.[6]

An example of feeling of not belonging anywhere anymore comes from Eva, who, after 18 years in Australia, had this to say:

> You never feel hundred percent belonging here. And when I go to my country, I don't belong there either. When I go there, I understand why I move here... but when I'm here, sometimes I say, "Oh! I wish I could be there." It's a very awkward situation. (Eva)

Some solved the "awkwardness" of no longer feeling at home in either nation by rejecting national belonging altogether. Some described themselves as "internationalists," who "can be at home anywhere I want to," as Milena put it. The self-descriptor "internationalist" occurs repeatedly in our data, but Paulo was even more creative when he called himself an "earthling" to describe the same transnational identity.

Migration constitutes a rupture of the self for two reasons. First, the daily routines, habits, and practices that make up our identity are subjected to a complete transformation, as we have seen throughout this book. Second, even though the 21st century has been dubbed "the age of migration," the normative life course continues to be imagined as lived in a single place.[7] This presents a double challenge for the construction of a new self, namely a practical and an imagined reconstruction. Identity and belonging then become something that needs figuring out. Crafting a new self requires perseverance, agility, and the ability to live with paradoxes and to solve unexpected problems.

Losing and Shedding Old Selves

An unexpected problem many participants faced was that they lost their former selves. The sense of loss of self is not just a vague feeling, but can be linked to concrete losses and absences in terms of daily habits, work, language, and social contacts, as the philosopher Hannah Arendt illuminates in her 1943 essay "We Refugees:"

> We lost our home, which means the familiarity of daily life. We lost our occupation, which means the confidence that we are of some use in this world. We lost our language, which means the naturalness of reactions, the simplicity of gestures, the unaffected expression of feelings. We left our relatives [. . .], and that means the rupture of our private lives.[8]

How close this reflection was to the hearts of our participants can be seen from conversations we had in April 2009 about a mass shooting in the United States.[9] The tragic incident took place in an English-language class for adult migrants in an American Civic Association Immigration Center in upstate New York. From a distance, the setting looked eerily like an AMEP class, and news of the shooting deeply affected many associated with the AMEP. Many in our circles could see themselves in the shooting victims—11 adult English-language learners, their teacher, and a receptionist. The students came from seven different countries, namely Brazil, China, Haiti, Iraq, Pakistan, the Philippines, and Vietnam. At the same time, they could also see themselves in the perpetrator, a 41-year-old immigrant from Vietnam. Many were asking themselves what could have motivated such a horrendous crime. The gunman also killed himself and so ultimately his motives remain unknown, but media speculations focused on the recent loss of his job, his poor English, his apparent loneliness, and his overall lack of obvious success in life. These were also reasons that participants imputed to the gunman: "because he doesn't speak any English," "because he cannot communicate," "because he lost his job," "because of the recession," or "because he felt low." Maria went further:

DONNA: But why would he kill his fellow students?
MARIA: Because we has a lot of background, like we- we miss our country, we miss a lot of things, so I remember and- I put my in his place. "Why he's doing this?" Because he's migrant like me, "Why he did this?" And he feels

> so frustrate. [. . .] "And why he killed these old peoples?" I think because all migrants very lonely, here in the new country. And sometimes we not be ourselves. Because we can't express. And we feel more depressed because this we can't express how- . . . erm . . . how to say? . . . erm, ours feelings.

In her response to Donna's question, Maria immediately switches from "he" to "we" and so puts herself into the murderer's shoes and channels his frustration, loneliness, sadness, depression, and experience of loss. These losses mean that, sometimes, "we are not ourselves" anymore. As in this example, participants explored severe mental ill health through the stories of others.[10] In addition to media reports, friends, acquaintances, and community members provided pivots to reflect on the dangers of lost selves. For example, Katja and Nicolas, a couple who had fled Communist Poland in the 1970s, were deeply affected by the suicide of an exiled Polish film director, Aleksander Ford.[11] They had not personally known Ford, but discovered from the news that he had lived only two blocks away from them during their time in Denmark. This had shocked them and led them to reflect on their own loss through the feelings they attributed to him:

KATJA: I liked to go to theater, and read books and- I enjoyed good conversation. So for me it was quite painful to change country.

NICOLAS: These problems are cross society. It doesn't matter, intelligent[12] people and non-intelligent people have the same problem. Because non-intelligent person, he also want to communicate. He is communicating maybe on some other level. But he will have the same problem. The way he communicated in Russia, Poland, or Korea, he's not able to do that anymore. But the- erm more intelligent person, who brilliant in language, who talk about the writers, who had this beautiful vocabulary=

KATJA: =I think maybe it's more painful.

NICOLAS: Painful! Yeah. [. . .]

KATJA: If we KNEW that he's [=Ford] so lonely, and- and is just so upset, you know? We could go and talk to him! And he could come to us, because we were MISSING contact with intelligent people.=

NICOLAS: =contact with people of this type. Yeah.

KATJA: And later we were reading that he was alone. Came from Poland, and erm couldn't come in contact because of people- because of language, and become depressed and at the end he become suicide.

NICOLAS: Was very good director. And made very good- few Polish films, which are part of Polish film history now.

KATJA: Yeah, REALLY, really good director. I think that people like that- erm these kind of people are suffering more. Because for them language is not only . . . erm . . . tools- tool of communication. It's just that is life, that is everything, you know?

The mourning for an earlier, more literary, intellectual life that is apparent in Katja's and Nicolas' conversation echoes through our data. Goudarz, for instance, felt like a nobody in Australia and therefore needed extended visits back to his country of origin to recuperate his sense of self: "*After you come back* [to Australia from a visit to Iran], *you feel like you're somebody. That is what's important.*" As we have documented throughout this book, most participants experienced their migration as a hardship at some point, whether related to arrival shocks, difficulties with finding work, establishing social networks, managing their familial roles and obligations, or suffering from racism. Combined with mourning for a lost self, these could lead to feelings of perpetual discomfort. Maria expressed this by stating "to be a foreigner is very hard. I feel so like the fish not in water." In her words, the slight deviation from the common expression "like a fish out of water" is almost emblematic of migrants not quite fitting in.[13]

Not all participants experienced the loss of pre-migration selves as problematic, though. Many found it liberating to be able to leave parts of their former identities behind. This was the case for Roxana. Roxana is from a well-to-do Iranian family, who wanted to avoid compulsory military service for their two sons. When the oldest son turned 17, the family applied for a business visa to come to Australia. This meant that they invested in a small shop, which needed to turn a profit for at least 2 years and create at least one job for an Australian citizen or permanent resident. Roxana's husband was the primary applicant, but he had no intention of residing in Australia because he held a position as a bank director in Iran, which was the family's main source of income. So, Roxana came to Australia on her own to look after her adult and teenaged sons. This proved liberating for Roxana in at least two ways. First, she no longer needed to defer to her husband in everyday life, and second, she was free to voice her anti-Islamic opinions. In Iran, Roxana's husband had tightly controlled her:

> I was very dependent in my country to my husband. After many years work, I didn't work. I was at home, and my husband decided about EVERYthing. Because he was out, every day, and whenever I wanted to say something, he said, "No, you don't know about the outside. I know better. And I'm twelve years older than you. You- you don't know." (Roxana)

On his visits to Australia, the power dynamic shifted: "Here it's very different. He comes, I can say, 'Oh, you don't know anything, because I was here four months more than you.'" She spoke gleefully about her husband's inability to drive in Australia because he could not get used to driving on the left side of the road. In Iran, he had always been the driver when they were together, but in Australia this changed. Roxana enjoyed how uncomfortable it made her husband to be her passenger and to have to take instructions from her. She was also glad to leave the public meekness required of Iranian women behind. Like many Iranian women, she had suffered from the requirement to wear proper hijab in public and had been pulled up by the country's notorious morality police on two occasions for showing too much hair under her headscarf.[14] Roxana took great pleasure in being able to dress as she liked, presenting a confident public self, and engaging in debates that might be considered blasphemous in Iran.[15] One of Roxana's most memorable English-language learning experiences in the AMEP was when she was partnered in class with a Muslim man whom she riled up during a pair-speaking practice activity:

> I ask him, "Do you believe that women are- and men are equal?" He said, "Yes, I believe." And I said, "Oh no, you don't believe!" He said, "Why do you say?" I said- erm I asked him, "Do you believe that man can have three wives together?" He said, "Yes, I believe." And I said, "So, you- you don't believe that men and women are equal, because the women can't have erm three husbands together. But the man can, so you don't believe." [. . .] It was another experience for me, that I could say whatever I want to say. "Oh no, you don't believe!" But in Iran, I can't say. In Australia, I could say, "But, oh it's- Sorry. It's bullshit!" [laughs] (Roxana)

Despite Roxana's relief at being able to get rid of undesirable parts of her pre-migration identity, she also felt the loss of aspects of her former self that she cherished. She thought of herself as an ebullient, humorous, and "cheeky" person in Persian, but she could not perform these aspects of her identity in English because she was not proficient enough to do so. This made her feel as if "sometimes I have a big lock on my lips."

The association of different languages with different identities was another common topic for participants.[16] Kumiko and Michiko, for example, both reported feeling more confident, more independent, more outgoing, and even more friendly in English. By contrast, they felt they had to hide these aspects of their identities in their native Japanese:

KUMIKO: In Australia, I can be more myself. In Japan, I- we have to- we always have to=

MICHIKO: =Yeah. Think too much.=

KUMIKO: =Yeah. To worry=

MICHIKO: =about life. If I don't get married before thirty years old, everyone, neighbors, friends, "Something wrong with her."

KUMIKO: Will judge you.

MICHIKO: Yeah, cos if things happen or if I don't get job, "What's wrong with her?" You know, everyone's talking, I can hear and then- . . . I shouldn't be worried. But I can't stop worrying about everything.

KUMIKO: [laughs] So, we all have- like, you know, in our drawers, we have three or five masks. "Today, I put this one."

MICHIKO: Yeah, yeah.

Both women cherished the sense of freedom they experienced in Australia, even if it conflicted with experiences of racism, as we saw in Chapter 6. Such tensions and conflicting emotions over the identities they had left behind were reported by most participants because migration is "both liberating and destroying," as Laura put it. Tina, for instance, had been a successful lawyer in China and was very career minded. She was not able to regain her career in Australia, as we saw in Chapter 3. Over time, she came to see some advantages to that, as it allowed her to re-evaluate her priorities:

> Before I came here, as far as I am concerned, career forever goes first. It is what I achieve in my work that can prove and fulfill myself. In China we used to judge a person successful or not according to what he has achieved from work. Consequently, we used to study hard and work hard to prove how capable and successful we are. Unfortunately, in most cases, with the development of our career, we will finally find out that the more we dedicate to our career, the more possible that we lose ourselves. (Tina)

In Australia, the absence of adequate career prospects allowed her to discover leisure activities and the pleasures of domesticity:

> The leisure lifestyle and how Australians cherish life changed [my husband] a lot. He has learned to slow down to enjoy what life gives us and to value what we currently have. He has learned that career is not the whole world. Furthermore, he hopes I could also feel the same. [. . .] I begin to pay my attention to other things besides career. For instance, I begin to study cooking, which was ever the last thing I wanted to do because I think spending too much time and energy on cooking is not worthwhile. Now I even begin to try to improve my skills in cooking to make my husband happy. (Tina)

The image of a successful career woman like Tina settling in a democratic society that promotes equality of opportunity for both genders, yet having to conform to a gender role reminiscent of the 1950s, is paradoxical. Tina was not alone, though, and domesticity featured prominently among some female participants' projects of rebuilding their post-migration selves.

Finding and Crafting New Selves

Isabella was another homemaker. In contrast to Tina, this was nothing new for her. Isabella had never been in paid employment in her whole life. In fact, she had never even gone to school. Born in the late 1950s in southern Sudan, Isabella's early life was typical for a Madi woman of her generation:[17] As a girl, she was prepared for a domestic life centered on the family, marriage, and motherhood. Attending formal schooling was not even an option. She was married in her early teens and bore and raised nine children. Two of these were born in a refugee camp in Uganda, where the family had fled from the war. By the time the family was selected for resettlement in Australia, Isabella was in her late 40s.

It takes little imagination to realize not only the grit and determination, but also the skills and capabilities Isabella must have demonstrated to ensure the survival and integrity of her family through war, flight, famine, and extended periods of extreme adversity. Yet, her strength and ability were almost completely erased when she came to Australia, where all anyone seemed to see in her was her illiteracy. When we first met her, she had been attending English-language classes, on and off, for 7 years. Initially, her English-language classes had been part of the settlement provision through the AMEP and, later, they became part of her obligations as a welfare recipient. During that time, Isabella had learned enough spoken English to cope with daily life, but she continued to struggle with literacy. She had learned how to spell her name and address, and that was about it. Her personal view was that she was too old to learn how to read and write because her life course had unfolded without ever being socialized into the practices of formal education: "I find very hard because I'm child, I'm not going to school. I grow just refugee like that."[18]

Instead of attending English-language classes, Isabella would have preferred to work. What she wanted most was to find a cleaning job or similar manual work to be able to have her own income. However, that proved impossible without some kind of educational certificate, as we showed in Chapter 3. As a result, Isabella found herself in a bureaucratic quandary. Nominally, Centrelink expected her to look for work. However, when she asked them to help her find a job, she was told, "No, no. No job. Go AMEP Center." Essentially, no representative of the

Australian state really expected Isabella to find work, and attending English-language classes was counted as the bureaucratic substitute to demonstrate her willingness to work. For Isabella, this was a deeply unsatisfactory state of affairs because she wanted the requirement to work to be real. She wanted a job that would secure her independence. Finally, on the recommendation of a friend, she took the initiative and found casual part-time cleaning work for a private household. Isabella loved the work because the money it brought in allowed her to fulfill a dream: As her family had been scattered long ago by the war, she wanted to see some of her brothers again in this life. She saved up all the money she earned for a visit to the United States, a journey she planned, financed, and took completely on her own—passing a real-life literacy test with bravado.

VERA: You went alone to America? [spoken in surprised, disbelieving voice]
ISABELLA: Uhmhu.
VERA: Were you able to speak English?
ISABELLA: No, yeah. Yeah, they help me.
VERA: And you found your way to America? [still surprised voice]
ISABELLA: Yeah.
VERA: You must be proud of yourself!
ISABELLA: Yeah. I find them. Yeah. I find my brother, my nephew living in Dallas. I live in Dallas there, one month and half. I go to Nebraska. My youngest brother's in Nebraska. Then I take the Christmas there, yeah.
VERA: Wow! So do you see that you are doing well? When you came, you couldn't speak English! Zero.
ISABELLA: No zero, zero.

The new self that Isabella was confronted with in Australia was one full of deficit positionings: a Black African woman from a refugee background with no literacy and no English. These positionings caused Isabella a lot of grief, but she did not let them rule her, and she took great, even if quiet, pride in her achievement of financing and making the trip of a lifetime all by herself so that she could be reunited with some members of her dispersed family.

Strength, resilience, and perseverance against the odds were an important part of crafting new selves for many of our participants. Like Isabella, others, too, found that the grit and determination that had brought them so far were often obscured in Australia, where their stories became untellable because they were lumped together under labels that were, at best, inadequate stereotypes, such as "African," "Asian," "CALD," "English-language learner," "low-literacy learner," "migrant," or "refugee." The "refugee" label was one that many of the humanitarian entrants found deeply troubling and stigmatizing. Franklin, for instance, lamented:

> What complicate life to me in Regional City is many time of course I'm identified as a refugee. Which increases or put- increases my doubt. "How long will I be continue being called refugee with this name?" Until when will a person be called a refugee? Because I have what- my- the Australian citizenship, and I have what- the so-called Australian passport. But still I'm called a refugee. (Franklin)

Stereotypical labels that lumped them all into one big group contributed to holding participants back from achieving their full potential. For many, that situation was further complicated by the fact that the identities that mattered to them were unknown and meaningless in Australia. Examples of aspects of identity that became untellable include minority backgrounds from back home. Our Sudanese participants alone, for instance, belonged to eight different ethnic groups, including Acholi, Arabic, Bari, Dinka, Kakwa, Madi, Moro, and Shilluk.[19] The nuances of these ethnicities, languages, and identities were completely lost in Australia, subsumed under labels such as "Sudanese" or even "African." Another identity aspect that was lost was multiple migrations. The move to Australia was not the first international migration for at least 58 out of 130 participants. Some had spent considerable time in countries other than their country of origin and Australia. Those intermediary spaces had become an important aspect of their identities, too. Yet, they usually had to edit these complexities out of their life-stories to make sense.[20]

Maria is a participant from an ethnic minority background in her country of origin and someone who spent considerable time in a third country. One of the ways in which Maria described herself was as "BBC" for "Brazilian-born Chinese." For her, that was a complicated identity she had inherited from her parents, who were both refugees. Her father had been born in Jilin province in northern China into a family of Chinese Christians. In the 1920s, when he was about 10 years old, his parents were killed for their beliefs by the Chinese National Army, Kuomintang (KMT), and he was drafted into their army as a child soldier. He fought for the KMT for many years until he fled to Brazil in the 1950s after the Communists won the war and established the People's Republic of China.[21] Maria's mother was a member of Indonesia's Chinese minority and came to Brazil a few years later with her family, fleeing the anti-Chinese laws of the Suharto era.[22] Maria's parents met in São Paolo in 1970 and Maria was the first of 10 children to be born over the next years. From an early age she remembered receiving conflicting messages about her identity:[23]

> Since I was a child, my mom said to me, I am not Brazilian but Chinese. I remember when I went to school, I was told I am not Chinese but Brazilian. However, I was a child and I believe in my mom words. (Maria)

These identity conflicts resulted in a difficult childhood, particularly as Maria's parents never learned to speak Portuguese and the children became Portuguese-dominant once they started school. Years later, as an adult, Maria strategically embraced both her Brazilian and Chinese identities, as required. For instance, when she wanted to paint herself as a spontaneous, passionate person, she explained that as a typical trait of Brazilian people, whose "heart is very impulsive." On the other hand, when she wanted to draw attention to her business savvy, her work ethic, her career mindedness, and her competitive streak, she described these as Chinese traits.

Identity became further complicated for Maria when her husband, a Japanese Brazilian, accepted a high-level corporate job in Japan.[24] The move turned Maria from an independent, successful businesswoman, who had run her own thriving import-export company, into a full-time housewife. Maria struggled not only with the language, but also with the narrow strictures placed on women in Japan. Placing a high value on women being confident, independent, and receiving respect as equals, she felt extremely limited by her positioning in Japan. Most challenging for her was her outsider status, which manifested not only in the absence of adequate opportunities to participate in paid employment and public life, but also within the immediate family. Maria was increasingly sidelined in family communications as her young daughter, Sabrina, quickly learned Japanese but began to struggle with Portuguese. A typical interaction would involve Sabrina coming home from school and wanting to tell her mother about her day. However, Sabrina had stopped speaking Portuguese within a short time of being in Japan, while Maria never gained enough Japanese to be able to communicate well. So, the two would get frustrated with each other and the impasse could only be resolved by dad after his return home from work in the evening. The increasing necessity for the father to interpret between mother and daughter placed a significant strain on Maria's relationship with Sabrina, who soon acquired a "totally Japanese mind."

While Sabrina fell in love with Japan, her parents never felt like they fully fit in. Maria's unhappiness was compounded by her husband's dissatisfaction with his work relationships. In their late 30s, after 8 years in Japan, they decided to make a fresh start and applied for an independent skilled visa to come to Australia. Maria was determined to make Australia home. To ease her daughter into the transition, she enrolled her in a Japanese-medium school and decided to support her Japanese identity as much as possible. For herself, she focused on creating new connections by immersing herself in a local Baptist church and community center. She spent a lot of time attending their events, which included church services, prayer meetings, playing card games, quilting sessions, and supporting the elderly in the community. Maria loved volunteering with the elderly because she valued their stories and took them as learning opportunities, both to practice

English and to learn about Australian life. For instance, she set up a vegetable chopping service for arthritic people, out of a genuine desire to be useful and to serve, but also to make connections. Within a year of her arrival in Perth, she played an important role in the management of church affairs and was elected treasurer "because they feel I'm very clever with money, and I'm very dedicated."

In short, Maria strategically invested the skills, grit, and determination she had acquired through her difficult childhood, her university education, her professional experience, and her migration trajectory to create a new self. It was a multifaceted self, as she suggested when she spoke about herself in the third person: "I feel Maria has to make many face." Her many faces allowed Maria to focus on her core self as wife, mother, and Christian, which brought her to a—at least partially self-made—happy place: "I am happy with me. [laughs] Yeah, I happy because I have a good married. I have a good daughter and, I thank God because I can come in here and settle down very well."

Building Community

Maria received tangible evidence of her inclusion and belonging in Australia when she had to have surgery and her church community rallied to support her:

> This week although painful for me, but it was a great time to find who is your friend. The ladies at Baptist Believers knew I was ill. Then the ladies organized a food schedule. Two weeks I didn't cook and they send food to me and my family. Yummy Ozzie[25] food, I ate lamb with beanettes, basmati rice (my first time), lasagne, fish casserole, . . . Wow, it was good. My first time in Oz I have been spoiled and the best is for Australian people. I am blessed for having a such good friends and specially Ozzie friends. (Maria)

Maria was not alone in drawing strength from her faith, and the practical and spiritual supports provided by churches.[26] Joining a church was a first-order priority for some participants. Abenet and Amot, for instance, had been Presbyterians back home. When they arrived in Sydney, they discovered that no Presbyterian church was within a convenient traveling distance. To meet their need to join a spiritual community, they switched denominations and joined a nearby Mormon church. Abenet explained his rationale:

> When I came here, my program was three things. Number one to get house which was very close to a station because I'm not driving. For shopping and whatever, and all those things. The second priority was to get a house also which is very close to schools, because we are very new in the country, so I don't

> want my children to go very far where they can get lost or whatever. The third one is to get church also, it was one of my priority. I know that I was a member of the Presbyterian church when I came here but I couldn't get even one near at that time. I was new in the country, and I need to be a part of the church. Because socialization is one the most important things in life. (Abenet)

While few were as strategic as Abenet, joining a church was the most straightforward way to social inclusion for Christian participants. In fact, even some non-Christian participants attended a church for the practical benefits it provided. Jessie, for instance, had been raised in a Buddhist family in Taiwan. In Sydney, she regularly attended not only a Buddhist temple but also a Pentecostal church. One of the church leaders there, an elderly Anglo man, took her and another prospective convert from China under his wing. For a few years, the three of them engaged in intensive Bible study sessions up to four times a week. Jessie never converted to Christianity, but remained in contact with the missionary and continued to count him among her close friends, even after her return to Taiwan.

While joining a church was an important source of strength for many participants, being unable to do so was an additional source of suffering for others. The latter is true of the Filipino families in Tiny Town, whom we first met in Chapter 5. These were a deeply religious group of people. When asked about what they missed about life in the Philippines, they would always include attending church with their families in the list. However, they found attending church in Tiny Town difficult for various reasons. Most of them were Catholics and two were Mormons. Unfortunately, neither denomination had a church in Tiny Town. To travel to the nearest Catholic or Mormon church was difficult. In addition to the distance, they explained that their shift work usually precluded church attendance. Even if Sunday happened to be their rostered day off, they were too tired and needed to sleep to recuperate in order to be able to face the rigors of their strenuous shifts for another week.

Where they are available—or if migrants are flexible with the denomination—churches have the strongest institutional structures to provide a ready-made community that newcomers can join. By contrast, non-faith-based community organizations that participants joined were more varied. For instance, some of our Iranian participants with school-aged children attended community language schools on Saturdays.[27] These provided both language maintenance support for their children and opportunities to socialize for themselves. In another example, Danica got involved in Russian community radio, both as a way for her to maintain the language and to provide a service to the community. In yet another case, Milena took up salsa dancing.[28] Soon, her whole life revolved around salsa dancing. She became a salsa instructor, learned Spanish, and fell in love with a fellow dancer, whom she married after divorcing her first husband.

Milena's dedication was an exception. Generally, communities of believers proved stronger and more durable than others, where involvement usually was less intense and often did not last long. Building community outside of faith organizations is inherently difficult in an individualistic, consumerist, capitalist society such as Australia. In this sense, the much-vaunted "Australian community" that migrants are often exhorted to join does not exist. For Daisy, this lack of communal values was the greatest loss she felt in the post-migration context:

> Everybody just concentrate on their life. They go to work, your children, you don't even think of your neighbor, your sister or whatever. That is the biggest problem with our people. Because they have mortgages, they want to build back home, they have children they are educating. (Daisy)

Daisy, like many others, had a deep sense of obligation to give back to Australia to prove herself a worthy member of the community. Early in her time in Australia, she had seen a recruitment ad for volunteers to visit lonely people in nursing homes. Daisy put her hand up and she kept visiting elderly people for 4 years. During that time, she visited with more people than she could remember because they all kept dying, and she became depressed herself. Also, Daisy began to suspect that the NGO that ran the program might be discriminating against her by allocating the oldest and most frail residents to her. Qasem had a similar experience when he volunteered as a parent helper in his daughter's school but was turned down. The teacher told him, "*Don't worry, the* volunteer *list is now complete. We don't need any further* volunteers *for now*." Like Daisy, who could not be sure that all nursing home residents were equally likely to die soon, Qasem was unsure whether he had really volunteered too late or whether he was intentionally excluded.[29] Daisy decided that volunteering in the nursing home was not the best way for her to give back to the community. Instead, she decided to serve by working with African communities:

> So I stopped doing that, and I started volunteering with the African communities. And I have worked with Africans from all sorts. Like help them do their resumes, helping them get jobs, empowering them, and encouraging them. And they are people who may be- for example they are lawyers and they can't get lawyer jobs. They don't want to do other jobs. They are so depressed. But I sit down with them, and I talk to them. And slowly, slowly they come out, and they are working. I have so many people that I have just talked to them, showed them how they can start, and now they have stood on their feet. (Daisy)

Daisy's service has been recognized with two of the strongest markers of recognition the Australian state has to offer, an Award as Australian of the Year and being made a member of the Order of Australia.[30] Migrants are often accused of lacking interest in volunteering.[31] Yet it is not easy for them to volunteer in mainstream organizations, as Daisy and Qasem discovered. On the other hand, the volunteering that they do within churches and ethnic communities may often go unnoticed. An example of a community role that is unknown in Australia is that of "elder," which relates to communal parenting and dispute resolution.[32] In Africa, cultural norms are such that older people are expected to look out for younger people in their community, guide them, support them, encourage them, and discipline them as necessary, regardless of whether they are related or institutionally licensed. This communal social organization clashes with Australian norms where only parents or institutionally sanctioned adults such as teachers are expected to take responsibility. Not only are elder roles invisible in Australia, some forms of communal parenting such as physical discipline are even illegal. Several participants fulfilled such roles but suffered from the fact that their service was not recognized. Mamuna, a woman in her 50s, for instance, was, like Isabella, expected to work or to seek work in order to receive welfare payments, although there were no jobs available that suited her education and qualifications. However, Mamuna was not sitting around doing nothing, as some people might imagine. She was, in fact, incredibly busy looking after her grandchildren. Her caregiving work enabled her adult children and in-laws to be in the workforce. The arrangement benefited her extended family and the wider society, yet Mamuna was made to feel like a welfare cheat by Centrelink. In her community, she was widely regarded as wise and as a leader. During an hour-long visit, for example, her phone rang no less than six times. Each time it was a different caller. Upon taking each call she would apologize and explain to Vera that these were calls from people within the community who had brought family issues to her as an elder and she was consulted regularly. Mamuna manages interpersonal conflicts and family problems in her extended network. This is a great help to the families involved and a valuable service to society at large. Yet her services remain invisible because they are not paid work, and the skills she employs are neither accredited nor easily discernible within a culture that only recognizes formalized skills, paid work, and the nuclear family.[33]

Another example of highly valuable yet unrecognized communal service provision comes from Sylvia. One day, on her way home in Regional City, Sylvia noticed an unaccompanied teenaged girl, Helen, who she felt should not be out and about alone at night. Sylvia offered her a lift. When Helen told her that she had nowhere to go, Sylvia took her home for what she expected to be a brief visit and called Helen's parents who, unlike herself, were not from South Sudan but Sierra Leone, to advise them of Helen's whereabouts. To her dismay, Helen's father told Sylvia that he had thrown her out of the house and was not inclined to take her back. A mother herself and a woman who had survived a war zone and knew the dangers to unprotected women from personal experience, Sylvia let Helen stay with her. Over the next few months, while Helen took up residence in Sylvia's house, Sylvia negotiated with the Department of Community Services (DOCS; the name of Australia's child protection agency at the time), the police, and Helen's parents to find a long-term solution for her.[34] As an elder, Sylvia considered it her duty to support Helen. In Australian terms, Sylvia provided foster care for Helen. Foster caregivers are paid for by DOCS. Yet because Sylvia was not a licensed foster caregiver, she was not entitled to any payment for her services and bore the cost of helping Helen out of her own meager income. Money was not Sylvia's motivation, though. Her motivation was community. She was adhering to African communal values such as sharing, mutual aid, caring for others, interdependence, solidarity, reciprocal obligation, and social harmony.[35]

We started this chapter with the observation that home is an individual's space of emotional attachment. Through the ensuing exploration of participants' multiple, complex, and shifting selves, we are now able to add a social dimension. Home is where we are needed and where we can contribute to community.

8
Rethinking Language and Migration

The Challenge of Migrant Language Learning Revisited

With this book, we set ourselves the goal of exploring the dual challenge of learning a new language while living one's life through the medium of that language. This is a challenge that remains poorly understood, and non-migrants tend to underestimate its severity and the hardships involved. First, there is the shock of finding oneself in a new linguistic environment where you may not understand much of what is going on around you, while all the time being cognizant of the fact that not understanding what is going on may have acute repercussions for your well-being. Second, there is the difficulty of finding work that will not only pay the bills, but also sustain your ambitions and self-worth. Most participants took years to recapture their careers; many never did. Third, to improve proficiency in the new language, migrants need to interact in the new language, a task that is made difficult by the frequent absence of interlocutors willing to indulge newcomers, a lack of common topics, and the pervasiveness of misunderstandings. Misunderstandings may go on to reverberate through future interactions, as each misunderstanding leads to a loss of confidence that needs to be reclaimed over time. Fourth, migration intrudes even into the most intimate domains of life and alters family roles and relationships. It is not only that familial obligations and duties are redistributed, but also that new family tasks emerge. Prominent among these are new ways of parenting, including setting an—implicit or explicit—family language policy, and managing child language learning of both new and heritage languages. As children usually learn the new language faster, the potential impact of their superior (oral) proficiency on parental authority can become another tribulation for adult migrants. Fifth, migration continues to be imagined as a point of difference from the idealized sedentary mainstream population of their destination. This difference often marks those with a migration history as perpetual outsiders to their new society. Difference may be audible in their ways of speaking and visible where they are differently racialized. Experiences of Othering, exclusion, discrimination, and racism based on such differences create another level of adversity, as migrants need to cope with micro-aggressions, invalidations, insults, and sometimes even assaults. Finally, migration severs the self into a "before" and "after."

Life in a New Language. Ingrid Piller, Donna Butorac, Emily Farrell, Loy Lising, Shiva Motaghi-Tabari, and Vera Williams Tetteh, Oxford University Press. © Oxford University Press 2024. DOI: 10.1093/oso/9780190084288.003.0008

As pre-migration habits and identities have disappeared, new selves with a new sense of belonging, home, and community need to be fashioned.

Through the voices of our participants, we have documented the magnitude and anatomy of these challenges. Understanding them leads to an appreciation of migrants' courage, perseverance, and resilience. Living one's life through a new language is not easy, but it is a challenge that an ever-increasing number of people in the 21st century voluntarily or involuntarily have to face. As a society, it is our joint responsibility and common interest to reduce barriers and build bridges, on local, national, and global levels. Our aim with this book has been not only to make migrants' struggles visible, but also to chart a path that will help calm the turbulent waters of the raging river in which they may find themselves. Therefore, in this concluding chapter, we broaden our perspective out from the participants in this research to address broader social questions raised by our age of migration.

In shifting the gaze away from mobile people to their contexts of reception, the pervasive deficit perspective that engulfs all aspects of migrant life stands out. More than 70 years ago, the eminent transcultural psychiatrist H. B. M. Murphy observed:

> Assimilation to a new culture, especially when so speeded up, may seem very like acquiring a new personality [. . .]. The D.P. [=Displaced Person] who feels that he must give up this old personality to obtain a new one may feel that he is losing the last thing in the world that is really his and be correspondingly resistant to the process. As the change starts to take place, with or without this resistance, the D.P. may feel very empty, with no roots, no possessions, not even intangible ones. And the emptiness is emphasized if he finds that people are always regarding him as someone who must be given things, never as someone who has something in him which he can give in his turn.[1]

Although we may scoff at the outmoded language and argue that things have changed with the advent of multiculturalism, globalization, and transnationalism, a key settlement challenge identified by Murphy has remained, as we have shown throughout this book. Migrants are widely seen for what they lack, rather than for what they have to offer. Migrants' settlement in their new society is complicated by the deficit lenses through which the new society frames them. Their language is viewed as deficient English, not as a multilingual repertoire. Their language learning experiences come to be seen as irrelevant, instead of as foundations to build on. Their lack of local experience is highlighted as an obstacle, while their international experience remains unrecognized. Their aspirations are not taken seriously, but are ridiculed as castles in the air. Their qualifications are demoted without due consideration to minimal pathways that could effectively and efficiently bridge any gaps between requirements. Their own children may come to see their parents as inadequate and embarrassing. Racist invalidations, insults, or worse, may rub these deficient perspectives in, every now and then, to maintain even long-ago arrivals as forever foreigners.

Our research has shown that these deficit perspectives remain as entrenched today as they were 70 years ago. These deficit perspectives cannot be changed by newcomers, and the responsibility for change therefore lies with the receiving society. We now address what such change might look like by elucidating the implications of our findings for the ways in which we do social sciences research, understand the migration-economy nexus, support migrants across the life span, and build communicative resilience.

Sharing Data, Pooling Resources

In this book, we have returned to the data from six previous sociolinguistic ethnographies. Our methodological approach was inspired by open science principles and the desire to share our data and to pool our existing resources to be able to paint a bigger picture of language and migration.[2] While most researchers now accept the value of data sharing and reuse, implementation and practice remain patchy, particularly when it comes to qualitative data in the humanities and social sciences. In fact, even in STEM (science, technology, engineering, and mathematics) fields and disciplines, "data sharing is still mostly an ideal, honored more in the breach than in practice."[3] In ethnographic research, data sharing and reuse are in their infancy as researchers struggle with questions on what open research might even mean for them and how to implement FAIR principles (i.e., making their data findable, accessible, interoperable, and reusable).[4] These problems are compounded by time pressures and the absence of tried and tested workflows for reanalyzing and bringing to publication shared datasets.

As such, we have ventured into uncharted methodological territory with the research presented here. Our motivation for doing so was partly the result of a clash between what we consider to be some of the most exciting language and migration research and what we observe is wanted by policymakers, media representatives, and in public debate. Regarding the former, we believe that some of the best research in this space is based on qualitative ethnographic inquiry that approaches migrants and the contexts in which they find themselves holistically to produce nuanced, rich, and humane accounts that honor the complexity of real life. However, the very depth, complexity, and richness of this research mean that it rarely speaks to stakeholders outside academia and outside the immediate context under investigation. To policymakers, it may seem anecdotal and non-generalizable. By contrast, large-scale quantitative data or commissioned reports following survey approaches carry more weight. The result of this tension, in Australia at least, has been a proliferation of migration research that has been readily ignored and has achieved surprisingly little impact.[5]

There is, collectively, now a significant number of small-scale ethnographic studies investigating specific aspects of the lived experience of migration. Yet, these tend to be drowned out by census data and surveys. The problem with findings from the latter is that they cannot, by their very nature, provide an understanding of the lived experience of a social issue or phenomenon. As a result, public debate may not be well-informed about actual people, nor about the most pressing issues they face. The reason for this knowledge gap is partly the product of the dynamics inherent in different methods of data collection. Surveys and other forms of quantitative data collection are researcher-led. The research will only find what the researcher is looking for, and respondents can only answer the questions that are posed. In contrast, ethnographic studies allow for greater agency on the part of research participants to determine what kind of information is provided, what topics are addressed, and which direction data-collection activities and analysis ultimately take.

This flexibility enables qualitative researchers to account for change, complexity, and intersectionality. However, it usually limits them to a handful of participants. Data sharing has significant potential to resolve this tension. In saying so, we are not suggesting that data sharing is a silver bullet. Nothing ever is. For instance, the valuable flexibility of ethnographic research in fact exacerbates the known challenges of data sharing, as concepts, categories, processes, and procedures rarely map onto each other across research projects. This has been true even under such favorable circumstances as ours, where one researcher on the team, Ingrid, was involved in the design and execution of each of the six studies brought together here. Even so, we have often wished that we had built considerations of data sharing and reuse into our studies from the beginning. We did not, as these debates have only emerged in the past decade and, in our field, continue to be neglected. With this book, we have taken a first step, and we hope that it will serve as an inspiration for other researchers in the humanities and social sciences to attend to the long-term fate of their data right from the start of their research design. We hope that the value of our initial effort challenges others to take this approach further.

Our project shows what can be done with linguistic ethnography and provides a working model for how to combine existing small datasets into larger longitudinal studies of a social phenomenon or practice. It also provides a framework for supervising academics and their doctoral students to create a research and publishing community of practice that connects separate higher-degree research projects under a single, post-award project umbrella. Similarly, our study provides a model for early career and experienced scholars to work together to create and analyze big datasets from qualitative methods of inquiry.

By combining data from 130 participants across six separate ethnographic studies conducted over a period of 20 years, we have been able to cover a range of themes in a single analysis. At the same time, we have, throughout the writing of this book, struggled with our ambition to tell a broad story about the lived experience of migration and our desire to do justice to each of our participants. It has not been possible to tell every story and bring to life every participant we interacted with, learned from, and came to care about. To keep the book to a manageable length, we have instead outlined in each chapter a small number of stories as representatives of a specific truth claim about language learning and use in a specific domain. There is an inherent tension between the desire to humanize and individuate research findings and the desire to make broad truth claims about social organization. We have attempted to manage this tension to tell a bigger story that will raise awareness of the issues collectively faced by migrants navigating life in a new language.

Migration and Decent Work

Australia's migration program is firmly embedded in its economic policy, as we outlined in Chapter 1. For instance, the terms of reference of a 2023 parliamentary inquiry into migration mostly relate to economic considerations, as they define "immigration as a strategic enabler of vibrant economies," seek to explore "attraction and retention strategies for working migrants," and find strategies for "strengthening labour market participation."[6] Given how central economic and labor market considerations are to Australian migration, migrants' struggles with finding work and establishing careers may seem surprising. There is clearly a deep misalignment, and it is important to ask how this mismatch can be resolved.

The usual approach is to consider migrants' human capital. Among our participants are two different cohorts whose levels of human capital can be considered to contrast sharply. First, there is a cohort of people with disrupted education whose formal qualifications do not go beyond a few years of primary school at best and who have concomitant low levels of literacy. By conventional economic measures, this cohort has low levels of human capital. On the other end of the spectrum, there is a cohort of participants with high levels of formal education who are tertiary educated and even hold postgraduate degrees. It is reasonable to expect that the experiences of these two groups would differ widely, particularly when it comes to finding work. However, as we have shown throughout this book and particularly in Chapter 3, this is not necessarily the case. What both groups have in common is that their qualifications are misrecognized, their experience erased, and their aspirations dashed. Both groups struggle to get a foot in the door to a pathway that would engage the full range of their capabilities and allow them to contribute their talents in the service of their personal development, their families, and the wider society.

These commonalities have implications for support in the early settlement phase and for the broader debate about decent work. One is practical, the other is systemic.

Taking practical implications first, most participants struggled with the lack of pathways in the early settlement phase that would take seriously what they brought with them and provide a route to upskilling if needed, or an entry into a position where they could gain local experience. Many floundered as they were misdiagnosed as incompetent English speakers and had to navigate a maze of educational options, none of which seemed particularly relevant to their needs. The oft-stated ambition of Australian politics to create "a seamless transition for new arrivals from the airport to the workplace"[7] may provide a good soundbite. But it is not working, as tailored needs assessments, short-term "onboarding" programs, and bridging programs are lacking. Skills recognition is too often an all-or-nothing game, where state actors who issue visas and professional bodies tasked with skills recognition operate in splendid isolation from each other. Redoing full degrees or leaving the profession entirely are too often the only options. Greater creativity with learning-on-the-job options and tailored bridging qualifications is needed. The design and implementation of these should be pursued by professional and industry bodies, and we will provide some examples in the next section.

Where that transition "from the airport to the workplace" is enforced by the necessity to earn an income, immediate employment without a supported transition period can be deeply damaging. As we showed, some migrants become trapped in jobs for which they are overqualified and which bar them from pursuing options that would (re)connect them to their aspirations and careers through relevant education and training. The broader problem here is the neoliberal assault on decent work.[8] Linking migration debates with debates about the future of work also requires us to stop reducing migrants to workers, to a bundle of skills contributing to the economy, a situation that has become pervasive in Australia as elsewhere. This reductionist view of migrants as workers is deeply vexing. In fact, it undergirds many of the problems our participants faced.

Around the world, valuing the national economy over people has resulted in an ever-increasing set of exploitative jobs that can only be filled through migration. This is particularly obvious from another distinct cohort among our participants: abattoir workers. Our participants include several butchers and meat packers in two separate abattoirs. Some of these had been hired from the

Philippines on temporary skilled visas to bring their knife-skills and the helping hands of their wives to Australia. Others had come to Australia as refugees from the postcolonial wars in Sierra Leone and Sudan. The former wanted to work as butchers, a trade they had learned back home and one they took pride in. They also wanted to provide for their families, share in the lives of their children, and lead a full life that was not just all about work, far away from their families. The latter did not want to be involved in meat work at all, but were forced to do so due to a lack of alternatives. Both suffered from the exploitative conditions in the industry. Meat processing is a prime example of an industry where work conditions have become so unfavorable that it is avoided by people who have other options. Since the late 1990s, concentration in the meat-processing industry, combined with state policies favoring employers, resulted in a weakening of the Australasian Meat Industry Employees Union (AMIEU), the institution of low-wage awards, the abolition of the "tally system" where workers had been paid per unit of throughput rather than per time worked, the expansion of work hours, and the disappearance of overtime penalties.[9] As such, the employment challenges of migrants need to be understood as part of a broader system designed to undermine the value of work and workers. Migration and the jobs that migrants fill are, in a way, the canary in the coal mine of societal inequality. To improve migrants' employment trajectories, the perspective needs to shift from migration to broader struggles for decent work and against labor exploitation.

Migration across the Lifespan

In many ways, migration constitutes a crisis in the life of an individual, as we have shown throughout this book. This crisis arises from a combination of the departure from a familiar context, the initial language barrier, economic insecurity, family problems such as parenting challenges, confrontation with racism, and a loss of self. These migration traumas were closely connected to the loss of social networks in migration. The absence of family and friendship networks itself was deeply unsettling.[10] In various degrees, all participants had to face practical challenges and struggled to find interactional opportunities, to re-establish community, and to connect their pre- and post-migration selves.

The key finding about migrant language learning, then, is that it is hard. This is in stark contrast to the facile assumption that adult language learning will happen naturally in an assumedly immersive target environment. Migrants are often cast as resisters to language learning and as shirking their responsibilities. This is a complete mirage. It flies in the face of the actual challenge of adult language learning and contrasts with our combined decades of experience, where we have never spoken with a single NESB migrant who did not want to learn English—not only among our 130 core participants, but never. On the contrary, participants were keen to practice English, suffered from their inability to do so, and felt embarrassment and shame for their linguistic difference from an idealized way of speaking the language.

To best recover from the crisis of migration, migrants need targeted instrumental support to address practical problems in the early settlement phase. The overarching problem is the difficulty with establishing new social networks. The provision of practical settlement support and human fellowship through new network building is vital and should be accessible to all new arrivals, regardless of visa type. To this end, the provision of culturally sensitive migrant-support services, in the initial settlement phase in particular, is of paramount importance. Early post-arrival experiences are formative and can boost or destroy confidence. Therefore, engaging new arrivals through dedicated meeting opportunities, mentoring schemes, and buddy systems is vital. These initiatives are widely recognized as being highly beneficial but remain underutilized.[11] Targeted transition support in the early arrival phase is critical to start newcomers on good language learning, work, and settlement trajectories. How well the early phase is managed and how well its challenges are addressed can have lifelong implications. Getting the foundations right is crucial and shapes migrants' trajectories for years to come, as path dependency kicks in.

Supporting newcomers also entails a more systematic focus on the life cycle. Not only is migration a distinct life-cycle event, but arrival experiences vary by life stage. Whether key life-cycle events such as high school graduation, university graduation, finding a partner and marriage, having children, or approaching retirement took place before or after migration significantly impacted participants' trajectories.[12] This has implications for migration policies in that life stage needs to be more consistently taken into account. Migrants are not generic units of forever single people. To separate families, as was the case for some of the temporary migrants among our participants, is unconscionable and contradicts aims directed at smooth settlement.[13]

A life-stage approach has implications for service provision and calls for closer collaboration between service providers. We need a whole-of-society recognition that linguistic diversity is a key facet of Australian society and mediates well-being. This recognition and attention to its practical implications are currently lacking, as can be seen, for example, from the fact that schools routinely fail to engage with linguistically diverse parents, or that medical research continues to neglect to include migrant populations in clinical trials.[14] How such a whole-of-society approach could work will now be exemplified with regard to language service provision, which we will discuss as an exemplar.

Building Inclusive Communication

There are many ways to think about language. Language may be thought of as a cognitive skill that rests within the individual, and the level of which can be measured through language-proficiency tests. Language may also be thought of as a communication tool that interactants share to collaboratively achieve common goals. Yet another way to understand language is to see it as an identity marker that signals to others who we are, where we come from, and whether we are members of an ingroup or an outgroup. Language can also be considered an asset that can be transformed into economic, social, and cultural capital. What all these different perspectives on language-—and there are others-—have in common is that language is both individuated and shared.

Yet when it comes to communicating in a linguistically diverse society, the shared aspects of language are routinely erased. Language suddenly becomes the sole problem of those who are audibly and visibly othered. Instead of successful communication being the responsibility of all interactants, shared responsibility is denied and offloaded almost exclusively onto the shoulders of the weakest members of society. Migrants' language then becomes subject to incessant scrutiny, both formal and informal. Formal scrutiny comes in the form of repeated language tests that need to be taken to receive a visa, to transform a visa into permanent residency, to be eligible for citizenship, to be admitted to university, to have overseas qualifications recognized, or to be allowed to practice in certain professions. Informal scrutiny may be applied at any interaction where language proficiency is explicitly brought up, whether in the form of criticism or compliments. As we have seen, migrants themselves internalize the perpetual scrutiny their language is under by attributing imagined judgments to their interlocutors, by becoming experts in language testing, and by constantly worrying about their English-language proficiency.

The pervasive scrutiny of migrants' English allows the destination society to evade responsibility for successful communication and ignore the barriers erected by the prevailing narrow understanding of what constitutes linguistic proficiency. That understanding is currently almost exclusively focused on English—an English that is abstract, decontextualized, and standardized to a testable entity. As we have seen, that tested entity did not necessarily enable those who had it to communicate. For those who did not have it, its absolutist yardstick created an insurmountable barrier to the jobs and the education they desired. This view of language proficiency as inherent to the learner overlooks that language proficiency is always context-dependent, and as such we need to ask what the linguistic requirements of a particular role and context are, instead of obsessing over a person's test score.

In Chapter 2, we identified two key cohorts of language learners. First, there are those who have been habituated to language learning as a school subject. Their experience contrasts with that of the second cohort: people for whom learning languages is a practical matter driven by achieving communicative purposes in multilingual contexts. Despite the vastly different language-learning experiences of these two groups, their differences were leveled in Australia, where both forms—tested English and street English, as we dubbed them—became enmeshed in a deficit perspective. Instead of foundations to build on, those who brought tested English came to think that English for everyday purposes was something completely different and that they needed to start their language-learning journeys afresh. Conversely, those who brought street English were judged on how it fell short vis-à-vis an abstract and idealized standard of well-balanced speaking, listening, reading, and writing skills.

The differences and similarities between the two cohorts have implications for language testing and language teaching. Regarding the former, we suggest that there is currently an excessive focus on language testing that divorces language proficiency from the contexts in which language is used and from the communicative purposes it is used for. This creates absurd barriers, as we saw in examples of participants who were turned away from cleaning jobs because of their supposedly poor English; of participants whose English was deemed insufficient to convert their temporary visas into permanent visas, although they were clearly capable of holding a job and supporting themselves; or of participants who had become experts in language testing and displayed an uncanny fluency in language test scores without being able to translate those test scores into everyday English.

The importance of understanding language as context-specific practices and multilingual repertoires, instead of an abstract all-encompassing proficiency in English, is also apparent when it comes to language teaching. Language-teaching programs that participants encountered had nothing to offer to those who had achieved specific test scores, even if they themselves clearly identified specific language-learning needs related to "everyday language," including aspects of Australian English, telephone talk, and casual interaction. Low-literacy participants, on the other hand, were treated as a tabula rasa without any language at all. Their impressive multilingual repertoires and their ability to learn new languages through interaction were neither recognized nor utilized to offer targeted language training. Significant opportunities exist to tailor language teaching to specific needs and align it with other educational programs, including workplace training. Building explicit attention to language into all educational programs promises benefits for all learners, in line with an understanding of language competences as fundamental to lifelong learning, as embraced by major international bodies such as the Organisation for Economic Co-operation and Development (OECD) and the United Nations.[15]

Through the wider window onto lived experience, our research has also explored the social construction of language proficiency in an officially monolingual but functionally multilingual society. Communication in Australia is perniciously reduced to monolingual proficiency in English. The focus on English often prohibits the full use of a person's repertoire. Beyond language testing and language teaching, which continue to focus on migrants' language, we also need to change the perspective and consider what it means to communicate well in a linguistically diverse society. Scholars of language and race have increasingly called for a shift in focus away from language learners to the powerful listeners who place them under so much scrutiny.[16] This entails an applied perspective on language services provision and the linguistic responsibilities of institutions to ensure fair and equitable access for all. Australia has engaged with the question of what this means since the 1980s when the "National Policy on Languages" was published.[17] The "National Policy on Languages" enshrined four guiding principles, related to achieving competence in English for all, maintenance and development of languages other than English, provision of services in languages other than English as needed, and opportunities for learning second languages. Implementations of the policy related to the strengthening of the AMEP, support for community language schools, the creation of a national telephone interpreting service and a multicultural broadcaster, and attention to language teaching in schools. The fortunes of these implementations have been highly variable, as they have been subject to political debates about and contestations of multiculturalism, at national, state, and local levels, within the general decline of the welfare state.[18]

That the national ideal of shared responsibility for successful communication has significant shortcomings and needs to be updated for the 21st century became painfully clear during the COVID-19 pandemic, when widespread failure to communicate effectively with NESB communities resulted in mortality rates of the overseas-born exceeding those of the native-born by three times.[19] This example plainly demonstrates that a communication strategy needs to be part of a public health strategy, just as it needs to be part of all aspects of our social, national, and institutional lives. This includes disaster preparation, response, and recovery, where effective communication plans are vital. While the government undoubtedly needs to take the lead to establish the overall framework, all institutions and communities are called upon to implement sound local communication plans.[20]

Holistic communication strategies and plans involve understanding language needs and language resources at all levels. Language needs relate to the languages, the mediums, and the platforms through which information is disseminated.

Language resources relate to multilingual speakers, logistics, and technologies needed. Multilingual speakers can broker communication across language barriers and provide language assistance in a timely and targeted manner as needed in the family and in local communities.[21] It is with regard to multilingual language brokers that the importance of a broad linguistic vision becomes clear. The parents whom we met in Chapter 5 are raising the multilingual speakers and communication mediators of the future. Supporting them holistically to achieve high levels of competence both in English and in the heritage language, through schools and the community, is therefore inherently beneficial to all. To achieve this, language professionals, educators, policymakers, and migrant service providers, as well as migrant communities and their members, need to work hand in hand. Schools and educational institutions need to find practical ways to make the advantages of children's bilingual skills more tangible to them and to others. In this way, children can become encouraged to maintain and extend their heritage languages, with positive impacts on their sense of self and their relationships with their parents. It is also desirable to make resources available to parents to address the challenges and opportunities of heritage-language maintenance in migration contexts. This may result in emotionally and psychologically healthier familial relationships and, ultimately, a healthier society.

It is our hope that this book will help move the conversation about migration out of the academy. As a multilingual, multiethnic nation of migrants in a globalizing world, Australia needs to better understand its sociocultural identity and how its dominant constructions of language proficiency and competence, as well as employability skills, need to be updated to build a more inclusive, tolerant, and egalitarian 21st century society.

This is a society that was founded and continues to be built on inward migration and, since the middle of the last century, on an imagined multiculturalism and a hopeful future of reconciliation between First Nations and non-Indigenous people. However, Australia's migration policy and its assertion of an inclusive multiculturalism are inconsistent with the exclusion and marginalization experienced by those who were not born in the country. Our book contributes to an informed understanding of how to address some of these disparities.

How to Use This Book in Teaching

This appendix provides suggestions of how to use this book in teaching in units related to language and migration, intercultural communication, and applied sociolinguistics. It does so by highlighting the key points made in each chapter and offering chapter-by-chapter discussion questions and interactive learning suggestions, as well as suggestions for further reading.

Chapter 1: Doing Things with Words in a New Language

Key Points

- The key challenge of migrant language learning is not only a linguistic one, but migrants also need to achieve things through a new language they are still learning. Many of the things they need to achieve through the new language are high stakes, such as finding a job, renting a house, or seeking healthcare.
- Migrant language learning is shaped by country of origin, level of education, occupation, visa stream, prior English-language learning, and other factors.
- Migrant language learning is not only multifaceted due to the diversity of migrants, but also embedded in the variety of language ideologies and policies of their destination. In Australia, these include a long-standing preferencing of immigration from the British Isles with a concomitant preferencing of English, combined with a newer orientation to multiculturalism. The latter is today embedded in a neoliberal migration program where migrants are primarily welcomed for their contributions to the economy, including their human and financial capital.
- The lived experience of English-language learning in Australia also needs to be understood against the background of using English as a legal instrument of migrant selection and as an economic asset in a human capital bundle.

- Full and equitable social inclusion has a linguistic dimension, which requires institutional arrangements that accommodate the diverse linguistic resources and needs of all its members, including new arrivals.

Discussion Questions

- Have you ever had to achieve a real-life goal through a language other than your native language? Can you share details of the experience? Who was involved? What was at stake? How did it go? How did you feel?
- What are the main differences between migrant language learning and child language learning, and between migrant language learning and classroom language learning? Can you think of differences other than those identified in the chapter?
- Summarize key phases in Australian migration policy and the ideologies specific to each period. Why do these ideologies matter for the experience of adult language learning?
- Identify key phases in migration policy and related ideologies in another country of your choice.
- Summarize the role of language as a legal instrument and as a form of human capital. What other roles of language can you identify?

Further Reading

A great way to orient to the lived experience of language learning and migration is through memoirs and fiction. We recommend the essays collected in the *Growing up in Australia* series (Beneba Clarke, 2019; Pung, 2008), and novels such as *Americanah* (Adichie, 2013) and *A Concise Chinese-English Dictionary for Lovers* (Guo, 2007). Some of our favorite migrant memoirs include *Heading South, Looking North* (Dorfman, 1999), *Lost in Translation* (Hoffman, 1990), *Out of Place* (Said, 2000) and *Solito* (Zamora, 2022).

Linguistic Diversity and Social Justice (Piller, 2016) provides a conceptual framework for the sociolinguistic exploration of language and migration. *Immigrant America* (Portes & Rumbaut, 2014) offers a detailed portrait of another society built on migration.

The research blog *Language on the Move* (Piller, 2009–) regularly publishes research in the broad fields of language and migration, intercultural communication, and multilingualism in an easy-to-read short format, and we recommend you subscribe to its newsfeed.

Chapter 2: Arriving in a New Language

Key Points

- Adult migrants do not arrive as linguistic blank slates in a new country. They bring their own linguistic repertoires, which are likely to include some English due to the global spread of English.
- "English," like all language names, is a deceptively simple label that glosses over the variation inherent in any language.
- Not understanding and not being understood in the early arrival phase can result in the experience of language shock.
- What we call "tested English" is closely tied to formal education and is focused on grammar, reading and writing, and rote learning. New arrivals with tested English usually experience a lack of communicative competence in everyday contexts.
- What we call "street English" is a form of English that has been learned informally while needing to communicate in English-speaking contexts. If street English goes hand in hand with little or no formal education, new arrivals may suffer from the lack of literacy skills needed to survive in a complex bureaucratic society where communication tends to be technologically mediated.
- Neither those with tested English nor those with street English are well catered to in English-language teaching programs and often miss out on targeted support.

Discussion Questions

- Put yourself in Lou's shoes when he arrived in Darwin. What could he have done differently? What would you do?
- Write a memoir of your own English-language learning journey. Where does your English fit within the circles model of English? How does your English-language learning trajectory fit on the continuum of tested and naturalistic language learning?

- Imagine you had to design a language-teaching program that caters to at least five of the language learners we met in Chapter 2. How would you go about it? Identify key pedagogical and resource considerations.

Further Reading

For background on the English-language learning experiences of new migrants, you might wish to extend your understanding of the role of English in specific national contexts. Choose a context that interests you and then select an ethnographic exploration of English-language teaching in that context. Some of our favorites include *Buying into English* (Prendergast, 2008), which is situated in Slovakia; *Interpreting English Language Ideologies in Korea* (J. Cho, 2017), situated in South Korea; and *Language Policy and Planning for the Modern Olympic Games* (J. Zhang, 2021), situated in China.

You should also read an ethnography of English-language learning in a migration context. Again, there are many excellent texts to choose from. We recommend the classic *Identity and Language Learning* (Norton, 2013) and examples such as *Constructing Inequality in Multilingual Classrooms* (Martín Rojo, 2010), *Mogadishu on the Mississippi* (Bigelow, 2010), or *The Language of Adult Immigrants* (E. R. Miller, 2014). *ESOL: A Critical Guide* (Cooke & Simpson, 2008) is aimed at teachers and policymakers and highlights diversity in the language classroom.

Chapter 3: Looking for Work in a New Language

Key Points

- Migrants are more likely to be unemployed or underemployed than their native-born peers. This is generally attributed to their limited English-language proficiency, their inferior qualifications, or their lack of local experience.
- Our research shows that these deficits are produced in the destination society where migrants' language proficiency, qualifications, and experience are devalued in the labor market.
- What new arrivals genuinely lack are high-value social networks to help them understand and navigate employment pathways, and (re)establish their careers. Creating such networks is a key area for targeted early arrival support.

Discussion Questions

- Reflect on Franklin's trajectory and identify intervention points. What could have been done when, and by whom, to achieve a better outcome?
- Identify a workplace you are familiar with and which has at least 10 employees and map their countries of origin on the jobs they do. Do you notice a pattern? Tip: this works well as a group project. If you do not have access to a workplace or personal knowledge, some companies will provide this information in their published annual reports. Research about the representation of NESB migrants in the Australian Public Service by Opare-Addo & Bertone (2021) could serve as a model.
- Debate Vesna's comment that "everywhere the medicine is the same." One side of the debate should speak to the proposition that the work of a midwife is the same internationally and that therefore the imposition of high levels of English-language proficiency constitutes an unfair barrier to employment for people like Vesna. The other side should speak to the proposition that the imposition of high levels of English-language proficiency before midwives are allowed to practice is vital to ensuring patient safety. Can you think of solutions that would satisfy both sides of the debate?

Further Reading

Select sociolinguistic ethnographies of communication in diverse workplaces in an industry that is of interest to you. We recommend *Communication That Counts* (Tenedero, 2022) about accounting, *Fresh Fruit, Broken Bodies* (Holmes, 2013) about farmworkers, *Paradise Laborers* (Adler & Adler, 2004) about hospitality, and *Scripts of Servitude* (Lorente, 2017) about domestic work.

Culture, Discourse, and the Workplace (Angouri, 2018) provides a systematic toolkit for the ethnographic exploration of language at work, with a focus on case studies in small and medium-sized enterprises.

Chapter 4: Finding a Voice in a New Language

Key Points

- Despite the common assumption that language learning in an immersion setting is easy, finding interlocutors, establishing common ground, and managing misunderstandings pose an underrecognized problem.

- Interactions that did not go well due to rejection, misunderstanding, or other factors often lead to an erosion of confidence.
- Reclaiming confidence in one's ability to communicate in the new environment was often linked to turning-point interactions where participants had their English and their identities validated by supportive interlocutors. In other cases, it happened gradually over time.

Discussion Questions

- List all the interactional strategies employed by Lou to improve his English. Can you think of other strategies? What are the affordances and difficulties of each strategy on the list?
- Have you ever found yourself in a situation like Qasem's? What could Qasem have done differently so that he would have been less isolated? What could the other parents have done differently to improve Qasem's experience? Who is responsible for Qasem's exclusion, and how could the situation be improved?
- Based on customer service interactions described in Chapter 4, develop a list of suggestions for inclusive communication strategies in customer service. Make sure to consider spoken, written, digital, material, and other aspects that are relevant to making a particular service accessible to linguistically diverse clients.

Further Reading

Achieving Understanding (Bremer et al., 2013 [1996]) is a classic exploration of linguistically diverse interactions. *Peer Interaction and Second Language Learning* (Philp, Adams, & Iwashita, 2013) provides a useful overview of the role of interaction in instructed language learning, and *Rethinking Second Language Learning* (Cordella & Huang, 2016) brings together a collection of studies related to interactions across generations in a diverse society.

The following journals regularly publish conversation analytic and/or interactional sociolinguistic research in linguistically diverse contexts and we recommend subscribing to their news feeds: *Anthropology and Education Quarterly*; *International Journal of Bilingual Education and Bilingualism*; *Journal of Multilingual and Multicultural Development*; *Journal of Sociolinguistics*; *Language in Society*; and *Multilingua*.

Chapter 5: Doing Family in a New Language

Key Points

- Migration is a catalyst for family change. New ways of allocating family tasks and responsibilities emerge, and new family concerns may appear that are specific to the migration context. Among the latter, questions of choosing a family language and rearing children bilingually stand out. Tensions are inevitable consequences of these changes and transformations.
- Family transformations do not take place in a vacuum. They are deeply shaped by the exclusions and inclusions that migrant families experience in their new society.
- While most migrant parents want their children to grow up bilingually, how to achieve that goal is unclear and raises tensions not only between partners, but also between children and parents.
- Decisions about language choices and practices in migrant families are influenced by parents' and children's language experiences, beliefs, and attitudes, which in turn are influenced by language ideologies and attitudes prevalent in the wider society.
- While there is a common assumption that children who grow up in homes where a language other than English is spoken will automatically become bilingual, the reality is far more complicated. Children's integration into the new school and environment and their language learning and practices are fraught with challenges for both children and their parents.

Discussion Questions

- Can you think of the time when you moved out of your parents' house or another occasion when there was a physical absence or addition to your family? How did the move or absence affect roles and responsibilities within the family? What changed, and how did members compensate for the physical absence?
- What can parents do to support their children's bilingualism? What can teachers and schools do to support family bilingualism? Who else can help? Write down a list of action points for these different groups.
- Put yourself in the shoes of the parents who noticed that their children were embarrassed about their English. How would you react? What strategies might relieve these tensions?

Further Reading

Growing up Bilingual (Zentella, 1997) is a classic ethnographic exploration of language issues in migrant families, and we also recommend *Bilingual Childcare* (Benz, 2017), *Culturally Contested Literacies* (G. Li, 2010), *Invisible Work* (Okita, 2002), *Linguistic Intermarriage in Australia* (Torsh, 2020), and *Raising Global Families* (Lan, 2018).

Family Language Policy (Spolsky, 2004) provides an excellent overview of the key issues from a sociolinguistic perspective, and "Transnational Families" (Baldassar et al., 2017) from a sociological perspective.

Chapter 6: Facing Discrimination in a New Language

Key Points

- In the context of migration, people experience being both audibly and visibly Othered. The intersection of both audible and visible difference can present significant challenges for creating a life in a new language and society.
- Difference is made relevant in forms of everyday racism, including selective incivility, micro-aggressions, invalidations, insults, and even assaults.
- White migrants who are audibly but not visibly Othered envisioned a trajectory toward future belonging, tied to increased language proficiency, reduced accent, and complete integration by the second generation. By contrast, racialized migrants did not necessarily see themselves on such a trajectory and most expected to be perpetual outsiders.
- Racist aggression was a heavy burden for those who experienced it, particularly if such experiences were recurring, severe, and/or occurred in the early settlement phase. Participants developed a variety of coping mechanisms.

Discussion Questions

- Have you ever observed selective incivility? Collect your observations in a group and create a typology. What are the observed characteristics of the persons who were treated favorably and unfavorably? What are the observed characteristics of the person who engaged in selective incivility? What are the characteristics of the context? Pool the group grids for the whole class and see what patterns, if any, emerge.

- Have you ever been asked where you are from? What was the context, and how did it make you feel? Have you ever asked anyone where they are from? What was the context, and how did the conversation unfold?
- List all the ways in which participants reacted to micro-aggressions. How would you have reacted? What other constructive reactions and coping strategies can you think of?
- Revisit Jaime's story and identify intervention points. Who could have done what to achieve a better outcome? Who, if anyone, should be held responsible? If you cannot agree, consider what processes and procedures would need to be put in place to achieve better outcomes for people like Jaime.

Further Reading

Audible Difference (J. Miller, 2003), *Linguistic Minorities and Modernity* (Heller, 2006), *Looking like a Language, Sounding like a Race* (Rosa, 2019), and *The Succeeders* (A. Flores, 2021) offer engaging school ethnographies with a focus on the intersection of language and race.

Race and America's Immigrant Press (Zecker, 2011) provides an illuminating investigation into how European migrants to the United States learned to think of themselves as White.

Two edited collections, *Raciolinguistics* (Alim, Rickford, & Ball, 2016) and *The Oxford Handbook of Language and Race* (Alim et al., 2020) comprise a wide range of studies examining the connection between language and race.

Chapter 7: Self-Making in a New Language

Key Points

- Migration constitutes a rupture of the self into a before and after, as old habits and ways of doing things disappear and a new sense of belonging and connection needs to be established.
- Pre-migration identities often are untranslatable and become untellable, particularly if they include minoritized identities from contexts that may not be widely known and/or multiple migrations.
- Acquiring new post-migration identities can be both liberating and constraining.
- To rebuild identities, inclusion in a community is vital. Participants experienced the greatest sense of inclusion in their families, in faith-based communities, and in some other voluntary associations.

Discussion Questions

- Think back to the gossiping event you engaged in most recently. How did gossiping create a sense of belonging, and for whom?
- Choose a short migrant memoir from a collection such as Beneba Clarke (2019); Coe (2012) or Shukla & Suleyman (2020) and identify any breaks in the author's self. What reflections about losing and finding the self in migration, belonging, and community building does the author share? Tip: Each student could read a different memoir and you could pool your findings under the headings "old self," "new self," "un/belonging," and "community" (not every memoir will have content related to each). Can you find any patterns?
- Maria was very strategic in building community. List her strategies and add your own suggestions for how newcomers might go about making friends and inserting themselves into a community.
- Work in a group and imagine you are the new Linguistic Inclusion Committee appointed by your school. Draft an action plan for the inclusion of students from non-dominant linguistic backgrounds. Tip: Pool your action plans, select the best ideas, identify a timeframe and the resources needed, and pitch the plan to your head of school (or another relevant decision-maker) for implementation.

Further Reading

Engaging ethnographic studies of self, belonging, and community-building in migration contexts include *Chinese Senior Migrants and the Globalization of Retirement* (Newendorp, 2020) about Chinese clubs and neighborhood associations in Boston; *Fighters, Girls and Other Identities* (Madsen, 2015) about a martial arts club in Denmark; or *Transnational Ruptures* (Nolin, 2006) about Guatemalan forced migrants in Canada.

Beyond the Mother Tongue (Yildiz, 2012) offers a comprehensive investigation into language and self, with a focus on German-language literature produced by diverse authors.

Chapter 8: Rethinking Language and Migration

Key Points

- The responsibility for successful language learning and settlement must be shared by mobile and sedentary people in the receiving society. This includes overcoming the pervasive deficit perspective that destination societies impose on migrants.

- Data sharing and reuse offer significant and largely untapped opportunities to broaden the findings and impact of ethnographic and other qualitative research.
- To improve employment outcomes for migrants, better pathways in the early arrivals phase are needed, and the reduction of migrants to workers must be overcome. Struggles for decent work and migrant rights are intertwined.
- A life-cycle perspective on migration can result in more targeted and effective policies and supports. Support in the early settlement phase is vital to ensure a smooth transition into the new society.
- Debates around migrant language learning need to be expanded to center on language services and resilient communication strategies in a diverse society.

Discussion Questions

- How would you go about designing a buddy program for new arrivals in a context you are familiar with?
- Read the research blogpost "Language Barriers to Social Participation" (Piller, 2022) and identify any language and communication barriers in an institution you are familiar with. What linguistic needs do you see? What linguistic resources are available? What are the risks and opportunities? What scope for improvement is there?

Further Reading

Linguistic Diversity in a Time of Crisis (2020b) and *The Language-on-the-Move Covid-19 Archives* (Piller, 2020–) provide a variety of case studies of language needs and inclusive communication strategies in a diverse society.

[illegible]

- [illegible] speakers impure or inadequate.
- [illegible]
- To improve employment outcomes for immigrants, [illegible] must be overcome [illegible] interviewed.
- [illegible]
- Debates [illegible] languages [illegible]

Discussion Questions

- How would [illegible]
- Read the [illegible]

Further Reading

[illegible]

Notes

List of Participants

1. Detailed profiles of some participants have previously been published in Butorac (2011); Farrell (2008); Motaghi-Tabari (2016); Piller & Lising (2014); Williams Tetteh (2015). A mini-portrait of each of the 130 participants in the form of a Twitter thread is available at Piller (2023).
2. f = female; m = male.
3. For an overview of visa types, see Chapter 1. A secondary visa holder is the spouse of a visa holder.
4. This includes formal education undertaken in Australia and so refers to the highest level of education at the time of the research. "≤Primary" includes up to 7 years of formal schooling. "≥Masters" refers to any postgraduate degree.
5. All our participants from Sudan are from the south of the country, which became an independent state, South Sudan, in 2011, after participants had left.
6. Yugoslavia ceased to exist in 1992, although that is the country where Goran described growing up. His home state is Bosnia.

Chapter 1

1. Müller (2001), p. 19; Ingrid's translation.
2. Adult-child interactions and socialization practices differ widely across cultures. For an overview, see Duranti, Ochs, & Schieffelin (2013).
3. For language barriers to accessing emergency services, see, e.g., Penn, Watermeyer, & Nattrass (2016); Piller (2017c); Raymond (2014).
4. T. Cho (2008), p. 15.
5. See Acknowledgments for details.
6. *2021 Census Quickstats* (2022); *Migration, Australia* (2021)
7. Moreton-Robinson (2015), p. 63.
8. According to 2021 census data (*Aboriginal and Torres Strait Islander people: Census*, 2022).
9. For the size of the Australian population in 2021, see *Population: Census* (2022). The size of the pre-colonial Indigenous population is unclear, and estimates range from as low as 300,000 to a few million (Bradshaw, Williams, Saltré, Norman, & Ulm, 2021; Rowse, 2004). While the larger estimates are gaining more credence, the Indigenous population was decimated by introduced diseases, genocidal warfare, and state child removal beginning in 1788 and continuing well into the 20th century (Crosby, 2004; Moses, 2004).
10. *Migration, Australia* (2021).
11. We recommend Hunt (2013, 2016) as an eminently readable history of Australia up to Federation in 1901. Hughes (1986) remains the most authoritative history of convict transportation to Australia. Black convicts made up 1%–2% of transportees but have been completely expunged from accounts of Australia's convict heritage (Pybus, 2006). South Asian indentured laborers were part of British Empire population transfers but have become a historical footnote as "Afghan cameleers" (Khatun, 2019). Although the historical record is clear and 19th-century authors had no qualms writing about the "Queensland slave trade," any mention of the fact that Pacific Islanders were kidnapped from their homes and enslaved in Australian sugar plantations, pearling stations, and brothels continues to be met with outrage, even today (Hunt, 2021). On the intersection of prostitution and race in colonial Australia, see Frances (1999). The main motivation for the Immigration Restriction Act was concerns about Australia being invaded by Asians, particularly Chinese, and by European colonial competitors such as the French and Germans (Hunt, 2021).
12. For a detailed historical overview of Australia's migration policy from Federation to the early years of the 21st century, see Jupp (2007).

13. See S. Martin (1998) for a history of the AMEP on its 50th anniversary.
14. For a review of economic migration schemes since the 1990s, see Hugo (2014).
15. At any one time during the 21st century, around 300 different visa types with work rights have been available, and policy details, rules, and regulations are constantly being tweaked. Our account of Australia's visa regime is based on *Cultural diversity of Australia* (2022); Love & Spinks (2020); Spinks & Sherrell (2019); C. F. Wright, Clibborn, Piper, & Cini (2022).
16. Up until the late 20th century, migration to Australia was predominantly conceived as permanent resettlement, and temporary visas with work rights were rare. This has since changed, and temporary visas with work rights now vastly outnumber permanent visas. In 2019, the year prior to COVID-19-related border closures, 37,600 people arrived on permanent skilled visas and 31,800 people entered on temporary skilled visas. The ranks of the latter were swelled by students with work rights (172,800 entrants) and working holiday makers (50,300 entrants) (*Migration, Australia*, 2020). Pathways from temporary to permanent visas have become increasingly arcane and time-consuming (Mares, 2016).
17. For example, in 2019, the year prior to COVID-19 related border closures, 292,500 people arrived on visas related to economic activities, including student visas; 23,400 arrived on family reunion visas; and 15,200 arrived as humanitarian entrants (*Migration, Australia*, 2020).
18. In fact, most of the Indigenous population today is also descended from Indigenous and non-Indigenous unions (Rowse, 2004).
19. Jupp (2007), p. 22.
20. *Australia 2021* (2022).
21. Our argument here draws on the work of Indigenous theorist Moreton-Robinson (2015).
22. Phenotype does mediate this promise in everyday interactions, of course. An ethnic hierarchy undoubtedly remains in place, which invests White-looking native-born people with more legitimacy and a greater sense of belonging than is the case for racial others and NESB overseas-born people. White-looking migrants may pass within the first generation and may be fully absorbed into the Anglo mainstream by the second generation. The promise of English to erase their migrancy and to ensure belonging may be more tenuous for those immigrants racialized as Others and their descendants, as we will discuss in Chapter 6, when we examine how racism and differential constructions of belonging inflect the language-learning experiences of our participants.
23. For intergenerational language shift in Australia, see Clyne (2005a). While the numeric dominance of English speakers among the original settler population is undoubtedly an important factor in ensuring the pre-eminence of English in Australia, potentially competing languages have also been actively suppressed, at times violently, for example, Irish in the early colony (Piller, 2011a, 2011b) and German in the early 20th century (Pennay, 2006).
24. For the political trope of Australia as the most successful multicultural nation, see, e.g., Bouma (2015); Busbridge (2019); Lim (2021); for the celebration of multiculturalism in public discourse, see Forbes-Mewett, Hegarty, & Wickes (2022); Hassanli, Walters, & Williamson (2021); Reid (2019); M. Watkins & Noble (2019); for the coexistence of multiculturalism with White supremacy, see Hage (1998).
25. C. A. Martin (2021a, 2021b); Rollo (2020).
26. For the framing of migration as a national security threat post–9/11, see, e.g., Hammerstad (2014); Léonard & Kaunert (2022). For details on the discursive construction of asylum seekers as both threats and victims through the "Children Overboard Affair" and its use in Australian politics, see Clyne (2005b); Haw (2023); Leroy (2023); Macken-Horarik (2003a, 2003b); Silverstein (2020).
27. For a legal discussion of Australia's mandatory detention scheme in international comparison, see Ghezelbash (2018). For a firsthand account of immigration detention, see the multi-award winning autobiography *No friend but the mountains* (Boochani, 2018).
28. From the speech to parliament by Labor MP King O'Malley during debate of the Act, as quoted in Hunt (2021), p. 607. O'Malley himself, incidentally, was US-born.
29. Kisch (1937); Mason (2014); Zogbaum (2004). Kisch eventually found refuge in Mexico.
30. For the use of English-language proficiency testing in the 2007 Australian citizenship test, see McNamara (2009a, 2009b); McNamara & Ryan (2011). For the broader international context, where proficiency in the national language has increasingly been made a citizenship requirement for those who do not have citizenship through birth, see, e.g., Bonotti & Willoughby (2022); Frost & McNamara (2018); Khan & McNamara (2017).

31. For fact-checks of claims emanating from the right-wing "One Nation" party that more than one million Australians did not speak English, see Piller (2018a, 2018c). The language test that was proposed in legislation passing the House of Representatives but defeated in the Senate was the IELTS (International English Language Testing System) with a proposed required achievement level of Band 6 (McDonald, Moyle, & Temple, 2019). IELTS recognizes nine language proficiency bands, with Band 1 ("non-user") the lowest and Band 9 ("Expert user") the highest. Band 6 describes a "competent user" (*How IELTS is scored*, 2022).
32. For a review of English-language proficiency debates targeting international students, see Bodis (2021a, 2021b). For humanitarian entrants, see Mayne-Davis, Wilson, & Lowrie (2020). For Muslim women, see Neelam (2022).
33. For an in-depth exploration of the proliferation of temporary visa schemes and their social and individual consequences, see Mares (2016).
34. Daniel (2020); Houghton (2020); Pupazzoni (2020).
35. Hawthorne (2005).
36. The concept of "linguistic entrepreneurship" is helpful to understand language learning as a form of human capital accumulation under neoliberal economic conditions; e.g., De Costa, Park, & Wee (2016, 2021); J. Li & Zheng (2023).
37. Our conceptual framework is built on Piller (2016).
38. Our approach to quality assurance in qualitative analysis is guided by the principles of theoretical analysis, comprehensive data treatment, constant comparison, and contrasting case analysis (Silverman, 2016).
39. We choose to share our locus of enunciation because we believe that the academic convention of hiding behind the cloak of objectivity is a major source of epistemological inequality (Diniz De Figueiredo & Martinez, 2021; Piller, Zhang, & Li, 2022).

Chapter 2

1. Arabic and English have been in competition for preeminence in multilingual Sudan since the 19th century. Sudan had been part of the Ottoman Empire until 1885. A successful Islamist rebellion resulted in a short-lived independent Sudanese state, which established Arabic as the national language. This state came to an end with the British-Egyptian invasion of 1898. The British colonial period, which lasted until 1956, favored English for official purposes. English spread widely through Christian mission schools, which were particularly active in the south of the country. After independence, Arabic-English competition remained high on the political and educational agenda and fed into the civil wars that have racked the country ever since, culminating in the establishment of South Sudan as an independent state in 2011, with English as sole official language (James, 2008; Karar, 2019; Laitin & Ramachandran, 2022; Sano, 2019).
2. We explore Franklin's trajectory in Australia in greater detail in Chapter 3.
3. For TOEFL performance descriptors and test comparisons, see *Comparing TOEFL iBT scores* (2022); *Performance descriptors for the TOEFL iBT test* (2021).
4. For selective mutism as a developmental disorder, see A. Hua & Major (2016); Johnson & Wintgens (2017).
5. Anyidoho & Dakubu (2008).
6. Numbers based on list of countries and territories where English is an official language, (2022).
7. For an overview of global TESOL, see Rose, Syrbe, Montakantiwong, & Funada (2020). For a historical and critical examination of its rise, see Phillipson (1992, 2009). There are numerous country studies of English in specific national contexts, such as J. Zhang (2021) for China; Borjian (2013) for Iran; and J. Cho (2017) for South Korea.
8. Zarb (2022).
9. E. W. Schneider (2020).
10. The circles model of Englishes was originally developed by Kachru (1986). The model has been criticized as simplistic but continues to serve as a useful shorthand for different language-learning trajectories and, even more so, for different ideological relationships between different forms of English and the identities they index (J. S.-Y. Park & Wee, 2009; Piller & Bodis, 2024). The field of study that deals with the different social roles of English is often referred to as "World Englishes," with English in the plural to indicate the diversity of the language (Capstick, 2020; Jenkins, 2015; E. W. Schneider, 2020).

11. As an example of these contestations in West African contexts, see Adejunmobi (2004, 2008); in the Philippines, see Lising & Bautista (2022).
12. Estimates for communicative English-language proficiency in outer-circle country populations range from as low as 10% in Sierra Leone (Oyètádé & Luke, 2008) to 20% in India (Azam, Chin, & Prakash, 2013) and to as high as 56% in the Philippines (Gonzalez, 2004).
13. Whether Sudan should be classified as belonging to the outer or expanding circle is a matter of debate (see note 1). All of our Sudanese participants hail from the southern stronghold of English.
14. Burundi, which had been a German and Belgian colony, adopted Kirundi and French as official languages after independence in 1959. In an example of the ever-increasing importance of English, English was added as the third official language in 2014 (English is now official language of Burundi, 2014; Nduwimana, 2020).
15. Competent English (2022).
16. Mobasher (2018).
17. *Australia's population by country of birth* (2022).
18. Boochani (2018); Boochani, Tofighian, & Mansoubi (2022).
19. The maximum age to be admitted under this scheme is 45. There are a variety of different visas in this stream, and details keep changing. Points may also be allocated for regional settlement, Australian degrees, and qualifications of spouses.
20. Points calculator (2022).
21. The five accepted tests are IELTS, TOEFL, Pearson Test of Academic English (PTE Academic), Occupational English Test (OET), and Cambridge C1 Advanced Test (*English language visa requirements*, 2022).
22. For English-language testing in university admission, see Piller & Bodis (2024).
23. *[National curriculum of the Islamic Republic of Iran]* (2013).
24. Published research echoes these observations and has found that English-language teaching in Iranian public schools fails to develop communicative and intercultural competence. Locally developed textbooks have been criticized for their narrow local content, including high levels of misogyny (Ansary & Babaii, 2003; J. F. K. Lee & Mahmoudi-Gahrouei, 2020).
25. For the burgeoning private English-language sector in Iran, see Aghagolzadeh & Davari (2017); Haghighi & Norton (2017).
26. The overall IELTS score is made up of four sub-scores—for reading, writing, listening, and speaking. Immigration requirements not only stipulate a specific overall score, but also specify minimum sub-scores. So, Amin needed an overall score of 6 with no sub-score below 6, which explains why he needed to retake the test despite his overall score being higher in previous attempts.
27. The fee for sitting an IELTS test in Iran is around USD 220 ([IELTS exam fee], 2022). To put this in context, the annual GDP per capita in the country in the first decade of the 21st century was USD 5,000–6,000 (Islamic Republic of Iran, 2022).
28. Deep familiarity with IELTS scores is not restricted to highly educated participants. Meatworkers from the Philippines on a temporary work visa who needed to achieve an IELTS score of 5 to convert their visa to permanent residency were equally obsessed with their IELTS scores (Piller & Lising, 2014).
29. There is also a racist dimension to the erasure and devaluation of African Englishes, as we will explore in Chapter 6.
30. For a general account of the accumulation of cultural capital through participating in institutional credentialing processes, see Bourdieu (1984, 1991).
31. For historical background on the conflict in South Sudan and its aftermath, see Martell (2018).
32. For historical background on the conflict in Sierra Leone and its aftermath, see Mitton (2015).
33. The following account is based on Cole (2013); Oyètádé & Luke (2008).
34. We stress that this was the first English-medium institution of higher learning in sub-Saharan Africa and do not wish to erase pre-colonial traditions of higher education (Kane, 2016).
35. For a detailed version of this argument, see Patel (2021).
36. Oyètádé & Luke (2008), p. 131.
37. In English, Klao is more commonly known as "Kru," a European confusion between the Indigenous language name "Klao" and "crew," as "Klaomen" frequently worked as "crew men" (Williamson & Blench, 2000).
38. "Thrown together from different corners of their respective countries, as neighbors, Africans are increasingly learning each other's languages, not in a planned, conscientious manner but as a

process of social symbiosis. [. . .] The process can be described as almost effortless" (Prah, 2010, p. 169). For further discussion of everyday multilingualism in Africa, see also Lüpke (2013).

39. For an anatomy of the long-running civil war in Ethiopia, see Tronvoll (2022).

Chapter 3

1. The main exception was a cohort of 12 participants from the Philippines, who had entered Australia on a temporary skilled visa, which requires sponsorship by an Australian employer. Their job search had taken place outside the country, and they had no experience looking for work in Australia.
2. Across OECD countries, migrants face disadvantage entering the labor market vis-à-vis the native-born (International migration outlook 1997–2020, 2021). In Australia, higher unemployment rates of the overseas-born than the Australia-born have been a feature of the labor market throughout the 21st century so far (Cheng, Wang, & Taksa, 2021; To, Grafton, & Regan, 2017). In 2019, when the unemployment rate for the Australia-born was 4.7, that of family reunion migrants was 14.2 and that of humanitarian entrants was 19.5 (*Characteristics of recent migrants*, 2020). At 4.8, the unemployment rate of economic migrants was almost identical to that of the Australia-born. However, the identical unemployment rate of this group still indicates disadvantage. This is because entrants in this group receive a visa precisely because they have qualifications that are lacking in the Australian labor market. Additionally, their visas are usually tied to an employment contract or evidence of financial self-sufficiency. Therefore, the unemployment rate of this group should be much lower than that of the general population.
3. See Chapter 2.
4. Work entails many goods and is a fundamental part of human societies, as the philosopher Deranty (2021) argues.
5. Research with migrant cleaners in Europe, such as Gonçalves & Schluter (2017) and Strömmer (2016a, 2016b), has consistently found that cleaning is one of the most accessible employment sectors for migrants with low levels of proficiency in the dominant language. This research has also found that cleaning work does not usually offer opportunities to practice the dominant language and to acquire new linguistic skills.
6. ELICOS stands for "English Language Intensive Courses for Overseas Students." Prior to the COVID-19 pandemic, international education constituted Australia's third largest export sector, with English-language teaching accounting for a substantial segment (*The value of international education to Australia*, 2015).
7. The reasons for migrant disadvantage in the labor market have been the focus of a substantial international research effort. Limited proficiency in the destination language—i.e., limited English-language proficiency in Australia—takes pride of place among the explanations proffered. The US economist Barry Chiswick has been particularly prolific in producing a body of work that demonstrates a correlation between target language proficiency, employment outcomes, and lifetime earnings. Drawing on large quantitative datasets from censuses and panel studies in various destination countries, including Australia, Canada, Germany, Israel, and the United States, the researcher and his associates have consistently found that "acquaintance with the local language increases the likelihood of being employed and has positive earnings outcomes" (Chiswick, Rebhun, & Beider, 2020, p. 1). See also Chiswick, Lee, & Miller (2006); Chiswick & Miller (1998); Chiswick & Miller (2001). That a correlation exists between English-language proficiency and employment outcomes has been replicated in numerous Australian studies, such as Cheng, Wang, Jiang, Taksa, & Tani (2021); Hebbani & Preece (2015); and Khawaja, Hebbani, Gallois, & MacKinnon (2019).
8. *No one teaches you to become an Australian: Report of the inquiry into migrant settlement outcomes* (2017), p. 82.
9. *AMEP and SEE programme alignment report* (2015); Yates et al. (2010); Yates et al. (2015).
10. Language proficiency is both a matter of performance and perception (Piller, 2017d; Piller & Bodis, 2022). Linguistic discrimination can sometimes serve as a proxy for racial discrimination, as we will discuss in detail in Chapter 6.
11. For conceptual analyses of the ways in which the discourse about migrants' alleged language deficit serves to hide systemic barriers and helps to form them as flexible neoliberal subjects, see Haque (2017) and Piller (2016).
12. The internalization of systems of oppression as individual feelings of inferiority is well-understood with regard to sexism and racism (de Beauvoir, 1949; Fanon, 1967).

13. See also Chapter 7 for an exploration of domesticity to establish a sense of home and belonging.
14. For explorations of the ways in which the desire for English may animate the migration trajectories of Japanese women, see Piller & Takahashi (2006); Takahashi (2013).
15. See Chapter 2.
16. Explicit grammar instruction is controversial in contemporary language teaching. Its earlier central role—stemming from the teaching of classical languages such as Ancient Greek, Latin, or Sanskrit—has been significantly reduced in modern language teaching since the second half of the 20th century under the influence of communicative language teaching methods (Ur, 2011).
17. J. Smith et al. (2008); Tusting (2010).
18. On the production of linguistic insecurity through measurement against an idealized, unrealistic standard, see also J. Cho (2015).
19. Indeed, the difference in the unemployment rate between the native-born and the overseas-born we noted above is particularly high in the first few years after arrival. In the first 2 years after arrival, the unemployment rate of new migrants is more than 15%–30% higher than the overall unemployment rate. For skilled migrants, the gap closes in the first 5 years, but for family reunion migrants and humanitarian entrants, it takes up to 10 years of labor market adjustments for their unemployment rate to come down to the level of the native-born (*Australia's migration trends 2017–18 highlights*, 2019).
20. E.g., *Australia's migration trends 2017–18 highlights* (2019); Hartley & Fleay (2016); To et al. (2017).
21. E.g., Charlesworth & Isherwood (2021); De Alwis, Parr, & Guo (2020); Kifle, Kler, & Fleming (2019); Rajendran, Ng, Sears, & Ayub (2020); Wen & Maani (2018).
22. Cebulla & Tan (2019). See also Riga (2019).
23. Kifle et al. (2019). Those classified as migrants from English-speaking backgrounds hail predominantly from the United Kingdom, New Zealand, Ireland, and South Africa.
24. De Alwis et al. (2020).
25. Australia has had a well-publicized shortage of health professionals for most of the 21st century (Schultz, 2020) and "midwife" has been on the list of occupations eligible for skilled migration throughout this period (Skilled occupation list, 2020).
26. Overseas Qualifications Unit (2020).
27. Jupp (2007), p. 147.
28. The English-language proficiency of migrant health professionals has received significant attention, both in Australia and other migrant-receiving countries. Many of these studies further reify the deficit discourse identified above. Studies that note significant differences between the linguistic proficiency needed to study for a nursing degree and those needed in actual practice include T. Crawford & Candlin (2013) and Starr (2009).
29. Early childhood education in Australia has long been undervalued. It is poorly paid and considered women's work. By contrast, some other countries, particularly in the socialist bloc, place a high value on engaging a child's full potential in the early years (Ailwood, 2007; Y. Liu & Boyd, 2020; Nuttall, 2018). Along with aged care, childcare is an industry into which migrants are channeled (Man, 2004; Webb, Faine, Pardy, & Roy, 2017; C. F. Wright & Clibborn, 2020).
30. We further explore the circumstances surrounding this stark decision, which involved leaving her little daughter behind in Australia, in Chapter 6.
31. The sociologist Pierre Bourdieu (1984, 1991) explains that institutional legitimation is vital for human capital (which he refers to as "cultural capital") to have value.
32. This was in contrast to the Filipino butchers and their wives, who had come to Australia with the express goal of working in the meat industry (Piller & Lising, 2014).
33. According to Australian Bureau of Statistics data (*2021 Census Quickstats*, 2022). Given its small African population, we refrain from providing a precise citation that would identify the town in order to protect our participants' anonymity.
34. TAFE stands for "Technical and Further Education" and refers to Australia's public vocational colleges.
35. The third "D" is sometimes also taken to stand for "*d*emeaning," "*d*ull," or "*d*emanding." For a discussion of the role of language in the funneling of migrant workers into 3D jobs internationally, see Piller (2016).
36. Martell (2018), p. 199.
37. MacDonald (2017); Majavu (2020).
38. The idea of the "fair go" is considered a stereotypical Australian value. With regard to immigration, Ozdowski (2012) distinguishes three different foundations: the progressive social justice

ethos of the early colonial days, the embrace of cosmopolitanism and multiculturalism after the Second World War, and the government-controlled immigration system since then.

39. There is a large body of literature on the establishment of migrants' social networks. Most note migrants' difficulties in establishing strong and diverse networks with native-born groups, and the negative consequences this can have for their labor market integration (e.g., Gomes, 2015; Kalfa & Piracha, 2018; Ryan, 2011). We explore our participants' social networks in more detail in Chapters 4 and 7.
40. See Creese (2011), p. 66.

Chapter 4

1. Wotherspoon (2016).
2. On Australian slang and swearing, see K. Allan & Burridge (2006); Burridge (2004); Goddard (2015); McLeod (2011); B. A. Taylor (1976, 1995).
3. The impression was confirmed by several people, including those conventionally deemed native speakers. Interestingly, the impression was dependent on interaction. The transcripts of Lou's speech give a very different impression, as they expose many grammatical inaccuracies that were not noticeable in conversation. For the passing study, see Piller (2002b).
4. In the psycholinguistic literature on additional language learning, motivation is usually conceptualized as a trait of the individual learner (Dörnyei, 1998; Dörnyei & Ushioda, 2013). We follow sociolinguistic approaches that have reconceptualized motivation as "investment" and "agency," and as inextricably linked to social context, including power structures, language ideologies, and learner identities and positionalities (Darvin, 2019; Darvin & Norton, 2015; Ensser-Kananen & Pettitt, 2017; Menard-Warwick, 2009; E. R. Miller, 2010, 2014, 2016; Norton, 2013; Norton & Toohey, 2011; Pavlenko & Norton, 2007; Peirce, 1995).
5. "Ocker" is a slang term for a stereotypical uncouth rural beer-guzzling lower-class Australian male with a heart of gold (Elder, 2007). The fictional character Crocodile Dundee is widely considered an ocker prototype (Rattigan, 1988) and the stereotype has been kept alive into the 21st century through the cultural industries and advertising (R. Crawford, 2007, 2010).
6. Xie & Peng (2018).
7. Redfern is an inner-city suburb in Sydney that used to have a ghetto-like reputation but has more recently been undergoing gentrification (Palin, 2019; Shaw, 2000).
8. See Chapter 3 for participants' job search experiences.
9. *Neighbours* (Watson, 1985–) and *Home and Away* (Bateman, 1988–) are, respectively, the longest and second-longest running soap operas on Australian TV. The shows have also been highly successful internationally. Weekly 20-minute episodes chronicle the lives of the residents of a fictional suburban street and of a fictional seaside town.
10. This is true in migration contexts (Bigelow, 2010; Bremer, Roberts, Vasseur, Simonot, & Broeder, 2013 [1996]; Norton, 2013; Pavlenko & Blackledge, 2004; Perdue, 1993a, 1993b), study abroad programs (Doerr, 2012, 2013; DuFon & Churchill, 2006; Freed, 1995; Goldoni, 2013; Kinginger, 2011; Vidal & Howard, 2012), and even virtual reality immersion (Blyth, 2018; Dhimolea, Kaplan-Rakowski, & Lin, 2022).
11. T. Scott (1986).
12. For explorations of the creation of desire for interactions with idealized native speakers through media discourses and promotional materials for international education, see Bailey (2006, 2007); J. Cho (2015, 2021a); Kelsky (2001); J. S.-Y. Park (2010, 2016, 2020); J. S.-Y. Park & Bae (2009); Piller & Takahashi (2006, 2012); Takahashi (2013).
13. The following summary of family and friendship making and communication across the life course is based on G. Allan (2008); Budgeon (2006); David-Barrett et al. (2016); R. J. Thomas (2019). Although these accounts are based on European and North American research, the patterns are applicable to Australia, which is culturally similar in these matters.
14. Of course, some people abandon their birth family completely, and others form new families through adoption and patchwork relationships. Our aim here is not to erase the complexity of modern families, but to outline the patterns that may limit the quantity and quality of new intimate relationships for adult migrants.
15. R. J. Thomas (2019).
16. On the frequent absence of interactional opportunities in manual work, see Gonçalves & Schluter (2017); Lising (2023); Söderlundh & Keevallik (2023); Strömmer (2016a, 2016b).

17. For detailed explorations of the interactional experiences of international PhD students, see Ai (2017); Bodis (2021a, 2021b); Chang (2015, 2018); Fotovatian (2012); Fotovatian & Miller (2014); Stracke, Jones, Bramley, Csizér, & Magid (2014); B. Yu & Wright, (2016).
18. For an introduction to language ideologies, see Kroskrity (2010); Piller (2015a). For language ideologies and native speakers as desired interlocutors, see Chau (2021); Choi (2016); Ferri & Magne (2021); Olivo (2003); M. Y. Park (2020); Subtirelu (2015); Wiese (2015); D. Wright & Brookes (2019). We examine the racialization of the ideal English speaker in further detail in Chapter 6.
19. For a lyrical meditation on the loss of history and future in migration, see Natonek (1943). A brief discussion of Natonek's autobiography can be found in Piller (2018b). For studies of identity transformations in migrant writing, see Komska (2017); Pavlenko (2001a, 2001b, 2001c, 2007a, 2007b). Untellable identities are further explored in Chapter 7.
20. For the valorization of language learning in the former Soviet Union, its successor states, and Eastern Europe more widely, see A. M. Miller et al. (2006); Pavlenko (2003, 2008, 2013). For Australia's monolingual mindset, see Clyne (2005a, 2008); Ellis, Gogolin, & Clyne (2010); Hajek & Slaughter (2015).
21. For overviews of the research on language anxiety, see Hashemi (2011); Horwitz (2001, 2010); Teimouri, Goetze, & Plonsky (2019); X. Zhang (2019). For an example of a therapeutic approach, see Lou & Noels (2020).
22. On the use of props to achieve interactional goals, see Broth, Cromdal, & Levin (2018); Canagarajah & Minakova (2023); Kimura & Canagarajah (2020); Scollon (2001).
23. *Royal Commission into the Robodebt Scheme Report* (2023), p. xiii.
24. Piller (2017d).
25. For the social role of shame in language learning, see Liyanage & Canagarajah (2019); Piller (2017a, 2017b).
26. Australia and New Zealand, where Elizabeth first arrived, both run volunteer schemes for English-language tutors who provide informal language-learning support to new arrivals. In Australia, the main volunteer English-language home tutor program is administered through the AMEP, but churches and other nongovernmental organizations (NGOs) run similar programs (*AMEP home tutor resources topic packs*, 2011; Dallimore, 2018; Kettle, 2018; Masters, Murray, & Lloyd, 2005; P. G. Watkins, Razee, & Richters, 2012).
27. The idea of situated learning where newcomers move from peripheral to central membership in communities of practice if they are supported to see themselves as legitimate and on a pathway to inclusion goes back to Lave & Wenger (1991) and Wenger (1998). The concept has been applied to language learning in Åhlund & Aronsson (2015); Baird, Kibler, & Palacios (2014); De Fina (2007); Faine (2008); Finn (2010); Iddings (2005); Kanno (1999); Oriyama (2016); Premier & Parr (2019); Taronna (2016); Vickers & Deckert (2013).
28. For introductions to turning-point narratives in autobiographic memory, see Enz & Talarico (2016); Grysman & Hudson (2011). For turning-point narratives in language learning specifically, see J. Lee (2016); Menard-Warwick (2022).

Chapter 5

1. Spouses of primary temporary skilled visa holders may receive a secondary temporary skilled visa if the company sponsoring the primary applicant also offers a job to the spouse. Furthermore, primary temporary skilled visa holders may sponsor their spouses and underage children on dependent visas if they meet certain financial conditions. The costs associated with dependent visas are considerable. In addition to visa fees and travel costs, they include all costs normally covered through taxes, such as needing to take out private health insurance and paying full school fees, even when attending public schools. Furthermore, accommodation in Tiny Town is scarce and the share accommodation in which workers live is not suitable for families. These factors, combined with the 4-year limit on their contracts and visas, make it virtually impossible to move children to Tiny Town. For a detailed exploration of the language learning and settlement experiences of the Filipino meat workers in Tiny Town, including their efforts to convert their temporary visas into permanent ones so that they would be able to bring their children, see Piller & Lising (2014).
2. On global care chains and the emotional labor involved, see Hochschild (2012, 2015); Hondagneu-Sotelo (2001).

3. The metaphor of "doing" family goes back to the foundational work of West & Zimmerman (1987). Key readings on family as performance and display include Blackstone (2014); Finch (2007); Sarkisian (2006); J. Wilson & Tonner (2020).
4. Although research into families separated by migration started early (W. I. Thomas & Znaniecki, 1927), it was long neglected. In recent years, research on transnational families has exploded, as Baldassar, Kilkey, Merla, & Wilding (2017) observe when they note that their chapter on "transnational families" was included only in the second edition of *The Sociology of Families* in 2017, but not in the first one in 2004. The focus of this booming research area has been on global care-chains (Parreñas, 2001, 2012; Yeates, 2012; Yeoh, Somaiah, Lam, & Acedera, 2020), the political economy of remittances (Armand, 2018; Binford, 2003; Della Puppa & Ambrosini, 2022; Fokkema, Cela, & Ambrosetti, 2013; Mahmud, 2021; Paerregaard, 2015; Sawyer, 2016), and the use of communication technologies in maintaining relationships (Fortunati, Pertierra, & Vincent, 2013; Kaufmann, 2018; Kaur & Shruti, 2016; Madianou, 2017; Nedelcu & Wyss, 2016). There is also a growing literature on the transformations experienced by "stayers," family members of migrants who themselves do not migrate (Chan, 2017; Dziekońska, 2023; Fuller, 2017; Kuépié, 2018; Somaiah, Yeoh, & Arlini, 2020).
5. Such a newspaper headline reporting results of the 2021 Australian census, which showed, as had every other census before, that women do substantially more housework than men (Lazy men lumping women with household chores, 2022). The pattern is not restricted to Australia, of course (Hochschild, 2003).
6. The following account is based on Gagnon (2005); Gebeyehu (2013); Mariam (2010); McGill, Iggers, & Cline (2007); Tadesse (2007).
7. See Chapter 3 for non-recognition of overseas qualifications.
8. See Chapter 7 for further exploration of changing gender roles.
9. Agirdag (2013).
10. The latter dilemma needs to be understood against the difficulties of finding interlocutors that we discussed in Chapter 4.
11. For the management of disagreement in couple talk, see Fishman (1978, 1980, 1983); Piller (2002a); Tannen (1984, 1989, 1994).
12. These considerations are similar to those raised by other groups of Australian parents (Ellis & Sims, 2022; Lising, 2022; Piller & Gerber, 2021; Torsh, 2020, 2022; Wang, 2020, 2022).
13. For overviews of family language policy, see Curdt-Christiansen (2018); King, Fogle, & Logan-Terry (2008); Schwartz (2010); Spolsky (2012). For intercultural communication and family bilingualism, see also Zhu (2019).
14. For further discussion on how this group constitutes a distinct cohort, see Chapter 2.
15. The figure is based on a meta-study of North American research and includes elementary and secondary school arrivals (Collier, 1989). More recent Israeli research found longer catch-up times of 9 to 11 years for elementary school students (Levin & Shohamy, 2007, 2008). Despite strong beliefs to the contrary, younger children have repeatedly been found to need more time to catch up than older ones (MacSwan & Pray, 2005). For an overview of relevant research and the differences that various school forms make, see Piller (2016).
16. There is, in fact, significant program variation (Davison, 2014; Oliver, Rochecouste, & Nguyen, 2017). ESL pull-out sessions and individual tutoring are the options experienced by our participants.
17. Harklau (1994); Talmy (2009).
18. See Chapter 2 for an exploration of the English-language proficiency of this cohort on arrival.
19. De Houwer (2020).
20. The title of an influential article in bilingualism studies is "When learning a second language means losing the first" (Wong Fillmore, 1991).
21. Although ignoring children if they speak the wrong language is often advised in the bilingual parenting advice literature, it has not been found to be very effective in other contexts, either (Doepke, 1992; Wang, 2022; S. Wilson, 2020).
22. The outcome of any language policy, in the family as elsewhere, is determined by a complex interplay of a multiplicity of contextual factors (Schwartz & Verschik, 2013; Smith-Christmas, 2016).
23. Bourdieu (1991).
24. For children feeling ashamed of the parents' language, see also De Houwer (2017). Generally, family is one of the main domains where vicarious shame and guilt are experienced, and women and children suffer these the most (Walker & Bantebya-Kyomuhendo, 2014).

25. For an overview of the languages of multilingual Iran, see Moradi (2020). For specific information on Azeri, see Floor & Javadi (2013); Mirvahedi (2016); Rezaei, Latifi, & Nematzadeh (2017).
26. For the role of emotions in bilingual parenting, see Pavlenko (2004, 2006a); Pavlenko & Piller (2001); Wang (2022).
27. For another examination of how children's and parents' differential linguistic capital in migration can result in role reversals in the parent-child relationship, see Luykx (2005).
28. For teachers' strategies to mitigate the face threat of error corrections, see Ergül (2021).
29. Goffman (1955).
30. There is, in fact, a whole genre of parenting advice that feeds on inculcating parental guilt, including guilt about guilt, as in the "mommy guilt" genre (Adams & Buttrose, 2006; Bort, Pflock, & Renner, 2005).
31. See Guardado & Becker (2014).

Chapter 6

1. Slovaks have constituted a significant minority in Vojvodina for about 200 years, when the territory was part of the Austro-Hungarian Empire (Surova, 2018). We use the term "Serbo-Croatian" for the language in keeping with Anna's usage, who described both her own language and that of her Croatian in-laws as "Serbo-Croatian." For a discussion of the disintegration of Serbo-Croatian into Bosnian, Croatian, Montenegrin, and Serbian during the Yugoslav wars of succession, see Bugarski (2012) or Greenberg (2004). Serbo-Croatian today is best understood as "one linguistic language in the guise of three or four political languages" (Bugarski, 2004, p. 18).
2. Since the institution of anti-Chinese policies in Malaysia in the late 1960s, many Chinese Malaysians have left the country. After Singapore, Australia has been their second most important destination (Hugo, 2011; Koh, 2015).
3. See Chapter 3 for an exploration of participants' job search experiences.
4. For the rights and responsibilities of Australian citizenship, see Australian citizenship (2023).
5. For details see *Australian Citizenship Act 2007* (2007) or Become an Australian citizen (by conferral) (2023).
6. The following summary is based on Basford, Offermann, & Behrend (2014); Embrick, Domínguez, & Karsak (2017); Estacio & Saidy-Khan (2014); Senter & Ling (2017); Solorzano (1998); Sue (2010); Sue et al. (2007); Yosso, Smith, Ceja, & Solórzano (2009).
7. For details, see Bliuc, McGarty, Hartley, & Muntele Hendres (2012); Itaoui & Dunn (2017); Johns, Noble, & Harris (2017); Soutphommasane (2012); Stratton (2011).
8. The party was founded in 2016 and deregistered by the Electoral Commission in 2022 ('Love Australia or Leave' is now a political party, 2016; *Notice of deregistration—Love Australia or Leave*, 2022).
9. Like most participants, and as is common in public discourse in Australia, Michiko used "Australian" as a synonym for "white-looking." We will discuss the racialization of "Australian" as White and native English-speaking in the section "Between Language and Race" below.
10. The term "selective incivility" is sometimes used as a synonym for micro-aggressions (Byrd, 2016; Cortina, Kabat-Farr, Leskinen, Huerta, & Magley, 2011; Fernando & Kenny, 2023; Krings, Johnston, Binggeli, & Maggiori, 2014; Ozturk & Berber, 2020). We prefer to reserve it for instances where an actual comparison is involved.
11. See note 6.
12. Sue et al. (2008), p. 331.
13. Fleras (2016).
14. *Drivers licences in Australia* (2017).
15. Recently, there has been increasing discussion in the literature that compliments about language proficiency also constitute a form of micro-invalidation (Kubota, Corella, Lim, & Sah, 2023). This is not how our participants perceived compliments about their English. Those who reported receiving compliments about their English either were pleased with the compliment and took it as an affirmation of their language-learning efforts, or they dismissed the compliment as insincere flattery.
16. For the "Where are you from?" question as a micro-aggression in other contexts, see also Ballinas (2017); Hatoss (2012); Z. Hua (2015); Z. Hua & Wei (2016); Kim (2020).

17. Daisy does not systematically distinguish between long and short i, o, and u, and rarely reduces full vowels to the schwa, even in unstressed positions. For an overview of English in Kenya and phonological features of Kenyan English in general, see Bobda (2000, 2001); Buregeya (2019) Michieka (2005).
18. Hill (1999, 2000, 2008).
19. Al-Saji (2010).
20. For the emerging field of raciolinguistics, see Alim, Reyes, & Kroskrity (2020); Alim & Smitherman (2012); Alim, Williams, Haupt, & Jansen (2021); Corona & Block (2020); N. Flores (2020); García et al. (2021); Khan (2020); Ramjattan (2019, 2022); Rosa (2016, 2019); Rosa & Flores (2017). For explorations of the intersection of audibility and visibility in differently racialized migrant groups, see Colic-Peisker (2002, 2005, 2009, 2011); Colic-Peisker & Tilbury (2008); Creese (2011); Creese & Kambere (2003); Creese & Wiebe (2012); Tankosić & Dovchin (2021); Tankosić, Dryden, & Dovchin (2021).
21. *Racial Discrimination Act 1975, Compilation No. 19* (2022). For the proxy role of language in racist discrimination in contexts including education, employment, before the law, and in other gatekeeping encounters such as finding housing, see also Baugh (2005); Du Bois (2019); Eades (2003, 2012); J. Li, Ai, & Xu (2021); Lippi-Green (2012); Piller (2016); Rosa (2019); Smith-Khan (2019a, 2019b, 2019c, 2019d).
22. On imagined identity in general, see B. Anderson (1991). On Australian identity imagined as White and English-speaking, see Chapter 1 and Hage (1998); Piller, Torsh, & Smith-Khan (2023).
23. On linguistic passing, see Piller (2002b).
24. This is known as the McGurk Effect (McGurk & MacDonald, 1976). For its application in intercultural communication, see Lindemann & Subtirelu (2013); Piller (2017d); Rubin (1992); Rubin & Smith (1990); Subtirelu (2013, 2015).
25. See note 15.
26. For confirmation of these perceptual patterns in experimental research, see Gnevsheva (2017, 2018a, 2018b).
27. Our European and Iranian participants certainly reported fewer instances of experiencing micro-aggressions, and those that they reported tended to be less serious. Ours is not a quantitative study and there could be other explanations. For instance, European and Iranian participants were, on the whole, better educated and more financially secure than their counterparts from Africa, who were mostly humanitarian entrants, or from the Philippines, who were mostly on temporary work visas. Of course, these patterns in themselves are testament to a racist and colonial global order (Andrews, 2021).
28. For background on the authoritarian military dictatorship under General Augusto Pinochet between 1973 and 1990, see Huneeus (2007); Politzer (1989); Stern (2006).
29. Davis & Stevenson (2006).
30. With reference to the US context, E. Anderson (2015) explains that Black people cannot avoid White spaces and must navigate them as best they can, while White people do not normally venture into Black spaces, which are limited to destitute and abject localities like urban ghettos. For a study of how Australian hospitals are constituted as White spaces for Black nurses, see Mapedzahama, Rudge, West, & Perron (2012).
31. Like all participant names, "Jaime" is a pseudonym, patterned on his real name, a Spanish name with a conventional, quite different-sounding, English version. Like "Jim" and "James," the English version has a conventional, quite different-sounding, abbreviation.
32. Mencken (1919, p. 280). For contemporary explorations of name anglicizing, see Chang (2011); Cotterill (2020); Fang & Fine (2020); Piller (2015b); Xu (2020).
33. On reverse stigmatization as a strategy for coping with racism, see Kusow (2004).
34. Interventions by bystanders have been found to be one of the most effective challenges to racism (J. K. Nelson, Dunn, & Paradies, 2011), yet remain rare (Roberts & Rizzo, 2021).
35. Quoted in Berenstain (2016, p. 570).

Chapter 7

1. There are many accounts of life in the divided city, and F. Taylor (2007) is a good starting point.
2. Bonegilla is often considered emblematic of postwar migration to Australia, both in its positive and negative aspects (Dellios, 2017; Wills, 2008). The site in rural Victoria today houses a migration museum (see https://www.bonegilla.org.au/). Over 300,000 migrants passed through

the reception center and over 1.2 million Australians today claim descent from someone who spent time in Bonegilla. Consequently, it features prominently in migrant memoires (Armstrong, 2001; Fitzpatrick, 2021; Licht, 2015; Moss, 1997; Schueller, 2012) and even fiction (Purman, 2018).

3. Talk about absent third parties can sometimes be exclusive and socially disruptive (Dytham, 2018), but none of the talk we recorded was malicious. None of the people talked about were known to everyone in the group. They were mostly exemplars of relationships, behaviors, or experiences. Anthropologists consider gossip essential to interaction and the creation of social worlds (Dunbar, 1998, 2004). Gossip serves a range of social purposes, including entertainment, information sharing, constructing, reinforcing, or challenging group norms and power relationships, and inclusion or exclusion in social groups (Blum-Kulka, 2000; Búriková, 2015; Coates, 2000, 2015; Dreby, 2009; Galasinska, 2010; McMichael & Manderson, 2004; Mohammad & Vásquez, 2015; S. K. Scott, 2017; Sun, Schilpzand, & Liu, 2023).
4. Jones (1980, p. 194), a famous definition of gossip.
5. The complexity and multiplicity of the meanings of home in migration contexts are widely acknowledged in the literature (Ahmed, 1999; Erdal, 2021; Hunter, 2016; S. Liu, 2015; Ralph & Staeheli, 2011; Shindo, 2021).
6. "Dag" is an affectionate Australian slang term for someone with questionable taste, poor style, and lacking self-consciousness about social appearances. The practice of decorating everyday objects in national flags, country shapes, or country names can be described as a form of banal nationalism (Billig, 1995). Sometime earlier, Laura had attended an intercultural communication class taught by Ingrid, where banal nationalism was one of the topics.
7. Now in its 6th edition, the immensely successful book with the title *The Age of Migration* was first published in 1993 (de Haas, Castles, & Miller, 2019). The sedentarist bias in imagining the life course is most obvious in legal structures that treat immobility as the norm, and mobility as deviation (McCollum, Keenan, & Findlay, 2020), but has even been shown to pervade graveyard plotting and funeral service provision (Hunter, 2016). There is a difference between countries of the Global North and the Global South. In the latter, migration may well have become a normalized option in the imagined life course (Capino, 2010; Coe, 2012; Dalgas, 2015; Hsu, 2000; Nyanzi, Rosenberg-Jallow, Bah, & Nyanzi, 2005; Rajan, Varghese, & Jayakumar, 2013; Somaiah et al., 2020; Teo, 2003).
8. Originally published in 1943, quoted from Arendt (2017, p. 3f).
9. Most of these conversations were with participants in another research project, who were studying English in the AMEP at the time. Their data are not included here, as we explain in the Acknowledgments. For news reports of the mass shooting in question, see Candiotti (2009); Chernoff & Candiotti (2009); Esposito, Thomas, Goldman, Potter, & Michels (2009); Fernandez & Hernández (2009); Fernandez & Schweber (2009); Hernández & Rivera (2009); Huynh & Chen (2009).
10. Mental ill health may be more prevalent in migrants generally, or in forced migrants only. The public health literature on the topic often does not distinguish between these different groups, or takes "refugee" to be synonymous with "migrant." Studies that suggest higher prevalence of mental ill health and greater severity of symptoms include Bhugra (2004); Cetin (2016); Dovchin (2020); Forte et al. (2018); Hameed, Sadiq, & Din (2018); Mwanri et al. (2022); Sullivan, Vaughan, & Wright (2020); Tilbury (2007); Wu et al. (2021). The suggestion that migrants are at greater risk of mental health issues is not uncontroversial, and some studies have found no differences between the native and non-native-born population (Hollander et al., 2020).
11. For a short biography of Ford, see Aleksander Ford (2017).
12. Katja and Nicolas consistently used "intelligent" to mean "intellectual."
13. For a detailed exploration of the sense of exclusion that motivated Maria's declaration, see Butorac (2014). The theme of "not fitting in" pervades studies of bilingual selves (Butcher, 2010; Ciriza-Lope, Shappeck, & Arxer, 2016; Dumenden & English, 2013; Heinz, 2001; Pavlenko, 2001a; Stracke et al., 2014; Viswanathan, Torelli, Yoon, & Riemer, 2010; Warriner, 2007).
14. In 2022, forced hijab in Iran and the strict policing of women's public appearance since the Islamic Revolution in 1979 gained renewed international attention with the death in custody of a young woman, Mahsa Amini, ensuing widespread protests, and their brutal repression (Ghaedi, 2022).
15. In Iran, blasphemy is a crime punishable by death. The Islamic Republic's penal code includes the crime of "waging war against God" (*moharebeh*), which covers a wide range of critical words

and deeds (*Iran: Chilling use of the death penalty to further brutally quell popular uprising*, 2022; *Iran: UN experts condemn execution of protestor, raise alarm about detained artists*, 2022).

16. For the real social and psychological effects of using different languages, or even different ways of speaking, on the sense of self, see Dewaele (2004, 2008, 2010); Koven (1998); Pavlenko (2002, 2006a, 2006b).
17. For a collection of studies about women's lives in South Sudan, see Bubenzer & Stern (2011).
18. Isabella may well be right. The literacy learning of adult language learners remains poorly understood (H. Moore, Nicholas, & Deblaquiere, 2008; S. H. Moore, 2007; Peyton & Young-Scholten, 2020) and knowledge of how best to teach and support them remains scarce (Chapman & Williams, 2015; Haznedar, Peyton, & Young-Scholten, 2018; Perry & Hart, 2012; Wienberg, Dutz, & Grotlüschen, 2021). On broader investigations of literacy and identity, see the research collected in Pitkänen-Huhta & Holm (2012).
19. For background on ethnic and linguistic diversity in South Sudan, see Beswick (2004); Frahm (2015).
20. On tellable and non-tellable life stories in migration contexts, see, e.g., Buitelaar (2006); Luibhéid (2021); Maydell (2020). Stories that do not fit the stereotypes and discourses of the destination can have dire consequences for asylum seekers, whose stories may be perceived as "incredible" (Blommaert, 2009; Smith-Khan, 2017a, 2017b, 2019a, 2019d).
21. For the KMT anti-Christian campaigns of the 1920s, see Lutz (1976). For a study of the experiences of the "homeless generation" of KMT veterans, see Fan (2012).
22. For background on anti-Chinese racism in Indonesia and Chinese emigration from Indonesia in the second half of the 20th century, see Cribb & Coppel (2009); Lindsey & Pausacker (2005); Sai & Hoon (2012); Tanasaldy (2022).
23. Chinese people have settled in Brazil in significant numbers at least since the early 19th century, but they continue to be widely perceived as outsiders to the nation (Lesser, 1999; Stenberg, 2012).
24. More numerous and better known than the Chinese diaspora in Brazil, the Japanese minority there dates from the early years of the 20th century when the Japanese state signed a labor export agreement with Brazil. In the 1980s and 1990s, many of the descendants of these migrants moved "back" to Japan in one of the world's largest and best-described ethnic return migrations (Lesser, 2003; Roth, 2002; Tsuda, 2003; Yamanaka, 2003). Maria's husband is somewhat exceptional in that most return migrants were working-class people, similar to the ancestral migration to Brazil.
25. "Ozzie" or "Aussie" is an Australian slang term for "Australian."
26. All the participants for whom religion was important or who spoke to us about their faith were Christians. For in-depth explorations of settlement support provided by churches, and the relationship between Christianity and migration more broadly, see Ambrosini, Bonizzoni, & Molli (2021); Burgess (2009); Chao & Kuntz (2013); Fresnoza-Flot (2010); Gray (2016); Han (2011, 2019); Heyer (2012); Nguyen, Taylor, & Chatters (2016); Peñalva (2017); Piller (2021); Snyder (2016); Village, Powell, & Pepper (2017); Wang & Piller (2022); Y. Yu & Moskal (2019). Perera (2022) is a highly readable examination of a diasporic Tamil Hindu temple.
27. On community language schools in NSW as a site of community building, see Cruickshank, Jung, & Li (2022).
28. On community making in salsa dance groups, see B. Schneider (2014).
29. These kinds of doubts about being oversensitive are a key characteristic of micro-aggressions, as we discussed in Chapter 6.
30. For details on the Australia Day Awards, see https://cms.australianoftheyear.org.au/.
31. Couton & Gaudet (2008); Qvist (2018); Ruiz Sportmann & Greenspan (2019).
32. Mwanri et al. (2022).
33. These identity challenges are inextricably linked to participants' difficulties with finding work, as we discussed in Chapter 3.
34. For African parenting in Australia's child protection context, see Mugadza, Williams Tetteh, Stout, & Renzaho (2020).
35. Gyekye (1996).

Chapter 8

1. Murphy (1952, p. 192). For an overview of Murphy's career, see Corin & Bibeau (1988).

2. See Christensen, Freese, & Miguel (2019); Miedema (2022); Ruediger et al. (2022); Wilkinson et al. (2016) for overviews of the open science movement, and Farrell, Schneider, & Horst (2021) for a preliminary exploration of open research in sociolinguistics.
3. Ruediger et al. (2022, p. 3). In the United States, at least, uptake is likely to accelerate with key policy settings mandating open science principles (*2023 NIH Data Management and Sharing Policy*, 2023; A. Nelson, 2022).
4. Wilkinson et al. (2016).
5. See Neumann, Gifford, Lems, & Scherr (2014) for a detailed analysis of Australian migration scholarship and its impact between 1952 and 2013. Of course, we acknowledge that reasons why migration scholarship has little impact on policy are not limited to methodological considerations. Migration policy is a highly politicized and contested environment, as we outlined in Chapter 1.
6. *Migration, pathway to nation building* (2023, n.p.).
7. These are the words of Labor politician Tony Burke in 2007, at a time when the ALP was in opposition; quoted in Hart (2007, n.p.).
8. For background reading, see Harvey (2005, 2011); Wise (2015).
9. For a detailed historical analysis of labor and industrial relations in the Australian meat processing industry, see O'Leary (2008); for a summary of how they relate to migration, see Piller & Lising (2014).
10. For an exploration of migration as trauma and the role of churches in providing support, see also Wang & Piller (2022).
11. For examples of community initiatives related to migrant mentoring and buddy support, see Cross (2023); *Mentor program* (2023); *Opening the school gate: Engaging migrant and refugee families* (2016); Stump (2022).
12. Life-stage considerations in language socialization have recently gained increasing attention under the Spanish term *muda* (Ciriza, 2019; Ghimenton & Riley, 2019; Puigdevall, Walsh, Amorrortu, & Ortega, 2018; Pujolar, 2019; Pujolar & Gonzàlez, 2013; Pujolar & Puigdevall, 2015). The importance of centering life stage in migration scholarship is also highlighted by Erdal & Ezzati (2015).
13. Temporary visas are not the only policies that separate families. Another widely discussed example includes the prohibitive cost of parent visas (Choahan 2023).
14. For schools' lack of attention to NESB parents, see J. Cho (2021b); Piller, Bruzon, & Torsh (2023). For underrepresentation of NESB populations in clinical trials, see Hughson et al. (2016); Murray, Nebeker, & Carpendale (2019); A. B. Smith et al. (2018); A. B. Smith et al. (2020).
15. An OECD report about 21st-century skills and competences, for instance, calls for an "innovative literacy concept related to the capacity of students to apply knowledge and skills in key subject areas and to analyze, reason and communicate effectively as they raise, solve and interpret problems in a variety of situations" (Ananiadou & Claro, 2009, p. 7). Quality education focused on the development of a broad range of literacy skills within lifelong learning is one of the United Nation's Sustainable Development Goals (*The sustainable development goals report 2022*, 2022).
16. For orientations to raciolinguistics as it developed in the US context, see Alim et al. (2020); Charity Hudley & N. Flores (2022); N. Flores (2020); N. Flores & Rosa (2019); García et al. (2021); Rosa & Flores (2017). For studies specific to Australia, see Dovchin (2020); Piller, Torsh, & Smith-Khan (2023); Tankosić & Dovchin, 2021; Tankosić, Dryden, & Dovchin (2021).
17. Lo Bianco (1987).
18. For overviews of Australian language policy, see Lo Bianco (1995, 2008, 2010, 2014); Lo Bianco & Slaughter (2009). For community interpreting, see Eser (2020); Hale (2007); Taibi & Ozolins (2016). For a history of multicultural broadcasting, see Ang, Hawkins, & Dabboussy (2008).
19. For excessive mortality rates of the overseas-born, see Davey & Nicholas (2022). For analyses of multilingual communication failures, see Grey & Severin (2021, 2022); Karidakis et al. (2022); Piller (2020–2022); Piller, Zhang, & Li (2020a).
20. For a systematic model of how to develop comprehensive language services, see Y. Li, Rao, Zhang, & Li (2020).
21. For the effective deployment of communication volunteers during the first COVID-19 outbreak in China, see J. Zhang & Wu (2020); Zheng (2020).

References

2021 Census Quickstats. (2022). Canberra: Australian Bureau of Statistics. Retrieved from http://www.abs.gov.au/websitedbs/censushome.nsf/home/quickstats.

2023 NIH data management and sharing policy. (2023). Washington, DC: National Institutes of Health. Retrieved from https://oir.nih.gov/sourcebook/intramural-program-oversight/intramural-data-sharing/2023-nih-data-management-sharing-policy.

Aboriginal and Torres Strait Islander people: Census. (2022). Canberra: Australian Bureau of Statistics. Retrieved from https://www.abs.gov.au/statistics/people/aboriginal-and-torres-strait-islander-peoples/aboriginal-and-torres-strait-islander-people-census/latest-release.

Adams, P., & Buttrose, I. (2006). *Motherguilt.* Camberwell, Vic: Penguin.

Adejunmobi, M. (2004). *Vernacular palaver: Imaginations of the local and non-native languages in West Africa.* Clevedon: Multilingual Matters.

Adejunmobi, M. (2008). Intercultural and transcultural literacy in contemporary Africa. *Language and Intercultural Communication, 8*(2), 72–90. doi:10.1080/14708470802270828.

Adichie, C. N. (2013). *Americanah.* London: HarperCollins.

Adler, P. A., & Adler, P. (2004). *Paradise laborers: Hotel work in the global economy.* Ithaca, NY: Cornell University Press.

Aghagolzadeh, F., & Davari, H. (2017). English education in Iran: From ambivalent policies to paradoxical practices. In R. Kirkpatrick (Ed.), *English language education policy in the Middle East and North Africa* (pp. 47–62). Cham: Springer International.

Agirdag, O. (2013). The long-term effects of bilingualism on children of immigration: Student bilingualism and future earnings. *International Journal of Bilingual Education and Bilingualism, 17*(4), 449–464. doi:10.1080/13670050.2013.816264.

Åhlund, A., & Aronsson, K. (2015). Stylizations and alignments in a L2 classroom: Multiparty work in forming a community of practice. *Language & Communication, 43*, 11–26. doi:https://doi.org/10.1016/j.langcom.2015.03.004.

Ahmed, S. (1999). Home and away: Narratives of migration and estrangement. *International Journal of Cultural Studies, 2*(3), 329–347.

Ai, B. (2017). Constructing an academic identity in Australia: An autoethnographic narrative. *Higher Education Research & Development, 36*(6), 1095–1107. doi:10.1080/07294360.2017.1303459.

Ailwood, J. (2007). Mothers, teachers, maternalism and early childhood education and care: Some historical connections. *Contemporary Issues in Early Childhood, 8*(2), 157–165.

Al-Saji, A. (2010). The racialization of Muslim veils: A philosophical analysis. *Philosophy & Social Criticism, 36*(8), 875–902.

Aleksander Ford. (2017). *Culture.Pl.* Warsaw: Adam Mickiewicz Institute. Retrieved from https://culture.pl/en/artist/aleksander-ford

Alim, H. S., Reyes, A., & Kroskrity, P. V. (Eds.). (2020). *The Oxford handbook of language and race.* New York and Oxford: Oxford University Press.

Alim, H. S., Rickford, J. R., & Ball, A. F. (Eds.). (2016). *Raciolinguistics: How language shapes our ideas about race.* New York: Oxford University Press.

Alim, H. S., & Smitherman, G. (2012). *Articulate while black: Barack Obama, language, and race in the U.S.* Oxford: Oxford University Press.

Alim, H. S., Williams, Q. E., Haupt, A., & Jansen, E. (2021). "Kom Khoi San, kry trug jou land": Disrupting white settler colonial logics of language, race, and land with Afrikaaps. *Journal of Linguistic Anthropology, 31*(2), 194–217. doi:https://doi.org/10.1111/jola.12308.

Allan, G. (2008). Flexibility, friendship, and family. *Personal Relationships, 15*(1), 1–16. doi:https://doi.org/10.1111/j.1475-6811.2007.00181.x.

Allan, K., & Burridge, K. (2006). *Forbidden words: Taboo and the censoring of language.* Cambridge: Cambridge University Press.

Ambrosini, M., Bonizzoni, P., & Molli, S. D. (2021). How religion shapes immigrants' integration: The case of Christian migrant churches in Italy. *Current Sociology, 69*(6), 823–842.

AMEP and SEE programme alignment report. (2015). Canberra: Department of Education and Training. Retrieved from https://docs.education.gov.au/node/39901.

AMEP home tutor resources topic packs. (2011). Canberra: Commonwealth of Australia. Retrieved from https://immi.homeaffairs.gov.au/amep-subsite/Files/amep-home-tutor-scheme-resources-topic-packs-overview.pdf.

Ananiadou, K., & Claro, M. (2009). *21st century skills and competences for new millennium learners in OECD countries.* Paris: OECD. Retrieved from https://www.oecd-ilibrary.org/education/21st-century-skills-and-competences-for-new-millennium-learners-in-oecd-countries_218525261154.

Anderson, B. (1991). *Imagined communities: Reflections on the origin and spread of nationalism* (2nd ed.). London: Verso.

Anderson, E. (2015). The white space. *Sociology of Race and Ethnicity, 1*(1), 10–21. doi:10.1177/2332649214561306.

Andrews, K. (2021). *The new age of empire: How racism and colonialism still rule the world.* London: Penguin Books.

Ang, I., Hawkins, G., & Dabboussy, L. (2008). *The SBS story: The challenge of diversity.* Sydney: UNSW Press.

Angouri, J. (2018). *Culture, discourse, and the workplace.* London: Routledge.

Ansary, H., & Babaii, E. (2003). Subliminal sexism in current ESL/EFL textbooks. *Asian EFL Journal, 5*(1), 1–15.

Anyidoho, A., & Dakubu, M. E. K. (2008). Ghana: Indigenous languages, English, and an emerging national identity. In A. Simpson (Ed.), *Language and national identity in Africa* (pp. 141–157). Oxford: Oxford University Press.

Arendt, H. (2017). We refugees. In H. Lambert (Ed.), *International refugee law* (pp. 3–12). London: Routledge.

Armand, G. (2018). Mediated remittances: Transnational economic contributions from second-generation Filipino Americans. *Global Networks, 18*(3), 500–517. doi:doi:10.1111/glob.12198.

Armstrong, D. (2001). *The voyage of their life: The story of the SS Derna and its passengers.* Sydney: HarperCollins.

Australia's population by country of birth. (2022). Canberra: Australian Bureau of Statistics. Retrieved from https://www.abs.gov.au/statistics/people/population/australias-population-country-birth/latest-release.

Australia 2021. (2022). Canberra: Australian Bureau of Statistics. Retrieved from https://www.abs.gov.au/census/find-census-data/quickstats/2021/AUS.

Australia's migration trends 2017–18: Highlights. (2019). Canberra: Australian Government, Department of Home Affairs. Retrieved from https://www.homeaffairs.gov.au/research-and-stats/files/migration-trends-highlights-2017-18.PDF.

Australian citizenship. (2023). Retrieved from https://immi.homeaffairs.gov.au/citizenship-subsite/pages/learn-about-being-an-australian.aspx.

Australian citizenship act 2007. (2007). Canberra: Australian Government. Retrieved from https://www.legislation.gov.au/Details/C2020C00309.

Azam, M., Chin, A., & Prakash, N. (2013). The returns to English-language skills in India. *Economic Development and Cultural Change, 61*(2), 335–367. doi:10.1086/668277.

Bailey, K. D. (2006). Marketing the eikaiwa wonderland: Ideology, akogare, and gender alterity in English conversation school advertising in Japan. *Environment and Planning D: Society and Space, 24*(1), 105–130.

Bailey, K. D. (2007). Akogare, ideology, and "charisma man" mythology: Reflections on ethnographic research in English language schools in Japan. *Gender Place and Culture, 14*(5), 585–608.

Baird, A. S., Kibler, A., & Palacios, N. (2014). "Yo te estoy ayudando; estoy aprendiendo también/I am helping you; I am learning too:" A bilingual family's community of practice during home literacy events. *Journal of Early Childhood Literacy, 15*(2), 147–176. doi:10.1177/1468798414551949.

Baldassar, L., Kilkey, M., Merla, L., & Wilding, R. (2017). Transnational families. In J. Treas, J. Scott, & M. Richards (Eds.), *The sociology of families* (2nd ed., pp. 155–175). Oxford: Wiley-Blackwell.

Ballinas, J. (2017). Where are you from and why are you here? Microaggressions, racialization, and Mexican college students in a new destination. *Sociological Inquiry, 87*(2), 385–410. doi:10.1111/soin.12181.

Basford, T. E., Offermann, L. R., & Behrend, T. S. (2014). Do you see what i see? Perceptions of gender microaggressions in the workplace. *Psychology of Women Quarterly, 38*(3), 340–349. doi:10.1177/0361684313511420.

Bateman, A. (Director). (1988–). *Home and away*. Australia: Southern Star.

Baugh, J. (2005). Linguistic profiling. In S. Makoni, G. Smitherman, A. F. Ball, & A. K. Spears (Eds.), *Black linguistics* (pp. 155–168). London and New York: Routledge.

Become an Australian citizen (by conferral). (2023). Retrieved from https://immi.homeaffairs.gov.au/citizenship/become-a-citizen/permanent-resident.

Beneba Clarke, M. (2019). *Growing up African in Australia*. Melbourne: Black.

Benz, V. (2017). *Bilingual childcare: Hitches, hurdles and hopes*. Bristol: Multilingual Matters.

Berenstain, N. (2016). Epistemic exploitation. *Ergo: An Open Access Journal of Philosophy, 3*(22), 569–590. doi:https://doi.org/10.3998/ergo.12405314.0003.022.

Beswick, S. (2004). *Sudan's blood memory: The legacy of war, ethnicity, and slavery in early South Sudan*. Rochester, NY: University of Rochester Press.

Bhugra, D. (2004). Migration and mental health. *Acta Psychiatrica Scandinavica, 109*(4), 243–258. doi:https://doi.org/10.1046/j.0001-690X.2003.00246.x.

Bigelow, M. H. (2010). *Mogadishu on the Mississippi: Language, racialized identity, and education in a new land*. Malden, MA: Wiley-Blackwell.

Billig, M. (1995). *Banal nationalism*. London: Sage.

Binford, L. (2003). Migrant remittances and (under)development in Mexico. *Critique of Anthropology, 23*(3), 305–336. doi:10.1177/0308275X030233004.

Blackstone, A. (2014). Doing family without having kids. *Sociology Compass, 8*(1), 52–62. doi:https://doi.org/10.1111/soc4.12102.

Bliuc, A.-M., McGarty, C., Hartley, L., & Muntele Hendres, D. (2012). Manipulating national identity: The strategic use of rhetoric by supporters and opponents of the "Cronulla riots" in Australia. *Ethnic and Racial Studies, 35*(12), 2174–2194. doi:10.1080/01419870.2011.600768.

Blommaert, J. (2009). Language, asylum, and the national order. *Current Anthropology, 50*(4), 415–441. doi:10.1086/600131.

Blum-Kulka, S. (2000). Gossipy events at family dinners: Negotiating sociability, presence and the moral order. In J. Coupland (Ed.), *Small talk* (pp. 213–240). London: Routledge.

Blyth, C. (2018). Immersive technologies and language learning. *Foreign Language Annals, 51*(1), 225–232. doi:https://doi.org/10.1111/flan.12327.

Bobda, A. S. (2000). Comparing some phonological features across African accents of English. *English Studies, 81*(3), 249–266.

Bobda, A. S. (2001). East and Southern African English accents. *World Englishes, 20*(3), 269–284. doi:https://doi.org/10.1111/1467-971X.00215.

Bodis, A. (2021a). The discursive (mis)representation of English language proficiency: International students in the Australian media. *Australian Review of Applied Linguistics, 44*(1), 37–64.

Bodis, A. (2021b). "Double deficit" and exclusion: Mediated language ideologies and international students' multilingualism. *Multilingua*, *40*(3), 367–392. doi:doi:10.1515/multi-2019-0106.

Bonotti, M., & Willoughby, L. (2022). Citizenship, language tests, and political participation. *Nations and Nationalism*, *28*(2), 449–464. doi:https://doi.org/10.1111/nana.12799.

Boochani, B. (2018). *No friend but the mountains: Writing from Manus Prison* (O. Tofighian, Trans.). Sydney: Picador.

Boochani, B., Tofighian, O., & Mansoubi, M. (Eds.). (2022). *Freedom, only freedom: The prison writings of Behrouz Boochani*. London: Bloomsbury.

Borjian, M. (2013). *English in post-revolutionary Iran: From indigenization to internationalization*. Bristol: Multilingual Matters.

Bort, J., Pflock, A., & Renner, D. (2005). *Mommy guilt: Learn to worry less, focus on what matters most, and raise happier kids*. New York: Amacom Books.

Bouma, G. D. (2015). The role of demographic and socio-cultural factors in Australia's successful multicultural society: How Australia is not Europe. *Journal of Sociology*, *52*(4), 759–771. doi:10.1177/1440783315584210.

Bourdieu, P. (1984). *Distinction: A social critique of the judgement of taste* (R. Nice, Trans.). Cambridge, MA: Harvard University Press.

Bourdieu, P. (1991). *Language and symbolic power* (G. Raymond & M. Adamson, Trans.). Cambridge: Polity.

Bradshaw, C. J. A., Williams, A. N., Saltré, F., Norman, K., & Ulm, S. (2021). The First Australians grew to a population of millions, much more than previous estimates. *Conversation*. Retrieved from https://theconversation.com/the-first-australians-grew-to-a-population-of-millions-much-more-than-previous-estimates-142371.

Bremer, K., Roberts, C., Vasseur, M.-T., Simonot, M., & Broeder, P. (2013 [1996]). *Achieving understanding: Discourse in intercultural encounters*. London: Routledge.

Broth, M., Cromdal, J., & Levin, L. (2018). Showing where you're going: Instructing the accountable use of the indicator in live traffic. *International Journal of Applied Linguistics*, *28*(2), 248–264. doi:https://doi.org/10.1111/ijal.12194.

Bubenzer, F., & Stern, O. (Eds.). (2011). *Hope, pain & patience: The lives of women in South Sudan*. Cape Town, SA: Jacana Media.

Budgeon, S. (2006). Friendship and formations of sociality in late modernity: The challenge of "post traditional intimacy." *Sociological Research Online*, *11*(3), 48–58. doi:10.5153/sro.1248.

Bugarski, R. (2004). What's in a name: The case of Serbo-Croatian. *Revue des études slaves*, *75*(1), 11–20.

Bugarski, R. (2012). Language, identity and borders in the former Serbo-Croatian area. *Journal of Multilingual and Multicultural Development*, *33*(3), 219–235. doi:10.1080/01434632.2012.663376.

Buitelaar, M. (2006). "I am the ultimate challenge": Accounts of intersectionality in the life-story of a well-known daughter of Moroccan migrant workers in the Netherlands. *European Journal of Women's Studies*, *13*(3), 259–276. Retrieved from http://www.informaworld.com/smpp/content~content=a777124546.

Buregeya, A. (2019). *Kenyan English*. Berlin: De Gruyter Mouton.

Burgess, R. (2009). African Pentecostal spirituality and civic engagement: The case of the Redeemed Christian Church of God in Britain. *Journal of Beliefs & Values*, *30*(3), 255–273. doi:10.1080/13617670903371563.

Búriková, Z. S. (2015). "Good families" and the shadows of servitude: Au pair gossip and norms of au pair employment. In R. Cox (Ed.), *Au pairs' lives in global context: Sisters or servants?* (pp. 36–52). London: Palgrave Macmillan.

Burridge, K. (2004). *Blooming English: Observations on the roots, cultivation and hybrids of the English language*. Cambridge: Cambridge University Press.

Busbridge, R. (2019). A multicultural success story? Australian integration in comparative focus. *Journal of Sociology, 56*(2), 263–270. doi:10.1177/1440783319869525.

Butcher, M. (2010). From "fish out of water" to "fitting in": The challenge of re-placing home in a mobile world. *Population, Space and Place, 16*(1), 23–36. doi:https://doi.org/10.1002/psp.575.

Butorac, D. (2011). *Imagined identity, remembered self: Settlement language learning and the negotiation of gendered subjectivity* (PhD dissertation). Macquarie University, Sydney. Retrieved from http://www.languageonthemove.com/wp-content/uploads/2012/03/DButorac_PhD.pdf.

Butorac, D. (2014). "Like a fish not in water": How language and race mediate the social and economic inclusion of women migrants to Australia. *Australian Review of Applied Linguistics, 37*(3), 234–248.

Byrd, M. Y. (2016). Selective incivility: A micro aggression targeting racial and ethnic groups in the workplace. In M. F. Karsten (Ed.), *Gender, race, and ethnicity in the workplace: Emerging issues and enduring challenges* (pp. 123–149). Santa Barbara, CA: Praeger.

Canagarajah, S., & Minakova, V. (2023). Objects in embodied sociolinguistics: Mind the door in research group meetings. *Language in Society, 52*(2), 183–214. doi:10.1017/S0047404522000082.

Candiotti, S. (2009). NY gunman fired 98 shots in about a minute, police chief says. *CNN*. Retrieved from https://edition.cnn.com/2009/CRIME/04/08/ny.shooting/index.html.

Capino, J. B. (2010). *Dream factories of a former colony: American fantasies, Philippine cinema*. Minneapolis: University of Minnesota Press.

Capstick, T. (2020). *Language and migration*. London: Routledge.

Cebulla, A., & Tan, G. (2019, October 24). There's one big problem with Australia's skilled migration program: Many employers don't want new migrants. *The Conversation*. Retrieved from https://theconversation.com/theres-one-big-problem-with-australias-skilled-migration-program-many-employers-dont-want-new-migrants-125569.

Cetin, U. (2016). Cosmopolitanism and the relevance of "zombie concepts": The case of anomic suicide amongst Alevi Kurd youth. *The British Journal of Sociology, 68*(2), 145–166. doi:10.1111/1468-4446.12234.

Chan, C. (2017). In between leaving and being left behind: Mediating the mobilities and immobilities of Indonesian non-migrants. *Global Networks, 17*(4), 554–573. doi:10.1111/glob.12161.

Chang, G. C.-L. (2011). Behind a name. *Language on the Move*. Retrieved from https://www.languageonthemove.com/behind-a-name/.

Chang, G. C.-L. (2015). *Language learning, academic achievement, and overseas experience: A sociolinguistic study of Taiwanese students in Australian higher education* (PhD dissertation). Macquarie University, Sydney. Retrieved from http://www.languageonthemove.com/wp-content/uploads/2016/02/Grace-Chu-Lin-Chang_Taiwanese-students-in-Australian-higher-ed.pdf.

Chang, G. C.-L. (2018). 發聲，發生：留學的真實人生 - *In between languages: The lived experiences of international students in Australia*. Taipeh: Readmoo.

Chao, X., & Kuntz, A. (2013). Church-based ESL program as a figured world: Immigrant adult learners, language, identity, power. *Linguistics and Education, 24*(4), 466–478. doi:https://doi.org/10.1016/j.linged.2013.06.001.

Chapman, L., & Williams, A. (2015). Connecting with community: Helping immigrant low literacy ESL learners in local contexts. In J. Simpson & A. Whiteside (Eds.), *Adult language education and migration* (pp. 35–48). London: Routledge.

Characteristics of recent migrants. (2020). Canberra: Australian Bureau of Statistics. Retrieved from https://www.abs.gov.au/statistics/people/people-and-communities/characteristics-recent-migrants/latest-release.

Charity Hudley, A. H., & Flores, N. (2022). Social justice in applied linguistics: Not a conclusion, but a way forward. *Annual Review of Applied Linguistics, 42*, 144–154. doi:10.1017/S0267190522000083.

Charlesworth, S., & Isherwood, L. (2021). Migrant aged-care workers in Australia: Do they have poorer-quality jobs than their locally born counterparts? *Ageing and Society, 41*(12), 2702–2722. doi:10.1017/S0144686X20000525.

Chau, D. (2021). Spreading language ideologies through social media: Enregistering the "fake ABC" variety in Hong Kong. *Journal of Sociolinguistics, 25*(4), 596–616. doi:https://doi.org/10.1111/josl.12486.

Cheng, Z., Wang, B. Z., Jiang, Z., Taksa, L., & Tani, M. (2021). English skills and early labour market integration: Evidence from humanitarian migrants in Australia. *International Migration*, . doi:https://doi.org/10.1111/imig.12889.

Cheng, Z., Wang, B. Z., & Taksa, L. (2021). Labour force participation and employment of humanitarian migrants: Evidence from the Building a New Life in Australia longitudinal data. *Journal of Business Ethics, 168*(4), 697–720. doi:10.1007/s10551-019-04179-8.

Chernoff, A., & Candiotti, S. (2009). Binghamton struggles to understand why gunman killed 13. *CNN*. Retrieved from http://edition.cnn.com/2009/CRIME/04/04/binghamton.shooting/.

Chiswick, B. R., Lee, Y. L., & Miller, P. W. (2006). Immigrants' language skills and visa category. *International Migration Review, 40*(2), 419–450. doi:10.2307/27645601.

Chiswick, B. R., & Miller, P. W. (1998). English language fluency among immigrants in the United States. *Research in Labour Economics, 17*, 151–200.

Chiswick, B. R., & Miller, P. W. (2001). A model of destination-language acquisition: Application to male immigrants in Canada. *Demography, 38*(3), 391–409. Retrieved from http://muse.jhu.edu/journals/demography/v038/38.3chiswick.pdf.

Chiswick, B. R., Rebhun, U., & Beider, N. (2020). Language acquisition, employment status, and the earnings of Jewish and non-Jewish immigrants in Israel. *International Migration, 58*(2), 205–232. doi:10.1111/imig.12634.

Cho, J. (2015). Sleepless in Seoul: Neoliberalism, English fever, and linguistic insecurity among Korean interpreters. *Multilingua, 34*(5), 687–710. doi:10.1515/multi-2013-0047.

Cho, J. (2017). *Interpreting English language ideologies in Korea: Dreams vs. realities*. Amsterdam: Springer.

Cho, J. (2021a). Constructing a white mask through English: The misrecognized self in Orientalism. *International Journal of the Sociology of Language, 2021*(271), 17–34. doi:10.1515/ijsl-2020-0037.

Cho, J. (2021b). *Intercultural communication in interpreting: Power and choices*. London: Routledge.

Cho, T. (2008). Learning English. In A. Pung (Ed.), *Growing up Asian in Australia* (pp. 15–16). Melbourne: Black.

Choahan, N. (2023, February 16). Skilled migrants in high demand, but roadblocks may stymie efforts to retain talent in Australia. *ABC News*. Retrieved from https://www.abc.net.au/news/2023-02-16/australia-skilled-migrant-cap-indian-racism-jobs-family-reunion/101726700.

Choi, J. (2016). "Speaking English naturally": The language ideologies of English as an official language at a Korean university. *Journal of Multilingual and Multicultural Development, 37*(8), 783–793. doi:10.1080/01434632.2016.1142550.

Christensen, G., Freese, J., & Miguel, E. (2019). *Transparent and reproducible social science research: How to do open science*. Oakland: University of California Press.

Ciriza-Lope, M., Shappeck, M., & Arxer, S. (2016). Emergent target language identities among Latino English language learners. *Journal of Latinos and Education, 15*(4), 287–302. doi:10.1080/15348431.2015.1134535.

Ciriza, M. d. P. (2019). Towards a parental muda for new Basque speakers: Assessing emotional factors and language ideologies. *Journal of Sociolinguistics, 23*(4), 367–385. doi:10.1111/josl.12363.

Clyne, M. (2005a). *Australia's language potential.* Sydney: University of New South Wales Press.

Clyne, M. (2005b). The use of exclusionary language to manipulate opinion: John Howard, asylum seekers and the reemergence of political incorrectness in Australia. *Journal of Language and Politics, 4*(2), 173–196.

Clyne, M. (2008). The monolingual mindset as an impediment to the development of plurilingual potential in Australia. *Sociolinguistic Studies, 2*(3), 347–366. doi:10.1558/sols.v2i3.347.

Coates, J. (2000). Small talk and subversion: Female speakers backstage. In J. Coupland (Ed.), *Small talk* (pp. 241–263). London: Routledge.

Coates, J. (2015). *Women, men and language: A sociolinguistic account of gender differences in language* (3rd ed.). London: Routledge.

Coe, C. (2012). Growing up and going abroad: How Ghanaian children imagine transnational migration. *Journal of Ethnic and Migration Studies, 38*(6), 913–931. doi:10.1080/1369183X.2012.677173.

Cole, G. R. (2013). *The Krio of West Africa: Islam, culture, creolization, and colonialism in the nineteenth century.* Athens: Ohio University Press.

Colic-Peisker, V. (2002). Croatians in Western Australia: Migration, language and class. *Journal of Sociology, 38*(2), 149–166.

Colic-Peisker, V. (2005). "At least you're the right colour": Identity and social inclusion of Bosnian refugees in Australia. *Journal of Ethnic and Migration Studies, 31*(4), 615–638. doi:10.1080/13691830500109720.

Colic-Peisker, V. (2009). Visibility, settlement success and life satisfaction in three refugee communities in Australia. *Ethnicities, 9*(2), 175–199. doi:10.1177/1468796809103459.

Colic-Peisker, V. (2011). "Ethnics" and "Anglos" in the labour force: Advancing Australia fair? *Journal of Intercultural Studies, 32*(6), 637–654. doi:10.1080/07256868.2011.618108.

Colic-Peisker, V., & Tilbury, F. (2008). Being black in Australia: A case study of intergroup relations. *Race & Class, 49*(4), 38–56. doi:10.1177/0306396808089286.

Collier, V. P. (1989). How long? A synthesis of research on academic achievement in a second language. *TESOL Quarterly, 23*(3), 509–531.

Comparing TOEFL iBT Scores. (2022). Princeton, NJ: Educational Testing Service. Retrieved from https://www.ets.org/toefl/score-users/ibt/compare-scores.html.

Competent English. (2022). Retrieved from https://immi.homeaffairs.gov.au/help-support/meeting-our-requirements/english-language/competent-english.

Cooke, M., & Simpson, J. (2008). *ESOL: A critical guide.* Oxford: Oxford University Pres.

Cordella, M., & Huang, H. (Eds.). (2016). *Rethinking second language learning: Using intergenerational community resources.* Bristol: Multilingual Matters.

Corin, E., & Bibeau, G. (1988). H. B. M. Murphy (1915–1987): A key figure in transcultural psychiatry. *Culture, Medicine and Psychiatry, 12*(3), 397–415. doi:10.1007/BF00051976.

Corona, V., & Block, D. (2020). Raciolinguistic micro-aggressions in the school stories of immigrant adolescents in Barcelona: A challenge to the notion of Spanish exceptionalism? *International Journal of Bilingual Education and Bilingualism, 23*(7), 778–788. doi:10.1080/13670050.2020.1713046.

Cortina, L. M., Kabat-Farr, D., Leskinen, E. A., Huerta, M., & Magley, V. J. (2011). Selective incivility as modern discrimination in organizations: Evidence and impact. *Journal of Management, 39*(6), 1579–1605. doi:10.1177/0149206311418835.

Cotterill, S. (2020). Call me Fei: Chinese-speaking students' decision whether or not to use English names in classroom interaction. *Language, Culture and Curriculum, 33*(3), 228–241. doi:10.1080/07908318.2019.1614598.

Couton, P., & Gaudet, S. (2008). Rethinking social participation: The case of immigrants in Canada. *Journal of International Migration and Integration/Revue de l'integration et de la migration internationale, 9*, 21–44.

Crawford, R. (2007). "Anyhow . . . where d'yer get it, mate?" Ockerdom in adland Australia. *Journal of Australian Studies, 31*(90), 1–15. doi:10.1080/14443050709388105.

Crawford, R. (2010). Learning to say g'day to the world: The development of Australia's marketable image in the 1980s. *Consumption Markets & Culture, 13*(1), 43–59. doi:10.1080/10253860903346757.

Crawford, T., & Candlin, S. (2013). A literature review of the language needs of nursing students who have English as a second/other language and the effectiveness of English language support programmes. *Nurse Education in Practice, 13*(3), 181–185.

Creese, G. (2011). *The new African diaspora in Vancouver: Migration, exclusion and belonging.* Toronto: University of Toronto Press.

Creese, G., & Kambere, E. N. (2003). What colour is your English? *Canadian Review of Sociology and Anthropology, 40*(5), 565–573.

Creese, G., & Wiebe, B. (2012). "Survival employment": Gender and deskilling among African immigrants in Canada. *International Migration, 50*(5), 56–76. doi:10.1111/j.1468-2435.2009.00531.x.

Cribb, R., & Coppel, C. A. (2009). A genocide that never was: Explaining the myth of anti-Chinese massacres in Indonesia, 1965–66. *Journal of Genocide Research, 11*(4), 447–465. doi:10.1080/14623520903309503.

Crosby, A. W. (2004). *Ecological imperialism: The biological expansion of Europe, 900–1900* (2nd ed.). Cambridge: Cambridge University Press.

Cross, C. (2023). *5 ways to engage non-English speakers with workplace safety.* Brisbane: Work Healthy Australia. Retrieved from https://www.whsshow.com.au/whssblogfeeder/5-ways-to-engage-non-english-speakers-with-workplace-safety.

Cruickshank, K., Jung, Y. M., & Li, E. B. (2022). *Parallel lines: Community languages schools and their role in growing languages and building communities.* Sydney: Sydney Institute for Community Languages Education (SICLE). Retrieved from https://www.sydney.edu.au/content/dam/corporate/documents/faculty-of-arts-and-social-sciences/research/research-centres-institutes-groups/sicle/parallel-lines-draft-report.pdf.

Cultural diversity of Australia. (2022). Canberra: Australian Bureau of Statistics. Retrieved from https://www.abs.gov.au/articles/cultural-diversity-australia.

Curdt-Christiansen, X. L. (2018). Family language policy. In J. W. Tollefson & M. Pérez-Milans (Eds.), *The Oxford handbook of language policy and planning* (pp. 420–441). Oxford: Oxford University Press.

Dalgas, K. M. (2015). Becoming independent through au pair migration: Self-making and social re-positioning among young Filipinas in Denmark. *Identities, 22*(3), 333–346. doi:10.1080/1070289X.2014.939185.

Dallimore, C. (2018). Improving Adult Migrant English Program (AMEP) outcomes for the Afghan community in South Australia. *International Journal of Training Research, 16*(2), 182–191. doi:10.1080/14480220.2018.1501891.

Daniel, Z. (2020, April 22). Restaurants feeding jobless international hospitality workers during coronavirus pandemic. *ABC News.* Retrieved from https://www.abc.net.au/news/2020-04-24/restaurants-feeding-jobless-hospitality-workers-coronavirus/12180624.

Darvin, R. (2019). L2 motivation and investment. In M. Lamb, K. Csizér, A. Henry, & S. Ryan (Eds.), *The Palgrave handbook of motivation for language learning* (pp. 245–264). Cham: Springer International.

Darvin, R., & Norton, B. (2015). Identity and a model of investment in applied linguistics. *Annual Review of Applied Linguistics, 35*, 36–56. doi:10.1017/S0267190514000191

Davey, M., & Nicholas, J. (2022, February 17). Covid death rate three times higher among migrants than those born in Australia. *Guardian.* Retrieved from https://www.theguardian.com/australia-news/2022/feb/17/covid-death-rate-three-times-higher-among-migrants-than-those-born-in-australia.

David-Barrett, T., Kertesz, J., Rotkirch, A., Ghosh, A., Bhattacharya, K., Monsivais, D., & Kaski, K. (2016). Communication with family and friends across the life course. *PloS ONE, 11*(11), e0165687.

Davis, G. Y., & Stevenson, H. C. (2006). Racial socialization experiences and symptoms of depression among Black youth. *Journal of Child and Family Studies, 15*(3), 293–307. doi:10.1007/s10826-006-9039-8.

Davison, C. (2014). ESL in Australian schools: From the margins to the mainstream. In C. Leung, C. Davison, & B. Mohan (Eds.), *English as a second language in the mainstream* (pp. 27–45). London: Routledge.

De Alwis, S., Parr, N., & Guo, F. (2020). The education–occupation (mis)match of Asia-born immigrants in Australia. *Population Research and Policy Review, 39*(3), 519–548. doi:10.1007/s11113-019-09548-9.

de Beauvoir, S. (1949). *Le deuxième sexe.* Paris: Gallimard.

De Costa, P., Park, J. S.-Y., & Wee, L. (2016). Language learning as linguistic entrepreneurship: Implications for language education. *The Asia-Pacific Education Researcher, 25*(5), 695–702. doi:10.1007/s40299-016-0302-5.

De Costa, P., Park, J. S.-Y., & Wee, L. (2021). Why linguistic entrepreneurship? *Multilingua, 40*(2), 139–153. doi:doi:10.1515/multi-2020-0037.

De Fina, A. (2007). Code-switching and the construction of ethnic identity in a community of practice. *Language in Society, 36*(3), 371–392. doi:10.1017/S0047404507070182.

de Haas, H., Castles, S., & Miller, M. J. (2019). *The age of migration: International population movements in the modern world* (6th ed.). London: Bloomsbury.

De Houwer, A. (2017). Minority language parenting in Europe and children's well-being. In N. J. Cabrera & B. Leyendecker (Eds.), *Handbook on positive development of minority children and youth* (pp. 231–246). Cham: Springer International.

De Houwer, A. (2020). Why do so many children who hear two languages speak just a single language? *Zeitschrift für Interkulturellen Fremdsprachenunterricht, 25*(1), 7–26.

Della Puppa, F., & Ambrosini, M. (2022). "Implicit" remittances in family relationships: The case of Bangladeshis in Italy and beyond. *Global Networks, 22*(1), 134–149. doi:https://doi.org/10.1111/glob.12335.

Dellios, A. (2017). *Histories of controversy: Bonegilla migrant centre.* Melbourne: Melbourne University Press.

Deranty, J.-P. (2021). Post-work society as an oxymoron: Why we cannot, and should not, wish work away. *European Journal of Social Theory, 25*(3), 422–439. doi:10.1177/13684310211012169.

Dewaele, J.-M. (2004). The emotional force of swearwords and taboo words in the speech of multilinguals. *Journal of Multilingual and Multicultural Development, 25*(2–3), 204–222.

Dewaele, J.-M. (2008). The emotional weight of I love you in multilinguals' languages. *Journal of Pragmatics, 40*(10), 1753–1780.

Dewaele, J.-M. (2010). *Emotions in multiple languages.* Basingstoke: Palgrave Macmillan.

Dhimolea, T. K., Kaplan-Rakowski, R., & Lin, L. (2022). A systematic review of research on high-immersion virtual reality for language learning. *TechTrends, 66*(5), 810–824. doi:10.1007/s11528-022-00717-w.

Diniz De Figueiredo, E. H., & Martinez, J. (2021). The locus of enunciation as a way to confront epistemological racism and decolonize scholarly knowledge. *Applied Linguistics, 42*(2), 355–359. doi:10.1093/applin/amz061.

Doepke, S. (1992). *One parent, one language: An interactional approach.* Amsterdam: Benjamins.

Doerr, N. M. (2012). Study abroad as "adventure": Globalist construction of host–home hierarchy and governed adventurer subjects. *Critical Discourse Studies, 9*(3), 257–268.

Doerr, N. M. (2013). Do "global citizens" need the parochial cultural other? Discourse of immersion in study abroad and learning-by-doing. *Compare: A Journal of Comparative and International Education, 43*(2), 224–243.

Dorfman, A. (1999). *Heading south, looking north: A bilingual journey.* London: Penguin.

Dörnyei, Z. (1998). Motivation in second and foreign language learning. *Language Teaching, 31*(3), 117–135. doi:10.1017/S026144480001315X.
Dörnyei, Z., & Ushioda, E. (2013). *Teaching and researching: Motivation.* London: Routledge.
Dovchin, S. (2020). The psychological damages of linguistic racism and international students in Australia. *International Journal of Bilingual Education and Bilingualism, 23*(7), 804–818. doi:10.1080/13670050.2020.1759504.
Dreby, J. (2009). Gender and transnational gossip. *Qualitative Sociology, 32*(1), 33–52. doi:10.1007/s11133-008-9117-x.
Drivers licences in Australia. (2017). Canberra: Australian Government: Department of Infrastructure and Regional Development. Retrieved from https://www.bitre.gov.au/sites/default/files/is_084.pdf.
Du Bois, I. (2019). Linguistic discrimination across neighbourhoods: Turkish, US-American and German names and accents in urban apartment search. *Journal of Language and Discrimination, 3*(2), 92–119.
DuFon, M. A., & Churchill, E. (Eds.). (2006). *Language learners in study abroad contexts.* Clevedon: Multilingual Matters.
Dumenden, I. E., & English, R. (2013). Fish out of water: Refugee and international students in mainstream Australian schools. *International Journal of Inclusive Education, 17*(10), 1078–1088. doi:10.1080/13603116.2012.732120.
Dunbar, R. (1998). *Grooming, gossip, and the evolution of language.* Cambridge, MA: Harvard University Press.
Dunbar, R. (2004). Gossip in evolutionary perspective. *Review of General Psychology, 8*(2), 100–110.
Duranti, A., Ochs, E., & Schieffelin, B. B. (Eds.). (2013). *The handbook of language socialization.* Oxford: Wiley-Blackwell.
Dytham, S. (2018). The construction and maintenance of exclusion, control and dominance through students' social sitting practices. *British Journal of Sociology of Education, 39*(7), 1045–1059. doi:10.1080/01425692.2018.1455494.
Dziekońska, M. (2023). Transnational families: The experiences of Polish stayers from a life-long perspective. *Global Networks, 23*(4), 849–863. doi:https://doi.org/10.1111/glob.12418
Eades, D. (2003). Participation of second language and second dialect speakers in the legal system. *Annual Review of Applied Linguistics, 23*, 113–133. doi:10.1017/S0267190503000229.
Eades, D. (2012). Communication with Aboriginal speakers of English in the legal process. *Australian Journal of Linguistics, 32*(4), 473–489. doi:10.1080/07268602.2012.744268.
Elder, C. (2007). *Being Australian: Narratives of national identity.* Sydney: Allen & Unwin.
Ellis, E. M., Gogolin, I., & Clyne, M. (2010). The Janus face of monolingualism: A comparison of German and Australian language education policies. *Current Issues in Language Planning, 11*(4), 439–460.
Ellis, E. M., & Sims, M. (2022). "It's like the root of a tree that I grew up from . . .": Parents' linguistic identity shaping family language policy in isolated circumstances. *Multilingua, 41*(5), 529–548. doi:10.1515/multi-2021-0100.
Embrick, D. G., Domínguez, S., & Karsak, B. (2017). More than just insults: Rethinking sociology's contribution to scholarship on racial microaggressions. *Sociological Inquiry, 87*(2), 193–206. doi:10.1111/soin.12184.
English is now official language of Burundi. (2014, September 17). *IWACU English News.* Retrieved from https://www.iwacu-burundi.org/englishnews/english-is-now-official-language-of-burundi/.
English language visa requirements. (2022). Canberra: Australian Government, Department of Home Affairs. Retrieved from https://immi.homeaffairs.gov.au/help-support/meeting-our-requirements/english-language.

Enner-Kananen, J., & Pettitt, N. (2017). "I want to speak like the other people": Second language learning as a virtuous spiral for migrant women? *International Review of Education, 63*(4), 583–604. doi:10.1007/s11159-017-9653-2.

Enz, K. F., & Talarico, J. M. (2016). Forks in the road: Memories of turning points and transitions. *Applied Cognitive Psychology, 30*(2), 188–195. doi:https://doi.org/10.1002/acp.3176.

Erdal, M. B. (2021). Migrants' multifocal sedentarism: Ambivalent belonging and desired recognition in transnational social fields connecting Pakistan and Norway. *Journal of Intercultural Studies, 42*(5), 643–659. doi:10.1080/07256868.2021.1971167.

Erdal, M. B., & Ezzati, R. (2015). "Where are you from" or "when did you come"? Temporal dimensions in migrants' reflections about settlement and return. *Ethnic and Racial Studies, 38*(7), 1202–1217. doi:10.1080/01419870.2014.971041.

Ergül, H. (2021). Mitigating oral corrective feedback through linguistic strategies and smiling. *Journal of Pragmatics, 183*, 142–153. doi:https://doi.org/10.1016/j.pragma.2021.07.018/

Eser, O. (2020). *Understanding community interpreting services: Diversity and access in Australia and beyond*. Cham: Palgrave Macmillan.

Esposito, R., Thomas, P., Goldman, R., Potter, N., & Michels, S. (2009, 2009-04-04). Binghamton rampage leaves 14 dead, police don't know motive. *ABC News*. Retrieved from https://abcnews.go.com/US/story?id=7249853.

Estacio, E. V., & Saidy-Khan, S. (2014). Experiences of racial microaggression among migrant nurses in the United Kingdom. *Global Qualitative Nursing Research, 1*, 2333393614532618. doi:10.1177/2333393614532618.

Faine, M. (2008). *At home in Australia: Identity, nation and the teaching of English as a second language to adult immigrants in Australia. Monash University* (PhD dissertation). Monash University, Melbourne. Retrieved from https://doi.org/10.4225/03/587835886243a.

Fan, J. (2012). *China's homeless generation: Voices from the veterans of the Chinese Civil War, 1940s–1990s*. London: Routledge.

Fang, J., & Fine, G. A. (2020). Names and selves: Transnational identities and self-presentation among elite Chinese international students. *Qualitative Sociology, 43*(4), 427–448. doi:10.1007/s11133-020-09468-7.

Fanon, F. (1967). *Black skin, white masks*. London: Pluto Press.

Farrell, E. (2008). *Negotiating identity: Discourses of migration and belonging* (PhD dissertation). Macquarie University, Sydney. Retrieved from http://www.languageonthemove.com/wp-content/uploads/2012/05/FarrellPhDMigrationBelonging.pdf.

Farrell, E., Schneider, B., & Horst, D. (2021). Open research in language and society. *Language on the Move*. Retrieved from https://www.languageonthemove.com/open-research-in-language-and-society/.

Fernandez, M., & Hernández, J. C. (2009, April 6). Binghamton victims shared a dream of living better lives. *New York Times*. Retrieved from https://www.nytimes.com/2009/04/06/nyregion/06victims.html.

Fernandez, M., & Schweber, N. (2009, April 11). Binghamton killer kept his fury private. *New York Times*. Retrieved from https://www.nytimes.com/2009/04/12/nyregion/12binghamton.html.

Fernando, D., & Kenny, E. (2023). The identity impact of witnessing selective incivility: A study of minority ethnic professionals. *Journal of Occupational and Organizational Psychology, 96*(1), 56–80. doi:https://doi.org/10.1111/joop.12408.

Ferri, G., & Magne, V. (2021). Exploring the language ideology of nativeness in narrative accounts of English second language users in Montreal. *Critical Inquiry in Language Studies, 18*(3), 229–246.

Finch, J. (2007). Displaying families. *Sociology, 41*(1), 65–81. doi:10.1177/0038038507072284.

Finn, H. B. (2010). Overcoming barriers: Adult refugee trauma survivors in a learning community. *TESOL Quarterly, 44*(3), 586–596. Retrieved from http://www.jstor.org/stable/27896747.

Fishman, P. (1978). What do couples talk about when they're alone? In D. Butturff & E. L. Epstein (Eds.), *Women's language and style* (pp. 11–22). Akron, OH: L&S Books.

Fishman, P. (1980). Conversational insecurity. In H. Giles, P. W. Robinson, & P. M. Smith (Eds.), *Language: Social psychological perspectives* (pp. 127–132). New York: Pergamon Press.

Fishman, P. (1983). Interaction: The work women do. In B. Thorne, C. Kramarae, & N. Henley (Eds.), *Language, gender and society* (pp. 89–101). Cambridge: Newbury House.

Fitzpatrick, S. (2021). *White Russians, red peril: A Cold War history of migration to Australia.* Melbourne: Black.

Fleras, A. (2016). Theorizing micro-aggressions as racism 3.0: Shifting the discourse. *Canadian Ethnic Studies, 48*(2), 1–19.

Floor, W., & Javadi, H. (2013). The role of Azerbaijani Turkish in Safavid Iran. *Iranian Studies, 46*(4), 569–581. doi:10.1080/00210862.2013.784516.

Flores, A. (2021). *The succeeders: How immigrant youth are transforming what it means to belong in America.* Oakland: University of California Press.

Flores, N. (2020). From academic language to language architecture: Challenging raciolinguistic ideologies in research and practice. *Theory into Practice, 59*(1), 22–31. doi:10.1080/00405841.2019.1665411.

Flores, N., & Rosa, J. (2019). Bringing race into second language acquisition. *The Modern Language Journal, 103*, 145–151.

Fokkema, T., Cela, E., & Ambrosetti, E. (2013). Giving from the heart or from the ego? Motives behind remittances of the second generation in Europe. *International Migration Review, 47*(3), 539–572. doi:10.1111/imre.12032.

Forbes-Mewett, H., Hegarty, K., & Wickes, R. (2022). Regional migration and the local multicultural imaginary: The uneasy governance of cultural difference in regional Australia. *Journal of Ethnic and Migration Studies, 48*(13), 3142–3159. doi:10.1080/1369183X.2021.1915120.

Forte, A., Trobia, F., Gualtieri, F., Lamis, D. A., Cardamone, G., Giallonardo, V., . . . Pompili, M. (2018). Suicide risk among immigrants and ethnic minorities: A literature overview. *International Journal of Environmental Research and Public Health, 15*(7), 1438. doi:10.3390/ijerph15071438.

Fortunati, L., Pertierra, R., & Vincent, J. (Eds.). (2013). *Migration, diaspora and information technology in global societies.* London: Taylor & Francis.

Fotovatian, S. (2012). Three constructs of institutional identity among international doctoral students in Australia. *Teaching in Higher Education, 17*(5), 577–588. doi:10.1080/13562517.2012.658557.

Fotovatian, S., & Miller, J. (2014). Constructing an institutional identity in university tea rooms: The international PhD student experience. *Higher Education Research & Development, 33*(2), 286–297. doi:10.1080/07294360.2013.832154.

Frahm, O. (2015). Making borders and identities in South Sudan. *Journal of Contemporary African Studies, 33*(2), 251–267. doi:10.1080/02589001.2015.1070461.

Frances, R. (1999). Sex workers or citizens? Prostitution and the shaping of "settler" society in Australia. *International Review of Social History, 44*(S7), 101–122. doi:10.1017/S0020859000115214.

Freed, B. F. (Ed.). (1995). *Second language acquisition in a study abroad context.* Amsterdam: John Benjamins.

Fresnoza-Flot, A. (2010). The Catholic Church in the lives of irregular migrant Filipinas in France: Identity formation, empowerment and social control. *The Asia Pacific Journal of Anthropology, 11*(3–4), 345–361. doi:10.1080/14442213.2010.511628.

Frost, K., & McNamara, T. (2018). Language tests, language policy and citizenship. In J. W. Tollefson & M. Pérez-Milans (Eds.), *The Oxford handbook of language policy and planning* (pp. 280–298). Oxford and New York: Oxford University Press.

Fuller, H. R. (2017). The emotional toll of out-migration on mothers and fathers left behind in Mexico. *International Migration, 55*(3), 156–172. doi:10.1111/imig.12324.

Gagnon, G. (2005). *Targeting the Anuak: Human rights violations and crimes against humanity in Ethiopia's Gambella region.* New York: Human Rights Watch.

Galasinska, A. (2010). Gossiping in the Polish club: An emotional coexistence of "old" and "new" migrants. *Journal of Ethnic and Migration Studies, 36*(6), 939–951. doi:10.1080/13691831003643363.

García, O., Flores, N., Seltzer, K., Wei, L., Otheguy, R., & Rosa, J. (2021). Rejecting abyssal thinking in the language and education of racialized bilinguals: A manifesto. *Critical Inquiry in Language Studies, 18*(3), 203–228. doi:10.1080/15427587.2021.1935957.

Gebeyehu, T. (2013). Ethnic conflict, interaction and cohabitation in Africa: The case of Nuer and Anuak. *Eastern Africa Social Science Research Review, 29*(2), 97–112.

Ghaedi, M. (2022, December 4). Who are Iran's "morality police"? *DW.* Retrieved from https://www.dw.com/en/who-are-irans-morality-police/a-63200711.

Ghezelbash, D. (2018). *Refuge lost: Asylum law in an interdependent world.* Cambridge: Cambridge University Press.

Ghimenton, A., & Riley, K. C. (2019). A language socialization account of translinguistic mudes. In J. Won Lee & S. Dovchin (Eds.), *Translinguistics: Negotiating innovation and ordinariness* (pp. 37–48). London: Routledge.

Gnevsheva, K. (2017). Within-speaker variation in passing for a native speaker. *International Journal of Bilingualism, 21*(2), 213–227.

Gnevsheva, K. (2018a). The expectation mismatch effect in accentedness perception of Asian and Caucasian non-native speakers of English. *Linguistics, 56*(3), 581–598.

Gnevsheva, K. (2018b). Variation in foreign accent identification. *Journal of Multilingual and Multicultural Development, 39*(8), 688–702.

Goddard, C. (2015). "Swear words" and "curse words" in Australian (and American) English: At the crossroads of pragmatics, semantics and sociolinguistics. *Intercultural Pragmatics, 12*(2), 189–218. doi:10.1515/ip-2015-0010.

Goffman, E. (1955). On face-work: An analysis of ritual elements in social interaction. *Psychiatry, 18*(3), 213–231.

Goldoni, F. (2013). Students' immersion experiences in study abroad. *Foreign Language Annals, 46*(3), 359–376. doi:https://doi.org/10.1111/flan.12047.

Gomes, C. (2015). Negotiating everyday life in Australia: Unpacking the parallel society inhabited by Asian international students through their social networks and entertainment media use. *Journal of Youth Studies, 18*(4), 515–536.

Gonçalves, K., & Schluter, A. (2017). "Please do not leave any notes for the cleaning lady, as many do not speak English fluently": Policy, power, and language brokering in a multilingual workplace. *Language Policy, 16*(3), 241–265.

Gonzalez, A. (2004). The social dimensions of Philippine English. *World Englishes, 23*(1), 7–16. doi:https://doi.org/10.1111/j.1467-971X.2004.00331.x.

Gray, B. (2016). The politics of migration, church, and state: A case study of the Catholic Church in Ireland. *International Migration Review, 50*(2), 315–351.

Greenberg, R. D. (2004). *Language and identity in the Balkans: Serbo-Croatian and its disintegration.* Oxford: Oxford University Press.

Grey, A., & Severin, A. A. (2021). An audit of NSW legislation and policy on the government's public communications in languages other than English. *Griffith Law Review, 30*(1), 122–147. doi:10.1080/10383441.2021.1970873.

Grey, A., & Severin, A. A. (2022). Building towards best practice for governments' public communications in languages other than English: A case study of New South Wales, Australia. *Griffith Law Review, 31*(1), 25–56. doi:10.1080/10383441.2022.2031526.

Grysman, A., & Hudson, J. A. (2011). The self in autobiographical memory: Effects of self-salience on narrative content and structure. *Memory, 19*(5), 501–513. doi:10.1080/09658211.2011.590502.

Guardado, M., & Becker, A. (2014). "Glued to the family": The role of familism in heritage language development strategies. *Language, Culture and Curriculum, 27*(2), 163–181.

Guo, X. (2007). *A concise Chinese-English dictionary for lovers*. London: Random House.

Gyekye, K. (1996). *African cultural values: An introduction*. Accra: Sankofa.

Hage, G. (1998). *White nation: Fantasies of white supremacy in a multicultural society*. London: Routledge.

Haghighi, F. M., & Norton, B. (2017). The role of English language institutes in Iran. *TESOL Quarterly, 51*(2), 428–438.

Hajek, J., & Slaughter, Y. (Eds.). (2015). *Challenging the monolingual mindset*. Bristol: Multilingual Matters.

Hale, S. B. (2007). *Community interpreting*. Basingstoke: Palgrave Macmillan.

Hameed, S., Sadiq, A., & Din, A. m. U. (2018). The increased vulnerability of refugee population to mental health disorders. *Kansas Journal of Medicine, 11*(1), 1–12.

Hammerstad, A. (2014). The securitization of forced migration. In E. Fiddian-Qasmiyeh, G. Loescher, K. Long, & N. Sigona (Eds.), *The Oxford handbook of refugee and forced migration studies* (pp. 265–277). Oxford: Oxford University Press.

Han, H. (2011). Social inclusion through multilingual ideologies, policies and practices: A case study of a minority church. *International Journal of Bilingual Education and Bilingualism, 14*(4), 383–398. Retrieved from http://www.informaworld.com/10.1080/13670050.2011.573063.

Han, H. (2019). Making "second generation," inflicting linguistic injuries: An ethnography of a mainland Chinese church in Canada. *Journal of Language, Identity & Education, 18*(1), 55–69. doi:10.1080/15348458.2019.1569524.

Haque, E. (2017). Neoliberal governmentality and Canadian migrant language training policies. *Globalisation, Societies and Education, 15*(1), 96–113. doi:10.1080/14767724.2014.937403.

Harklau, L. (1994). ESL versus mainstream classes: Contrasting L2 learning environments. *TESOL Quarterly, 28*(2), 241–272. doi:https://doi.org/10.2307/3587433.

Hart, C. (2007, May 14). Refugees' job hunt time halved. *The Australian*.

Hartley, L., & Fleay, C. (2016, February 15). FactCheck Q&A: Do refugees cost Australia $100m a year in welfare, with an unemployment rate of 97%? *The Conversation*. Retrieved from https://theconversation.com/factcheck-qanda-do-refugees-cost-australia-100m-a-year-in-welfare-with-an-unemployment-rate-of-97-54395.

Harvey, D. (2005). *A brief history of neoliberalism*. Oxford: Oxford University Press.

Harvey, D. (2011). *The enigma of capital and the crises of capitalism*. London: Profile Books.

Hashemi, M. (2011). Language stress and anxiety among the English language learners. *Procedia—Social and Behavioral Sciences, 30*, 1811–1816. doi:https://doi.org/10.1016/j.sbspro.2011.10.349.

Hassanli, N., Walters, T., & Williamson, J. (2021). "You feel you're not alone": How multicultural festivals foster social sustainability through multiple psychological sense of community. *Journal of Sustainable Tourism, 29*(11–12), 1792–1809. doi:10.1080/09669582.2020.1797756.

Hatoss, A. (2012). Where are you from? Identity construction and experiences of "othering" in the narratives of Sudanese refugee-background Australians. *Discourse & Society, 23*(1), 47–68. doi:10.1177/0957926511419925.

Haw, A. L. (2023). "Hapless victims" or "making trouble": Audience responses to stereotypical representations of asylum seekers in Australian news discourse. *Journalism Practice, 17*(1), 5–23. doi:10.1080/17512786.2021.1930574.

Hawthorne, L. (2005). "Picking winners": The recent transformation of Australia's skilled migration policy. *International Migration Review, 39*(3), 663–696.

Haznedar, B., Peyton, J. K., & Young-Scholten, M. (2018). Teaching adult migrants: A focus on the languages they speak. *Critical Multilingualism Studies, 6*(1), 155–183.

Hebbani, A., & Preece, M. (2015). Spoken English does matter: Findings from an exploratory study to identify predictors of employment among African refugees in Brisbane. *The Australasian Review of African Studies, 36*(2), 110–129.

Heinz, B. (2001). "Fish in the river": Experiences of bilingual bicultural speakers. *Multilingua, 20*(1), 85–108.

Heller, M. (2006). *Linguistic minorities and modernity: A sociolinguistic ethnography* (2nd ed.). London: Continuum.

Hernández, J. C., & Rivera, R. (2009, April 5). Gunman had lost job, felt "degraded." *Seattle Times*. Retrieved from https://web.archive.org/web/20090406183655/http://seattletimes.nwsource.com/html/nationworld/2008986728_shoot05.html.

Heyer, K. E. (2012). *Kinship across borders: A Christian ethic of immigration*. Washington, DC: Georgetown University Press.

Hill, J. H. (1999). Language, race, and white public space. *American Anthropologist, 100*(3), 680–689.

Hill, J. H. (2000). The racializing function of language panics. In R. D. González & I. Melis (Eds.), *Language ideologies: Critical perspectives on the official English movement* (Vol. 2, *History, theory, and policy*, pp. 245–267). Mahwah, NJ: Lawrence Erlbaum Associates.

Hill, J. H. (2008). *The everyday language of white racism*. Malden, MA: Wiley-Blackwell.

Hochschild, A. R. (2003). *The second shift*. New York: Penguin.

Hochschild, A. R. (2012). *The outsourced self: What happens when we pay others to live our lives for us*. New York: Henry Holt.

Hochschild, A. R. (2015). Global care chains and emotional surplus value. In D. Engster & T. Metz (Eds.), *Justice, politics, and the family* (pp. 249–261). London: Routledge.

Hoffman, E. (1990). *Lost in translation: A life in a new language*. London: Penguin.

Hollander, A.-C., Pitman, A., Sjöqvist, H., Lewis, G., Magnusson, C., Kirkbride, J. B., & Dalman, C. (2020). Suicide risk among refugees compared with non-refugee migrants and the Swedish-born majority population. *The British Journal of Psychiatry, 217*(6), 686–692. doi:10.1192/bjp.2019.220.

Holmes, S. (2013). *Fresh fruit, broken bodies: Migrant farmworkers in the United States*. Berkeley: University of California Press.

Hondagneu-Sotelo, P. (2001). *Doméstica: Immigrant workers cleaning and caring in the shadows of affluence*. Berkeley: University of California Press.

Horwitz, E. (2001). Language anxiety and achievement. *Annual Review of Applied Linguistics, 21*, 112–126. doi:10.1017/S0267190501000071.

Horwitz, E. (2010). Foreign and second language anxiety. *Language Teaching, 43*(2), 154–167. doi:10.1017/S026144480999036X.

Houghton, N. (2020, April 22). Australia's migrant workers face serious financial hardship during coronavirus crisis. *SBS*. Retrieved from https://www.sbs.com.au/news/article/australias-migrant-workers-face-serious-financial-hardship-during-coronavirus-crisis/at7gi19i4.

How IELTS is scored. (2022). Retrieved from https://www.ielts.org/for-test-takers/how-ielts-is-scored.

Hsu, M. Y. (2000). *Dreaming of gold, dreaming of home: Transnationalism and migration between the United States and South China, 1882–1943*. Stanford, CA: Stanford University Press.

Hua, A., & Major, N. (2016). Selective mutism. *Current Opinion in Pediatrics, 28*(1), 114–120.

Hua, Z. (2015). "Where are you from?": Interculturality and interactional practices. In A. Komisarof & Z. Hua (Eds.), *Crossing boundaries and weaving intercultural work, life, and scholarship in globalizing universities* (pp. 167–179). London: Routledge.

Hua, Z., & Wei, L. (2016). "Where are you really from?": Nationality and Ethnicity Talk (NET) in everyday interactions. *Applied Linguistics Review, 7*(4), 449–470. doi:10.1515/applirev-2016-0020.

Hughes, R. (1986). *The fatal shore: A history of the transportation of convicts to Australia, 1787–1868*. London: Harvill Press.

Hughson, J.-A., Woodward-Kron, R., Parker, A., Hajek, J., Bresin, A., Knoch, U., . . . Story, D. (2016). A review of approaches to improve participation of culturally and linguistically diverse populations in clinical trials. *Trials, 17*(1), 263. doi:10.1186/s13063-016-1384-3.

Hugo, G. (2011). Migration and development in Malaysia. *Asian Population Studies, 7*(3), 219–241. doi:10.1080/17441730.2011.608983.

Hugo, G. (2014). Change and continuity in Australian international migration policy. *International Migration Review, 48*(3), 868–890. doi:10.1111/imre.12120.

Huneeus, C. (2007). *The Pinochet regime* (L. Sagaris, Trans.). Boulder, CO: Lynne Rienner.

Hunt, D. (2013). *Girt: The unauthorised history of Australia.* Melbourne: Black.

Hunt, D. (2016). *True girt.* Melbourne: Black.

Hunt, D. (2021). *Girt nation.* Melbourne: Black.

Hunter, A. (2016). Deathscapes in diaspora: Contesting space and negotiating home in contexts of post-migration diversity. *Social & Cultural Geography, 17*(2), 247–261. doi:10.1080/14649365.2015.1059472.

Huynh, N., & Chen, P. (2009, April 13). Jiverly Wong's father: What prompted mass killing in Binghamton remains a mystery. *Syracuse.com.* Retrieved from https://www.syracuse.com/news/2009/04/jiverly_wongs_father_our_son_w.html.

Iddings, A. C. D. (2005). Linguistic access and participation: English language learners in an English-dominant community of practice. *Bilingual Research Journal, 29*(1), 165–183. doi:10.1080/15235882.2005.10162829.

[IELTS exam fee]. (2022). Retrieved from https://iran-oxford.com/ielts-test-fee/#ielts-fee-in-dollar.

International migration outlook 1997–2020. (2021). Retrieved from https://www.oecd-ilibrary.org/social-issues-migration-health/international-migration-outlook_1999124x.

Iran: Chilling use of the death penalty to further brutally quell popular uprising. (2022). London: Amnesty International. Retrieved from https://www.amnesty.org/en/latest/news/2022/11/iran-chilling-use-of-the-death-penalty-to-further-brutally-quell-popular-uprising/.

Iran: UN experts condemn execution of protestor, raise alarm about detained artists. (2022). Geneva: United Nations, Human Rights, Office of High Commissioner. Retrieved from https://www.ohchr.org/en/press-releases/2022/12/iran-un-experts-condemn-execution-protestor-raise-alarm-about-detained.

Islamic Republic of Iran. (2022). Retrieved from https://data.worldbank.org/country/IR.

Itaoui, R., & Dunn, K. (2017). Media representations of racism and spatial mobility: Young Muslim (un)belonging in a post-Cronulla riot Sutherland. *Journal of Intercultural Studies, 38*(3), 315–332. doi:10.1080/07256868.2017.1314257.

James, W. (2008). Sudan: Majorities, minorities, and language interactions. In A. Simpson (Ed.), *Language and national identity in Africa* (pp. 61–78). Oxford: Oxford University Press.

Jenkins, J. (2015). *World Englishes: A resource book for students* (3rd ed.). London: Routledge.

Johns, A., Noble, G., & Harris, A. (2017). After Cronulla: "Where the Bloody Hell Are We Now?" *Journal of Intercultural Studies, 38*(3), 249–254. doi:10.1080/07256868.2017.1314243.

Johnson, M., & Wintgens, A. (2017). *The selective mutism resource manual* (2nd ed.). London: Routledge.

Jones, D. (1980). Gossip: Notes on women's oral culture. In C. Kramarae (Ed.), *The voices and words of women and men* (pp. 193–198). Oxford: Pergamon Press.

Jupp, J. (2007). *From White Australia to Woomera: The story of Australian immigration.* Melbourne: Cambridge University Press.

Kachru, B. B. (1986). The power and politics of English. *World Englishes, 5*(2–3), 121–140. doi:10.1111/j.1467-971X.1986.tb00720.x.

Kalfa, E., & Piracha, M. (2018). Social networks and the labour market mismatch. *Journal of Population Economics, 31*(3), 877–914.

Kane, O. (2016). *Beyond Timbuktu: An intellectual history of Muslim West Africa.* Cambridge, MA: Harvard University Press.

Kanno, Y. (1999). Comments on Kelleen Toohey's "'Breaking them up, taking them away': ESL students in grade 1": The use of the community-of-practice perspective in language minority research. *TESOL Quarterly, 33*(1), 126–132. doi:10.2307/3588195.

Karar, H. (2019). The implications of socio-politics and political economy on education policy in Sudan: 1900 to 2000. *Italian Journal of Sociology of Education, 11*(1), 428–447. doi:10.14658/pupjijse-2019-2-21.

Karidakis, M., Woodward-Kron, R., Amorati, R., Hu, B., Pym, A., & Hajek, J. (2022). Enhancing COVID-19 public health communication for culturally and linguistically diverse communities: An Australian interview study with community representatives. *Qualitative Health Communication, 1*(1), 61–83. doi:https://doi.org/10.7146/qhc.v1i1.127258.

Kaufmann, K. (2018). Navigating a new life: Syrian refugees and their smartphones in Vienna. *Information, Communication & Society, 21*(6), 882–898. doi:10.1080/1369118X.2018.1437205.

Kaur, R., & Shruti, I. (2016). Mobile Technology and "doing family" in a global world: Indian migrants in Cambodia. In S. S. Lim (Ed.), *Mobile communication and the family* (pp. 73–91). Dordrecht: Springer Netherlands.

Kelsky, K. (2001). *Women on the verge: Japanese women, Western dreams.* Durham, NC, and London: Duke University Press.

Kettle, M. (2018). Connecting digital participation and informal language education: Home Tutors and migrants in an Australian regional community. In M. Dezuanni, M. Foth, K. Mallan, & H. Hughes (Eds.), *Digital participation through social living labs* (pp. 173–190). Cambridge, MA: Chandos.

Khan, K. (2020). Raciolinguistic border-making and the elasticity of assessment and believeability in the UK citizenship process. *Ethnicities, 21*(2), 333–351. doi:10.1177/1468796820971441.

Khan, K., & McNamara, T. (2017). Citizenship, immigration laws, and language. In A. S. Canagarajah (Ed.), *The Routledge handbook of migration and language* (pp. 451–467). London: Routledge.

Khatun, S. (2019). *Australianama: The South Asian odyssey in Australia.* Brisbane: University of Queensland.

Khawaja, N. G., Hebbani, A., Gallois, C., & MacKinnon, M. (2019). Predictors of employment status: A study of former refugee communities in Australia. *Australian Psychologist, 54*(5), 427–437.

Kifle, T., Kler, P., & Fleming, C. M. (2019). The assimilation of Australian immigrants: Does occupation matter? *Applied Economics, 51*(17), 1841–1854. doi:10.1080/00036846.2018.1529398.

Kim, H. J. (2020). "Where are you from? Your English is so good": A Korean female scholar's autoethnography of academic imperialism in US higher education. *International Journal of Qualitative Studies in Education, 33*(5), 491–507.

Kimura, D., & Canagarajah, S. (2020). Embodied semiotic resources in research group meetings: How language competence is framed. *Journal of Sociolinguistics, 24*(5), 634–655. doi:https://doi.org/10.1111/josl.12435.

King, K. A., Fogle, L., & Logan-Terry, A. (2008). Family language policy. *Language and Linguistics Compass, 2*(5), 907–922. doi:10.1111/j.1749-818X.2008.00076.x.

Kinginger, C. (2011). Enhancing language learning in study abroad. *Annual Review of Applied Linguistics, 31*, 58–73. doi:10.1017/S0267190511000031.

Kisch, E. E. (1937). *Landung in Australien [Australian landfall].* Amsterdam: Allert de Lange.

Koh, S. Y. (2015). How and why race matters: Malaysian-Chinese transnational migrants interpreting and practising Bumiputera-differentiated citizenship. *Journal of Ethnic and Migration Studies, 41*(3), 531–550. doi:10.1080/1369183X.2014.937327.

Komska, Y. (2017). Trade publisher archives: Repositories of monolingualism? Race, language, and rejected refugee manuscripts in the age of total war. *Seminar: A Journal of Germanic Studies, 53*(3), 275–296.

Koven, M. (1998). Two languages in the self/the self in two languages: French-Portuguese bilinguals' verbal enactments and experiences of self in narrative discourse. *Ethos, 26*(4), 410–455.

Krings, F., Johnston, C., Binggeli, S., & Maggiori, C. (2014). Selective incivility: Immigrant groups experience subtle workplace discrimination at different rates. *Cultural Diversity and Ethnic Minority Psychology, 20*, 491–498. doi:10.1037/a0035436

Kroskrity, P. V. (2010). Language ideologies: Evolving perspectives. In J. Jaspers, J.-O. Őstman, & J. Verschueren (Eds.), *Society and language use* (pp. 192–211). Amsterdam: John Benjamins.

Kubota, R., Corella, M., Lim, K., & Sah, P. K. (2023). "Your English is so good": Linguistic experiences of racialized students and instructors of a Canadian university. *Ethnicities, 23*(5), 758–778. doi:10.1177/14687968211055808.

Kuépié, M. (2018). Is international migration always good for left behind households members? Evidence from children education in Cameroon. *International Migration, 56*(6), 120–135. doi:https://doi.org/10.1111/imig.12503.

Kusow, A. M. (2004). Contesting stigma: On Goffman's assumptions of normative order. *Symbolic Interaction, 27*(2), 179–197. doi:https://doi.org/10.1525/si.2004.27.2.179.

Laitin, D. D., & Ramachandran, R. (2022). Linguistic diversity, official language choice and human capital. *Journal of Development Economics, 156*, 102811. doi:https://doi.org/10.1016/j.jdeveco.2021.102811.

Lan, P.-C. (2018). *Raising global families: Parenting, immigration, and class in Taiwan and the US.* Stanford, CA: Stanford University Press.

Lave, J., & Wenger, E. (1991). *Situated learning: Legitimate peripheral participation.* Cambridge: Cambridge University Press.

Lazy men lumping women with household chores. (2022, July 14). *Sun Herald.*

Lee, J. (2016). *Asian migrant women's identity negotiation as language learners: Significant events towards imagined identities* (PhD dissertation). University of Waikato, Hamilton, New Zealand. Retrieved from https://hdl.handle.net/10289/10698.

Lee, J. F. K., & Mahmoudi-Gahrouei, V. (2020). Gender representation in instructional materials: A study of Iranian English language textbooks and teachers' voices. *Sexuality & Culture, 24*(4), 1107–1127. doi:10.1007/s12119-020-09747-z.

Léonard, S., & Kaunert, C. (2022). Refugee flows and terrorism in the European Union: Securitization through association. *International Politics, 59*(3), 562–576. doi:10.1057/s41311-021-00359-4.

Leroy, M. (2023). An island under siege: Negative Australian media narratives of asylum seekers and the opportunity for counter-discourses. *Interventions, 25*(1), 81–99. doi:10.1080/1369801X.2022.2080578.

Lesser, J. (1999). *Negotiating national identity: Immigrants, minorities, and the struggle for ethnicity in Brazil.* Durham, NC, and London: Duke University Press.

Lesser, J. (2003). *Searching for home abroad: Japanese Brazilians and transnationalism.* Durham, NC, and London: Duke University Press.

Levin, T., & Shohamy, E. (2007). The role of academic language in understanding the mathematics achievements of immigrant students in Israel. In C. S. Sunal & K. Mutua (Eds.), *The enterprise of education: Research on education in Africa, the Caribbean, and the Middle East* (pp. 313–336). Tuscaloosa, AL: Information Age.

Levin, T., & Shohamy, E. (2008). Achievement of immigrant students in mathematics and academic Hebrew in Israeli school: A large scale evaluation study. *Studies in Educational Evaluation, 34*, 1–14.

Li, G. (2010). *Culturally contested literacies: America's "rainbow underclass" and urban schools.* London: Routledge.

Li, J., Ai, B., & Xu, C. L. (2021). Examining Burmese students' multilingual practices and identity positionings at a border high school in China. *Ethnicities, 22*(2), 233–252. doi:10.1177/14687968211018881.

Li, J., & Zheng, Y. (2023). Enacting multilingual entrepreneurship: An ethnography of Myanmar university students learning Chinese as an international language. *International Journal of Multilingualism, 20*(3), 1234–1249. doi:10.1080/14790718.2021.1976785.

Li, Y., Rao, G., Zhang, J., & Li, J. (2020). Conceptualizing national emergency language competence. *Multilingua, 39*(5), 617–623. doi:https://doi.org/10.1515/multi-2020-0111.

Licht, H. (2015). *By the scruff of the neck: A suitcase of memories.* Adelaide, SA: Digital Print Australia.

Lim, L. L. (2021). *Australia as "the most successful multicultural society in the world"* (PhD dissertation). University of Technology Sydney, Retrieved from https://opus.lib.uts.edu.au/handle/10453/151036.

Lindemann, S., & Subtirelu, N. C. (2013). Reliably biased: The role of listener expectation in the perception of second language speech. *Language Learning, 63*(3), 567–594. doi:10.1111/lang.12014.

Lindsey, T., & Pausacker, H. (2005). *Chinese Indonesians: Remembering, distorting, forgetting.* Singapore: Institute of Southeast Asian Studies.

Lippi-Green, R. (2012). *English with an accent: Language, ideology, and discrimination in the United States* (2nd ed.). London: Routledge.

Lising, L. (2023). "Speak English!": Social acceleration and language learning in the workplace. *International Journal of Bilingual Education and Bilingualism, 26*(10), 1183–1196. doi:10.1080/13670050.2021.1955499.

Lising, L. (2022). "I want her to be able to think in English": Challenges to heritage language maintenance in a monolingual society. *Multilingua, 41*(5), 549–569. doi:10.1515/multi-2021-0106.

Lising, L., & Bautista, M. L. S. (2022). A tale of language ownership and identity in a multilingual society: Revisiting functional nativeness. *Journal of English and Applied Linguistics, 1*(1). Retrieved from https://animorepository.dlsu.edu.ph/jeal/vol1/iss1/1.

List of countries and territories where English is an official language. (2022). *Wikipedia.* Retrieved from List_of_countries_and_territories_where_English_is_an_official_language.

Liu, S. (2015). *Identity, hybridity and cultural home: Chinese migrants and diaspora in multicultural societies.* London: Rowman & Littlefield International.

Liu, Y., & Boyd, W. (2020). Comparing career identities and choices of pre-service early childhood teachers between Australia and China. *International Journal of Early Years Education, 28*(4), 336–350.

Liyanage, I., & Canagarajah, S. (2019). Shame in English language teaching: Desirable pedagogical possibilities for Kiribati in neoliberal times. *TESOL Quarterly, 53*(2), 430–455. doi:https://doi.org/10.1002/tesq.494.

Lo Bianco, J. (1987). *National policy on languages.* Canberra: Australian Government Publishing Service. Retrieved from http://www.multiculturalaustralia.edu.au/doc/lobianco_2.pdf.

Lo Bianco, J. (1995). Australian experiences: Multiculturalism, language policy and national ethos. *European Journal of Intercultural Studies, 5*(3), 26–43. doi:10.1080/0952391950050304.

Lo Bianco, J. (2008). Language policy and education in Austalia. In S. May & N. H. Hornberger (Eds.), *Encyclopedia of language and education* (Vol. 1, *Language policy and political issues in education*, pp. 343–353). New York: Springer.

Lo Bianco, J. (2010). The importance of language policies and multilingualism for cultural diversity. *International Social Science Journal, 61*(1), 37–67.

Lo Bianco, J. (2014). Domesticating the foreign: Globalization's effects on the place/s of languages. *The Modern Language Journal, 98*(1), 312–325. doi:10.1111/j.1540-4781.2014.12063.x.

Lo Bianco, J., & Slaughter, Y. (2009). *Second languages and Australian schooling.* Melbourne: Australian Council for Educational Research. Retrieved from http://research.acer.edu.au/cgi/viewcontent.cgi?article=1007&context=aer.

Lorente, B. P. (2017). *Scripts of servitude: Language, labor migration and transnational domestic work.* Bristol: Multilingual Matters.

Lou, N. M., & Noels, K. A. (2020). Breaking the vicious cycle of language anxiety: Growth language mindsets improve lower-competence ESL students' intercultural interactions. *Contemporary Educational Psychology, 61*, 101847. doi:https://doi.org/10.1016/j.cedpsych.2020.101847.

"Love Australia or Leave" is now a political party. (2016, October 17). *Crikey*. Retrieved from https://www.crikey.com.au/2016/10/17/love-australia-leave-now-political-party/.

Love, S., & Spinks, H. (2020). *Immigration: Budget review 2020–21 index.* Canberra: Parliament of Australia. Retrieved from https://www.aph.gov.au/About_Parliament/Parliamentary_Departments/Parliamentary_Library/pubs/rp/BudgetReview202021/Immigration.

Luibhéid, E. (2021). *Lives that resist telling: Migrant and refugee lesbians.* London: Routledge.

Lüpke, F. (2013). Multilingualism on the ground. In F. Lüpke & A. Storch (Eds.), *Repertoires and choices in African languages* (pp. 13–76). Berlin: De Gruyter Mouton.

Lutz, J. G. (1976). Chinese nationalism and the anti-Christian campaigns of the 1920s. *Modern Asian Studies, 10*(3), 395–416. Retrieved from http://www.jstor.org/stable/311913.

Luykx, A. (2005). Children as socializing agents: Family language policy in situations of language shift. In J. Cohen, K. T. McAlister, K. Rolstad, & J. MacSwan (Eds.), *ISB4: Proceedings of the 4th International Symposium on Bilingualism* (pp. 1407–1414). Somerville, MA: Cascadilla Press.

MacDonald, F. (2017). Positioning young refugees in Australia: Media discourse and social exclusion. *International Journal of Inclusive Education, 21*(11), 1182–1195. doi:10.1080/13603116.2017.1350324.

Machado, A. (1917). *Poesías completas*. Madrid: Publicaciones de la residencia de estudiantes.

Macken-Horarik, M. (2003a). A telling symbiosis in the discourse of hatred: Multimodal news texts about the "Children Overboard" affair. *Australian Review of Applied Linguistics, 26*(2), 1–16. doi:https://doi.org/10.1075/aral.26.2.01mac.

Macken-Horarik, M. (2003b). Working the borders in racist discourse: The challenge of the "Children Overboard Affair" in news media texts. *Social Semiotics, 13*(3), 283–303. doi:10.1080/1035033032000167024.

MacSwan, J., & Pray, L. (2005). Learning English bilingually: Age of onset of exposure and rate of acquisition among English language learners in a bilingual education program. *Bilingual Research Journal, 29*(3), 653–678.

Madianou, M. (2017). "Doing family" at a distance: Transnational family practices in polymedia environments. In L. Hjorth, H. Horst, A. Galloway, & G. Bell (Eds.), *The Routledge companion to digital ethnography* (pp. 128–137). London: Routledge.

Madsen, L. M. (2015). *Fighters, girls and other identities: Sociolinguistics in a martial arts club.* Bristol: Multilingual Matters.

Mahmud, H. (2021). Beyond economics: The family, belonging and remittances among the Bangladeshi migrants in Los Angeles. *International Migration, 59*(5), 134–148. doi:https://doi.org/10.1111/imig.12809.

Majavu, M. (2020). The "African gangs" narrative: Associating Blackness with criminality and other anti-Black racist tropes in Australia. *African and Black Diaspora: An International Journal, 13*(1), 27–39. doi:10.1080/17528631.2018.1541958.

Man, G. (2004). Gender, work and migration: Deskilling Chinese immigrant women in Canada. *Women's Studies International Forum, 27*(2), 135–148.

Mapedzahama, V., Rudge, T., West, S., & Perron, A. (2012). Black nurse in white space? Rethinking the in/visibility of race within the Australian nursing workplace. *Nursing Inquiry, 19*(2), 153–164. doi:https://doi.org/10.1111/j.1440-1800.2011.00556.x.

Mares, P. (2016). *Not quite Australian: How temporary migration is changing the nation.* Melbourne: Text.

Mariam, A. G. (2010, December 11). Ethiopia: The Anuak's forgotten genocide. *HuffPost*. Retrieved from https://www.huffpost.com/entry/ethiopia-the-anuaks-forgo_b_795330.

Martell, P. (2018). *First raise a flag: How South Sudan won the longest war but lost the peace.* New York: Oxford University Press.

Martin, C. A. (2021a). The backward stock of the South: The metaphoric structuring of Italian racial difference in 1920s Australia. *Journal of Intercultural Studies, 42*(4), 440–459. doi:10.1080/07256868.2021.1939275.

Martin, C. A. (2021b). The Chinese invasion: Settler colonialism and the metaphoric construction of race. *Journal of Australian Studies, 45*(4), 543–559. doi:10.1080/14443058.2021.1992480.

Martín Rojo, L. (2010). *Constructing inequality in multilingual classrooms.* Berlin: Mouton de Gruyter.

Martin, S. (1998). *New life, new language: The history of the Adult Migrant English Program.* Sydney: NCELTR Publications.

Mason, K. (2014). The saga of Egon Kisch and the White Australia Policy. *Bar News: The Journal of the New South Wales Bar Association, 64.* Retrieved from https://nswbar.asn.au/docs/webdocs/BN_032014_kisch.pdf.

Masters, J., Murray, D. E., & Lloyd, R. (2005). *Recruitment of volunteer home tutors for the AMEP home tutor scheme: Strategies to improve recruitment.* Sydney: NCELTR Publications. Retrieved from http://www.ameprc.mq.edu.au/__data/assets/pdf_file/0007/241459/Recruitment133HTS.pdf.

Maydell, E. (2020). "And in Israel we became Russians straight away": Narrative analysis of Russian-Jewish identity in the case study of double migration. *Narrative Inquiry, 30*(2), 404–426. doi:https://doi.org/10.1075/ni.19011.may.

Mayne-Davis, J., Wilson, J., & Lowrie, D. (2020). Refugees and asylum seekers in Australian print media: A critical discourse analysis. *Journal of Occupational Science, 27*(3), 342–358. doi:10.1080/14427591.2020.1754279.

McCollum, D., Keenan, K., & Findlay, A. (2020). The case for a lifecourse perspective on mobility and migration research. In J. Falkingham, M. Evandrou, & A. Vlachantoni (Eds.), *Handbook on demographic change and the lifecourse* (pp. 200–212). Cheltenham, UK, and Northampton, MA: Edward Elgar.

McDonald, P., Moyle, H., & Temple, J. (2019). English proficiency in Australia, 1981 to 2016. *Australian Journal of Social Issues, 54*(2), 112–134. doi:https://doi.org/10.1002/ajs4.67.

McGill, D., Iggers, J., & Cline, A. R. (2007). Death in Gambella: What many heard, what one blogger saw, and why the professional news media ignored it. *Journal of Mass Media Ethics, 22*(4), 280–299. doi:10.1080/08900520701583560.

McGurk, H., & MacDonald, J. (1976). Hearing lips and seeing voices. *Nature, 264*, 746–748.

McLeod, L. (2011). Swearing in the "tradie" environment as a tool for solidarity. *Griffith Working Papers in Pragmatics and Intercultural Communication, 4*(1–2), 1–10.

McMichael, C., & Manderson, L. (2004). Somali women and well-being: Social networks and social capital among immigrant women in Australia. *Human Organization, 63*(1), 88–99. Retrieved from http://sfaa.metapress.com/app/home/contribution.asp?referrer=parent&backto=issue,8,11;journal,22,269;linkingpublicationresults,1:113218,1.

McNamara, T. (2009a). Australia: The dictation test redux? *Language Assessment Quarterly, 6*(1), 106–111. doi:10.1080/15434300802606663.

McNamara, T. (2009b). The spectre of the dictation test: Language testing for immigration and citizenship in Australia. In G. Extra, M. Spotti, & P. Van Avermaet (Eds.), *Language testing, migration and citizenship: Cross-national perspectives on integration regimes* (pp. 224–241). London: Continuum.

McNamara, T., & Ryan, K. (2011). Fairness versus justice in language testing: The place of English literacy in the Australian citizenship test. *Language Assessment Quarterly, 8*(2), 161–178. doi:10.1080/15434303.2011.565438.

Menard-Warwick, J. (2009). *Gendered identities and immigrant language learning.* Bristol: Multilingual Matters.

Menard-Warwick, J. (2022). Narratives of multilingual becoming: The co-construction of solidarity as a language ideology. *Journal of Language, Identity & Education*, 1–16. doi:10.1080/15348458.2021.2008251.

Mence, V., Gangell, S., & Tebb, R. (2015). *A history of the Department of Immigration: Managing migration to Australia.* Canberra: Australian Government: Department of Immigration and Border Protection.

Mencken, H. L. (1919). *The American language* (4th ed.). New York: Alfred Knopf.

Mentor program. (2023). Bondi Junction: City East Community College. Retrieved from https://www.cec.edu.au/mentor-program.

Michieka, M. M. (2005). English in Kenya: A sociolinguistic profile. *World Englishes, 24*(2), 173–186. doi:https://doi.org/10.1111/j.1467-971X.2005.00402.x.

Miedema, F. (2022). *Open science: The very idea.* Dordrecht: Springer Nature.

Migration, Australia. (2020). Canberra: Australian Bureau of Statistics. Retrieved from https://www.abs.gov.au/statistics/people/population/migration-australia/2018-19.

Migration, Australia. (2021). Canberra: Australian Bureau of Statistics. Retrieved from https://www.abs.gov.au/statistics/people/population/migration-australia/latest-release.

Migration, pathway to nation building. (2023). Canberra: Parliament of Australia. Retrieved from https://www.aph.gov.au/Parliamentary_Business/Committees/Joint/Migration/MigrationPathway.

Miller, A. M., Sorokin, O., Wang, E., Feetham, S., Choi, M., & Wilbur, J. (2006). Acculturation, social alienation, and depressed mood in midlife women from the former Soviet Union. *Research in Nursing & Health, 29*(2), 134–146. doi:https://doi.org/10.1002/nur.20125.

Miller, E. R. (2010). Agency in the making: Adult immigrants' accounts of language learning and work. *TESOL Quarterly, 44*(3), 465–487. doi:10.5054/tq.2010.226854.

Miller, E. R. (2014). *The language of adult immigrants: Agency in the making.* Bristol: Multilingual Matters.

Miller, E. R. (2016). The ideology of learner agency and the neoliberal self. *International Journal of Applied Linguistics, 26*(3), 348–365. doi:10.1111/ijal.12129.

Miller, J. (2003). *Audible difference: ESL and social identity in schools.* Clevedon: Multilingual Matters.

Mirvahedi, S. H. (2016). Exploring family language policies among Azerbaijani-speaking families in the city of Tabriz, Iran. In J. Macalister & S. H. Mirvahedi (Eds.), *Family language policies in a multilingual world* (pp. 84–105). London: Routledge.

Mitton, K. (2015). *Rebels in a rotten state: Understanding atrocity in the Sierra Leone civil war.* Oxford: Oxford University Press.

Mobasher, M. M. (Ed.). (2018). *The Iranian diaspora: Challenges, negotiations, and transformations.* Austin: University of Texas Press.

Mohammad, A., & Vásquez, C. (2015). "Rachel's not here": Constructed dialogue in gossip. *Journal of Sociolinguistics, 19*(3), 351–371. doi:10.1111/josl.12125.

Moore, H., Nicholas, H., & Deblaquiere, J. (2008). *"Opening the Door" provision for refugee youth with minimal/no schooling in the Adult Migrant English Program Project 2.1: Modes of delivery for SPP youth.* Canberra: Australian Government: Department of Immigration and Citizenship. Retrieved from http://www.ameprc.mq.edu.au/docs/research_reports/research_report_series/Opening_the_door.pdf.

Moore, S. H. (2007). Researching appropriate assessment for low/pre-literacy adult ESL learners: Results, issues and challenges. *Prospect, 22*(2), 25–38.

Moradi, S. (2020). Languages of Iran: Overview and critical assessment. In *Handbook of the changing world language map* (pp. 1171–1202). Cham: Springer.

Moreton-Robinson, A. (2015). *The white possessive: Property, power, and indigenous sovereignty.* Minneapolis: University of Minnesota Press.

Moses, A. D. (2004). *Genocide and settler society: Frontier violence and stolen Indigenous children in Australian history.* New York and Oxford: Berghahn Books.

Moss, M. (Ed.). (1997). *Taking a punt: First stop Bonegilla.* Preston, Vic: City of Darebin.

Motaghi-Tabari, S. (2016). *Bidirectional language learning in migrant families* (PhD dissertation). Macquarie University, Sydney. Retrieved from http://www.languageonthemove.com/

wp-content/uploads/2017/03/Thesis_Shiva_Motaghi-Tabari_BidirectionalLanguageLearning.pdf.

Mugadza, H. T., Williams Tetteh, V., Stout, B., & Renzaho, A. M. N. (2020). Parenting in a new environment: Implications for raising sub-Saharan African children within the Australian child protection context. *The Australasian Review of African Studies, 41*(1), 166–194.

Müller, H. (2001). *Heimat ist das, was gesprochen wird.* Saarbrücken: Gollenstein.

Murphy, H. B. M. (1952). The assimilation of refugee immigrants in Australia. *Population Studies, 5*(3), 179–206.

Murray, K., Nebeker, C., & Carpendale, E. (2019). Responsibilities for ensuring inclusion and representation in research: A systems perspective to advance ethical practices. *Australian & New Zealand Journal of Psychiatry, 53*(9), 835–838.

Mwanri, L., Fauk, N. K., Ziersch, A., Gesesew, H. A., Asa, G. A., & Ward, P. R. (2022). Post-migration stressors and mental health for African migrants in South Australia: A qualitative study. *International Journal of Environmental Research and Public Health, 19*(13). doi:10.3390/ijerph19137914.

[National curriculum of the Islamic Republic of Iran]. (2013). Tehran: Ministry of Education of the Islamic Republic of Iran. Retrieved from http://cfu.ac.ir/file/2/attach201404326047545426747.pdf.

Natonek, H. (1943). *In search of myself* (B. Fles, Trans.). New York: G. P. Putnam's Sons.

Nduwimana, A. (2020). Should Burundians care about English as a global language? *LSE.* Retrieved from https://blogs.lse.ac.uk/africaatlse/2020/08/07/should-burundians-care-about-english-global-language-politics/.

Nedelcu, M., & Wyss, M. (2016). "Doing family" through ICT-mediated ordinary co-presence: Transnational communication practices of Romanian migrants in Switzerland. *Global Networks, 16*(2), 202–218. doi:10.1111/glob.12110.

Neelam, M. (2022). *Muslim women as speakers of English.* Cham: Palgrave Macmillan.

Nelson, A. (2022). *Memorandum on ensuring free, immediate, and equitable access to federally funded research.* Washington, DC: Executive Office of the President. Retrieved from https://www.whitehouse.gov/wp-content/uploads/2022/08/08-2022-OSTP-Public-Access-Memo.pdf.

Nelson, J. K., Dunn, K. M., & Paradies, Y. (2011). Bystander anti-racism: A review of the literature. *Analyses of Social Issues and Public Policy, 11*(1), 263–284. doi:https://doi.org/10.1111/j.1530-2415.2011.01274.x.

Neumann, K., Gifford, S. M., Lems, A., & Scherr, S. (2014). Refugee settlement in Australia: Policy, scholarship and the production of knowledge, 1952– 2013. *Journal of Intercultural Studies, 35*(1), 1–17.

Newendorp, N. D. (2020). *Chinese senior migrants and the globalization of retirement.* Stanford, CA: Stanford University Press.

Nguyen, A. W., Taylor, R. J., & Chatters, L. M. (2016). Church-based social support among Caribbean Blacks in the United States. *Review of Religious Research, 58*(3), 385–406. doi:10.1007/s13644-016-0253-6.

No one teaches you to become an Australian: Report of the inquiry into migrant settlement outcomes. (2017). Canberra: Parliament of the Commonwealth of Australia. Retrieved from https://parlinfo.aph.gov.au/parlInfo/download/committees/reportjnt/024098/toc_pdf/NooneteachesyoutobecomeanAustralian.pdf;fileType=application%2Fpdf.

Nolin, C. (2006). *Transnational ruptures: Gender and forced migration.* Aldershot: Ashgate.

Norton, B. (2013). *Identity and language learning: Extending the conversation* (2nd ed.). Bristol: Multilingual Matters.

Norton, B., & Toohey, K. (2011). Identity, language learning, and social change. *Language Teaching, 44*(4), 412–446. doi:10.1017/S0261444811000309.

Notice of deregistration—Love Australia or leave. (2022). Canberra: Australian Electoral Commission. Retrieved from https://www.aec.gov.au/Parties_and_Representatives/

Party_Registration/Deregistered_parties/files/web-notice-to-deregister-love-australia-or-leave.pdf.

Nuttall, J. (2018). Engaging with ambivalence: The neglect of early childhood teacher education in initial teacher education reform in Australia. In Claire Wyatt-Smith and Lenore Adie (Eds.) *Innovation and accountability in teacher education* (pp. 155–169). Cham: Springer.

Nyanzi, S., Rosenberg-Jallow, O., Bah, O., & Nyanzi, S. (2005). Bumsters, big black organs and old white gold: Embodied racial myths in sexual relationships of Gambian beach boys. *Culture, Health & Sexuality, 7*(6), 557–569. doi:10.1080/13691050500245687.

O'Leary, P. J. (2008). *Employers and industrial relations in the Australian meat processing industry: An historical analysis* (PhD dissertation). University of New South Wales.

Okita, T. (2002). *Invisible work: Bilingualism, language choice and childrearing in intermarried families.* Amsterdam: Benjamins.

Oliver, R., Rochecouste, J., & Nguyen, B. (2017). ESL in Australia: A chequered history. *TESOL in Context, 26*(1), 7–26.

Olivo, W. (2003). "Quit talking and learn English!": Conflicting language ideologies in an ESL classroom. *Anthropology & Education Quarterly, 34*(1), 50–71. doi:10.1525/aeq.2003.34.1.50.

Opare-Addo, J., & Bertone, S. (2021). Slow and uneven progress: The representation of non-English-speaking background employees in the Australian Public Service. *Australian Journal of Public Administration, 80*(3), 385–406. doi:https://doi.org/10.1111/1467-8500.12484.

Opening the school gate: Engaging migrant and refugee families. (2016). Melbourne: Centre for Multicultural Youth. Retrieved from https://www.cmy.net.au/wp-content/uploads/2019/11/Opening-the-School-Gate_Victorian-Schools_2016-1.pdf.

Oriyama, K. (2016). Community of practice and family language policy: Maintaining heritage Japanese in Sydney—ten years later. *International Multilingual Research Journal, 10*(4), 289–307. doi:10.1080/19313152.2016.1198977.

Overseas Qualifications Unit. (2020). Retrieved from https://migration.wa.gov.au/services/overseas-qualification-unit.

Oyètádé, B. A., & Luke, V. F. (2008). Sierra Leone: Krio and the quest for national integration. In A. Simpson (Ed.), *Language and national identity in Africa* (pp. 122–140). Oxford: Oxford University Press.

Ozdowski, S. (2012). Australia-Emergence of a modern nation built on diversity and 'Fair Go'. *Political Crossroads, 19*(1), 25–46. doi:10.7459/pc/19.1.03.

Ozturk, M. B., & Berber, A. (2020). Racialised professionals' experiences of selective incivility in organisations: A multi-level analysis of subtle racism. *Human Relations, 75*(2), 213–239. doi:10.1177/0018726720957727.

Paerregaard, K. (2015). The resilience of migrant money: How gender, generation and class shape family remittances in Peruvian migration. *Global Networks, 15*(4), 503–518. doi:10.1111/glob.12075.

Palin, M. (2019, January 23). Housing hell: Inside one of Australia's worst addresses. *news.com.au.* Retrieved from https://www.news.com.au/national/nsw-act/news/housing-hell-one-of-australias-worst-addresses-like-a-lunatic-asylum/news-story/c8a7edaccdbbf896cea30f657976f258.

Park, J. S.-Y. (2010). Naturalization of competence and the neoliberal subject: Success stories of English language learning in the Korean conservative press. *Journal of Linguistic Anthropology, 20*(1), 22–38. doi:10.1111/j.1548-1395.2010.01046.x.

Park, J. S.-Y. (2016). Language as pure potential. *Journal of Multilingual and Multicultural Development, 37*(5), 453–466. doi:10.1080/01434632.2015.1071824.

Park, J. S.-Y. (2020). Translating culture in the global workplace: Language, communication, and diversity management. *Applied Linguistics, 41*(1), 109–128.

Park, J. S.-Y., & Bae, S. (2009). Language ideologies in educational migration: Korean jogi yuhak families in Singapore. *Linguistics and Education, 20*(4), 366–377. doi:10.1016/j.linged.2009.09.001.

Park, J. S.-Y., & Wee, L. (2009). The three circles redux: A market-theoretic perspective on World Englishes. *Applied Linguistics, 30*(3), 389–406. doi:10.1093/applin/amp008.

Park, M. Y. (2020). "I want to learn Seoul speech!": Language ideologies and practices among rural marriage-migrants in South Korea. *International Journal of Bilingual Education and Bilingualism, 23*(2), 227–240. doi:10.1080/13670050.2017.1351419.

Parreñas, R. S. (2001). *Servants of globalization: Women, migration and domestic work.* Stanford, CA: Stanford University Press.

Parreñas, R. S. (2012). The reproductive labour of migrant workers. *Global Networks, 12*(2), 269–275. doi:10.1111/j.1471-0374.2012.00351.x.

Patel, I. (2021). *We're here because you were there: Immigration and the end of empire.* London: Verso Books.

Pavlenko, A. (2001a). "How am I to become a woman in an American vein?": Transformations of gender performance in second language learning. In A. Pavlenko, A. Blackledge, I. Piller, & M. Teutsch-Dwyer (Eds.), *Multilingualism, second language learning and gender* (pp. 133–174). Berlin and New York: Mouton de Gruyter.

Pavlenko, A. (2001b). "In the world of the tradition, I was unimagined": Negotiation of identities in cross-cultural autobiographies. *International Journal of Bilingualism, 5*(3), 317–344.

Pavlenko, A. (2001c). Language learning memoirs as a gendered genre. *Applied Linguistics, 22*(2), 213–240.

Pavlenko, A. (2002). Bilingualism and emotions. *Multilingua, 21*(1), 45–78.

Pavlenko, A. (2003). "Language of the enemy": Foreign language education and national identity. *International Journal of Bilingual Education and Bilingualism, 6*(5), 313–331. doi:10.1080/13670050308667789.

Pavlenko, A. (2004). Stop doing that, ia komu skazala!: Emotions and language choice in bilingual families. *Journal of Multilingual and Multicultural Development, 25*(2–3), 179–203.

Pavlenko, A. (2006a). *Emotions and multilingualism.* Cambridge: Cambridge University Press.

Pavlenko, A. (2007a). Autobiographic narratives as data in applied linguistics. *Applied Linguistics, 28*(2), 163–188.

Pavlenko, A. (2007b). Multilingual living: Explorations of language and subjectivity. *Language in Society, 36*(3), 448–451..

Pavlenko, A. (2008). Multilingualism in post-Soviet countries: Language revival, language removal, and sociolinguistic theory. *International Journal of Bilingual Education and Bilingualism, 11*(3–4), 275–314. doi:10.1080/13670050802271517.

Pavlenko, A. (2013). Multilingualism in post-Soviet successor states. *Language and Linguistics Compass, 7*(4), 262–271. doi:https://doi.org/10.1111/lnc3.12024.

Pavlenko, A. (Ed.). (2006b). *Bilingual minds: Emotional experience, expression and representation.* Clevedon: Multilingual Matters.

Pavlenko, A., & Blackledge, A. (Eds.). (2004). *Negotiation of identities in multilingual contexts.* Clevedon: Multilingual Matters.

Pavlenko, A., & Norton, B. (2007). Imagined communities, identity, and English language learning. In J. Cummins & C. Davison (Eds.), *International handbook of English language teaching* (pp. 669–680). Boston, MA: Springer.

Pavlenko, A., & Piller, I. (2001). New directions in the study of multilingualism, second language learning, and gender. In A. Pavlenko, A. Blackledge, I. Piller, & M. Teutsch-Dwyer (Eds.), *Multilingualism, second language learning and gender* (pp. 17–52). Berlin and New York: Mouton de Gruyter.

Peirce, B. N. (1995). Social identity, investment, and language learning. *TESOL Quarterly, 29*(1), 9–31. Retrieved from http://www.jstor.org/stable/3587803.

Peñalva, S. L. (2017). An ethnographic portrait of translingual/transcultural navigation among immigrant children and youth: Voices during Sunday school at a Latino Church. *Journal of Multilingual and Multicultural Development, 38*(5), 438–452. doi:10.1080/01434632.2016.1186683.

Penn, C., Watermeyer, J., & Nattrass, R. (2016). Managing language mismatches in emergency calls. *Journal of Health Psychology*, *22*(14), 1769–1779. doi:10.1177/1359105316636497.

Pennay, B. (2006). An Australian Berlin and hotbed of disloyalty: Shaming Germans in a country district during two world wars. *Journal of the Royal Australian Historical Society*, *92*(1), 15–28. Retrieved from https://search.informit.org/doi/10.3316/ielapa.200606885.

Perdue, C. (Ed.). (1993a). *Adult language acquisition: Cross-linguistic perspectives* (Vol. 1, *Field methods*). Cambridge: Cambridge University Press.

Perdue, C. (Ed.). (1993b). *Adult language acquisition: Cross-linguistic perspectives* (Vol. 2, *The results*). Cambridge: Cambridge University Press.

Perera, N. (2022). *Negotiating linguistic and religious diversity: A Tamil Hindu temple in Australia*. London: Routledge.

Performance descriptors for the TOEFL iBT Test. (2021). Princeton, NJ: Educational Testing Service. Retrieved from https://www.ets.org/content/dam/ets-org/pdfs/toefl/toefl-ibt-performance-descriptors.pdf.

Perry, K. H., & Hart, S. J. (2012). "I'm just kind of winging it": Preparing and supporting educators of adult refugee learners. *Journal of Adolescent & Adult Literacy*, *56*(2), 110–122. doi:https://doi.org/10.1002/JAAL.00112.

Peyton, J. K., & Young-Scholten, M. (Eds.). (2020). *Teaching adult immigrants with limited formal education: Theory, research and practice*. Bristol: Multilingual Matters.

Phillipson, R. (1992). *Linguistic imperialism*. Oxford: Oxford University Press.

Phillipson, R. (2009). *Linguistic imperialism continued*. London: Routledge.

Philp, J., Adams, R., & Iwashita, N. (2013). *Peer interaction and second language learning*. London: Routledge.

Piller, I. (2002a). *Bilingual couples talk: The discursive construction of hybridity*. Amsterdam: John Benjamins.

Piller, I. (2002b). Passing for a native speaker: Identity and success in second language learning. *Journal of Sociolinguistics*, *6*(2), 179–206.

Piller, I. (2011a). Can foreign languages drive you crazy? *Language on the Move*. Retrieved from https://www.languageonthemove.com/can-foreign-languages-drive-you-crazy/.

Piller, I. (2011b). Muslims, Catholics, foreign language speakers and other traitors. *Language on the Move*. Retrieved from https://www.languageonthemove.com/muslims-catholics-foreign-language-speakers-and-other-traitors/.

Piller, I. (2015a). Language ideologies. In *The international encyclopedia of language and social interaction* (pp. 917–927). Oxford: Wiley Online. doi:10.1002/9781118611463.wbielsi140.

Piller, I. (2015b). What's in a name? *Language on the Move*. Retrieved from https://www.languageonthemove.com/whats-in-a-name/.

Piller, I. (2016). *Linguistic diversity and social justice*. Oxford and New York: Oxford University Press.

Piller, I. (2017a). Anatomy of language shaming. *Language on the Move*. Retrieved from http://www.languageonthemove.com/anatomy-of-language-shaming/.

Piller, I. (2017b). Explorations in language shaming. *Language on the Move*. Retrieved from http://www.languageonthemove.com/explorations-in-language-shaming/.

Piller, I. (2017c). "I'm not listening to you!" Interacting in a linguistically diverse society. *Language on the Move*. Retrieved from https://www.languageonthemove.com/im-not-listening-to-you-interacting-in-a-linguistically-diverse-society/.

Piller, I. (2017d). *Intercultural communication: A critical introduction* (2nd ed.). Edinburgh: Edinburgh University Press.

Piller, I. (2018a). Factcheck: Do "over a million" people in Australia not speak English "well or at all"? *Conversation*. Retrieved from https://theconversation.com/factcheck-do-over-a-million-people-in-australia-not-speak-english-well-or-at-all-101461.

Piller, I. (2018b). In search of myself. *Language on the Move*. Retrieved from https://www.languageonthemove.com/in-search-of-myself/.

Piller, I. (2018c). The politicisation of English language proficiency, not poor English itself, creates barriers. *Conversation.* Retrieved from https://theconversation.com/the-politicisation-of-english-language-proficiency-not-poor-english-itself-creates-barriers-98475.

Piller, I. (2021). What can churches teach us about migrant inclusion? *Language on the Move.* Retrieved from https://www.languageonthemove.com/what-can-churches-teach-us-about-migrant-inclusion/.

Piller, I. (2022). Language barriers to social participation. *Language on the Move.* Retrieved from https://www.languageonthemove.com/language-barriers-to-social-participation/.

Piller, I. (2023). Meet the people behind "Life in a new language." *Language on the Move.* Retrieved from https://www.languageonthemove.com/meet-the-people-behind-life-in-a-new-language/.

Piller, I. (Ed.). (2020–2022). *Language-on-the-Move COVID-19 archives.* https://www.languageonthemove.com/covid-19/.

Piller, I. (Ed.). (2009–). *Language-on-the-Move.* Retrieved from https://www.languageonthemove.org/.

Piller, I., & Bodis, A. (2024). Marking and unmarking the (non)native speaker through English language proficiency requirements for university admission. *Language in Society, 53*(1), 1–23. https://doi.org/10.1017/S0047404522000689.

Piller, I., Bruzon, A. S., & Torsh, H. (2023). Monolingual school websites as barriers to parent engagement. *Language and Education, 37*(3), 328–345. doi:10.1080/09500782.2021.2010744.

Piller, I., & Gerber, L. (2021). Family language policy between the bilingual advantage and the monolingual mindset. *International Journal of Bilingual Education and Bilingualism, 24*(5), 622–635. doi:10.1080/13670050.2018.1503227.

Piller, I., & Lising, L. (2014). Language, employment and settlement: Temporary meat workers in Australia. *Multilingua, 33*(1–2), 35–59.

Piller, I., & Takahashi, K. (2006). A passion for English: Desire and the language market. In A. Pavlenko (Ed.), *Bilingual minds: Emotional experience, expression, and representation* (pp. 59–83). Clevedon: Multilingual Matters.

Piller, I., & Takahashi, K. (Producer). (2012). Japanese on the move: Life stories of transmigration. *Language on the Move.* Retrieved from www.languageonthemove.com/japanese-on-the-move.

Piller, I., Torsh, H., & Smith-Khan, L. (2023). Securing the borders of English and Whiteness. *Ethnicities, 23*(5), 706–725. doi:10.1177/14687968211052610.

Piller, I., Zhang, J., & Li, J. (2020a). Linguistic diversity in a time of crisis. *Multilingua, 39*(5), 503–515. doi:https://doi.org/10.1515/multi-2020-0136.

Piller, I., Zhang, J., & Li, J. (2022). Peripheral multilingual scholars confronting epistemic exclusion in global academic knowledge production: A positive case study. *Multilingua, 41*(6), 639–662. doi:10.1515/multi-2022-0034.

Piller, I., Zhang, J., & Li, J. (Eds.). (2020). *Linguistic diversity in a time of crisis [Special issue of Multilingua]* (Vol. 39).

Pitkänen-Huhta, A., & Holm, L. (Eds.). (2012). *Literacy practices in transition: Perspectives from the Nordic countries* (Vol. 28). Bristol: Multilingual Matters.

Points calculator. (2022). Retrieved from https://immi.homeaffairs.gov.au/help-support/tools/points-calculator.

Politzer, P. (1989). *Fear in Chile: Lives under Pinochet* (D. Wachtell, Trans.). New York: Pantheon Books.

Population: Census. (2022). Canberra: Australian Bureau of Statistics. Retrieved from https://www.abs.gov.au/statistics/people/population/population-census/2021.

Portes, A., & Rumbaut, R. G. (2014). *Immigrant America: A portrait* (4th ed.). Berkeley: University of California Press.

Prah, K. K. (2010). Multilingualism in urban Africa: Bane or blessing. *Journal of Multicultural Discourses, 5*(2), 169–182. doi:10.1080/17447143.2010.491916.

Premier, J., & Parr, G. (2019). Towards an EAL community of practice: A case study of a multicultural primary school in Melbourne, Australia. *The Australian Journal of Language and Literacy, 42*(1), 58–68.

Prendergast, C. (2008). *Buying into English: Language and investment in the new capitalist world.* Pittsburgh: University of Pittsburgh Press.

Puigdevall, M., Walsh, J., Amorrortu, E., & Ortega, A. (2018). "I'll be one of them": Linguistic mudes and new speakers in three minority language contexts. *Journal of Multilingual and Multicultural Development, 39*(5), 445–457. doi:10.1080/01434632.2018.1429453.

Pujolar, J. (2019). Linguistic mudes: An exploration over the linguistic constitution of subjects. *International Journal of the Sociology of Language, 257*, 165–189. doi:10.1515/ijsl-2019-2024.

Pujolar, J., & Gonzàlez, I. (2013). Linguistic "mudes" and the de-ethnicization of language choice in Catalonia. *International Journal of Bilingual Education and Bilingualism, 16*(2), 138–152.

Pujolar, J., & Puigdevall, M. (2015). Linguistic mudes: How to become a new speaker in Catalonia. *International Journal of the Sociology of Language 231*, 167–187.

Pung, A. (Ed.). (2008). *Growing up Asian in Australia.* Melbourne: Black.

Pupazzoni, R. (2020, April 8). Calls for migrant workers to be included in JobKeeper subsidy amid coronavirus crisis. *ABC News.* Retrieved from https://www.abc.net.au/news/2020-04-08/migrant-workers-are-struggling-due-to-coronavirus-jobseeker/12129798.

Purman, V. (2018). *The last of the Bonegilla girls.* Sydney: Harlequin.

Pybus, C. (2006). *Black founders: The unknown story of Australia's first Black settlers.* Sydney: University of New South Wales Press.

Qvist, H.-P. Y. (2018). Secular and religious volunteering among immigrants and natives in Denmark. *Acta Sociologica, 61*(2), 202–218.

Racial Discrimination Act 1975, compilation no. 19. (2022). Canberra: Australian Government. Retrieved from https://www.legislation.gov.au/Details/C2022C00366.

Rajan, S. I., Varghese, V. J., & Jayakumar, M. S. (2013). *Dreaming mobility and buying vulnerability: Overseas recruitment practices in India.* New Delhi: Routledge.

Rajendran, D., Ng, E. S., Sears, G., & Ayub, N. (2020). Determinants of migrant career success: A Study of recent skilled migrants in Australia. *International Migration, 58*(2), 30–51. doi:10.1111/imig.12586.

Ralph, D., & Staeheli, L. A. (2011). Home and migration: Mobilities, belongings and identities. *Geography Compass, 5*(7), 517–530. doi:https://doi.org/10.1111/j.1749-8198.2011.00434.x.

Ramjattan, V. A. (2019). Racist nativist microaggressions and the professional resistance of racialized English language teachers in Toronto. *Race Ethnicity and Education, 22*(3), 374–390. doi:10.1080/13613324.2017.1377171.

Ramjattan, V. A. (2022). Racializing the problem of and solution to foreign accent in business. *Applied Linguistics Review, 13*(4), 527–544. doi:https://doi.org/10.1515/applirev-2019-0058

Rattigan, N. (1988). Apotheosis of the Ocker. *Journal of Popular Film and Television, 15*(4), 148–155.

Raymond, C. W. (2014). Negotiating entitlement to language: Calling 911 without English. *Language in Society, 43*(01), 33–59. doi:10.1017/S0047404513000869.

Reid, D. (2019). Sharing the halal snack-pack: Multiculturalism as neo-assimilation in Australia. *Continuum, 33*(1), 77–92. doi:10.1080/10304312.2018.1537391.

Rezaei, S., Latifi, A., & Nematzadeh, A. (2017). Attitude towards Azeri language in Iran: A large-scale survey research. *Journal of Multilingual and Multicultural Development, 38*(10), 931–941. doi:10.1080/01434632.2017.1342652.

Riga, R. (2019, October 16). New Australians feel abandoned as they battle social isolation, struggle to find employment. *ABC News.* Retrieved from https://www.abc.net.au/news/2019-10-16/social-isolation-refugee-immigration/11586114.

Roberts, S. O., & Rizzo, M. T. (2021). The psychology of American racism. *American Psychologist, 76*, 475–487. doi:10.1037/amp0000642.

Rollo, S. (2020). The "Asia threat" in the US–Australia relationship: Then and now. *International Relations of the Asia-Pacific, 20*(2), 225–252. doi:10.1093/irap/lcy023.

Rosa, J. (2016). Standardization, racialization, languagelessness: Raciolinguistic ideologies across communicative contexts. *Journal of Linguistic Anthropology, 26*(2), 162–183. doi:10.1111/jola.12116.

Rosa, J. (2019). *Looking like a language, sounding like a race.* New York: Oxford University Press.

Rosa, J., & Flores, N. (2017). Unsettling race and language: Toward a raciolinguistic perspective. *Language in Society, 46*(5), 621–647. doi:10.1017/S0047404517000562.

Rose, H., Syrbe, M., Montakantiwong, A., & Funada, N. (2020). *Global TESOL for the 21st century.* Multilingual Matters. Bristol.

Roth, J. H. (2002). *Brokered homeland: Japanese Brazilian migrants in Japan.* Ithaca, NY: Cornell University Press.

Rowse, T. (2004). Notes on the history of Aboriginal population of Australia. In A. D. Moses (Ed.), *Genocide and settler society: Frontier violence and stolen Indigenous children in Australian history* (pp. 312–325). New York and Oxford: Berghahn.

Royal Commission into the Robodebt Scheme Report. (2023). Canberra: Commonwealth of Australia. Retrieved from https://robodebt.royalcommission.gov.au/publications/report.

Rubin, D. L. (1992). Nonlanguage factors affecting undergraduates' judgements of nonnative English-speaking teaching assistants. *Research in Higher Education, 33*(4), 511–531.

Rubin, D. L., & Smith, K. A. (1990). Effects of accent, ethnicity, and lecture topic on undergraduates' perceptions of non-native English speaking teaching assistants. *International Journal of Intercultural Relations, 14*, 337–353.

Ruediger, D., MacDougall, R., Cooper, D., Carlson, J., Herndon, J., & Johnsto, L. (2022). Leveraging data communities to advance open science: Findings from an incubation workshop series. *Ithaka S+R.* doi:https://doi.org/10.18665/sr.317145.

Ruiz Sportmann, A. S., & Greenspan, I. (2019). Relational interactions between immigrant and native-born volunteers: Trust-building and integration or suspicion and conflict? *VOLUNTAS: International Journal of Voluntary and Nonprofit Organizations, 30*, 932–946.

Ryan, L. (2011). Migrants' social networks and weak ties: Accessing resources and constructing relationships post-migration. *The Sociological Review, 59*(4), 707–724. doi:10.1111/j.1467-954X.2011.02030.x.

Sai, S.-M., & Hoon, C.-Y. (2012). *Chinese Indonesians reassessed: History, religion and belonging.* London: Routledge.

Said, E. W. (2000). *Out of place: A memoir.* London: Granta.

Sano, K. (2019). "One" but divided: Tribalism and grouping among secondary school students in South Sudan. *Anthropology & Education Quarterly, 50*(2), 189–204. doi:https://doi.org/10.1111/aeq.12288.

Sarkisian, N. (2006). "Doing family ambivalence": Nuclear and extended families in single mothers' lives. *Journal of Marriage and Family, 68*(4), 804–811.

Sawyer, A. (2016). Is money enough?: The effect of migrant remittances on parental aspirations and youth educational attainment in rural Mexico. *International Migration Review, 50*(1), 231–266. doi:10.1111/imre.12103.

Schneider, B. (2014). *Salsa, language and transnationalism.* Bristol: Multilingual Matters.

Schneider, E. W. (2020). *English around the world: An introduction* (2nd ed.). Cambridge: Cambridge University Press.

Schueller, W. (2012). *Memoirs of a German boyhood: The Wehrmacht and the Australian odyssey.* Sydney: xlibris.

Schultz, A. (2020, December 7). Australia needs an extra 205,900 healthcare workers. Where will they come from? *Crikey.* Retrieved from https://www.crikey.com.au/2020/12/07/healthcare-worker-shortage/.

Schwartz, M. (2010). Family language policy: Core issues in an emerging field. *Applied Linguistics Review, 1*(11), 171–191.

Schwartz, M., & Verschik, A. (Eds.). (2013). *Successful family language policy: Parents, children and educators in interaction*. Dordrecht: Springer.
Scollon, R. (2001). *Mediated discourse: The nexus of practice*. London: Routledge.
Scott, S. K. (2017). The politics of commiseration: On the communicative labors of "co-mothering" in El Alto. *Journal of Linguistic Anthropology, 27*(2), 171–189. doi:10.1111/jola.12151.
Scott, T. (Director). (1986). *Top gun* [Film]. USA: Paramount Pictures.
Senter, M. S., & Ling, D. A. (2017). "It's almost like they were happier when you were down": Microaggressions and overt hostility against Native Americans in a community with gaming. *Sociological Inquiry, 87*(2), 256–281. doi:10.1111/soin.12171.
Shaw, W. S. (2000). Ways of Whiteness: Harlemising Sydney's Aboriginal Redfern. *Australian Geographical Studies, 38*(3), 291–305. doi:https://doi.org/10.1111/1467-8470.00117.
Shindo, R. (2021). Home, sweet home? Community and the dilemma of belonging. *Geopolitics, 26*(2), 425–443. doi:10.1080/14650045.2019.1626829.
Shukla, N., & Suleyman, C. (2020). *The good immigrant: 26 writers reflect on America*. New York, Boston, and London: Little, Brown.
Silverman, D. (2016). *Qualitative research* (4th ed.). Los Angeles: Sage.
Silverstein, J. (2020). Refugee children, boats and drownings: A history of an Australian "humanitarian" discourse. *History Australia, 17*(4), 728–742. doi:10.1080/14490854.2020.1840287.
Skilled occupation list. (2020). Retrieved from https://immi.homeaffairs.gov.au/visas/working-in-australia/skill-occupation-list.
Smith, A. B., Agar, M., Delaney, G., Descallar, J., Dobell-Brown, K., Grand, M., . . . Girgis, A. (2018). Lower trial participation by culturally and linguistically diverse (CALD) cancer patients is largely due to language barriers. *Asia-Pacific Journal of Clinical Oncology, 14*(1), 52–60. doi:https://doi.org/10.1111/ajco.12818.
Smith, A. B., Niu, A. Y., Descallar, J., Delaney, G. P., Wu, V. S., Agar, M. R., & Girgis, A. (2020). Clinical trials knowledge and attitudes of Vietnamese- and Anglo-Australian cancer patients: A cross-sectional study. *Asia-Pacific Journal of Clinical Oncology, 16*(5), e242–e251. doi:https://doi.org/10.1111/ajco.13388.
Smith, J., Satchwell, C., Edwards, R., Miller, K., Fowler, Z., Gaechter, J., . . . Young, R. (2008). Literacy practices in the learning careers of childcare students. *Journal of Vocational Education & Training, 60*(4), 363–375. doi:10.1080/13636820802591764.
Smith-Christmas, C. (2016). *Family language policy: Maintaining an endangered language in the home*. London: Palgrave.
Smith-Khan, L. (2017a). Different in the same way? Language, diversity, and refugee credibility. *International Journal of Refugee Law, 29*(3), 389–416. doi:10.1093/ijrl/eex038.
Smith-Khan, L. (2017b). Telling stories: Credibility and the representation of social actors in Australian asylum appeals. *Discourse & Society, 28*(5), 512–534. doi:10.1177/0957926517710989.
Smith-Khan, L. (2019a). Communicative resources and credibility in public discourse on refugees. *Language in Society, 48*(3), 403–427. doi:10.1017/S0047404519000186.
Smith-Khan, L. (2019b). Debating credibility: Refugees and rape in the media. *Australian Review of Applied Linguistics, 42*(1), 4–36. doi:https://doi.org/10.1075/aral.18002.smi.
Smith-Khan, L. (2019c). Migration practitioners' roles in communicating credible refugee claims. *Alternative Law Journal, 45*(2), 119–124. doi:10.1177/1037969X19884205.
Smith-Khan, L. (2019d). Why refugee visa credibility assessments lack credibility: A critical discourse analysis. *Griffith Law Review, 28*(4), 406–430. doi:10.1080/10383441.2019.1748804.
Snyder, S. (2016). *Asylum-seeking, migration and church*. London: Routledge.
Söderlundh, H., & Keevallik, L. (2023). Labour mobility across the Baltic Sea: Language brokering at a blue-collar workplace in Sweden. *Language in Society, 52*(5), 783–804. doi:10.1017/S0047404522000392.

Solorzano, D. G. (1998). Critical race theory, race and gender microaggressions, and the experience of Chicana and Chicano scholars. *International Journal of Qualitative Studies in Education, 11*(1), 121–136. doi:10.1080/095183998236926.

Somaiah, B. C., Yeoh, B. S. A., & Arlini, S. M. (2020). "Cukup for me to be successful in this country": "Staying" among left-behind young women in Indonesia's migrant-sending villages. *Global Networks, 20*(2), 237–255.

Soutphommasane, T. (2012). *Don't go back to where you came from: Why multiculturalism works.* Sydney: NewSouth.

Spinks, H., & Sherrell, H. (2019). *Immigration: Budget review 2019–20 index.* Canberra: Parliament of Australia. Retrieved from https://www.aph.gov.au/About_Parliament/Parliamentary_Departments/Parliamentary_Library/pubs/rp/BudgetReview201920/Immigration.

Spolsky, B. (2004). *Language policy.* Cambridge: Cambridge University Press.

Spolsky, B. (2012). Family language policy: The critical domain. *Journal of Multilingual and Multicultural Development, 33*(1), 3–11. doi:10.1080/01434632.2011.638072.

Starr, K. (2009). Nursing education challenges: Students with English as an additional language. *Journal of Nursing Education, 48*(9), 478–487.

Stenberg, J. (2012). The Chinese of São Paulo: A case study. *Journal of Chinese Overseas, 8*(1), 105–122. doi:https://doi.org/10.1163/179325412X634328.

Stern, S. J. (2006). *Battling for hearts and minds: Memory struggles in Pinochet's Chile, 1973–1988.* Durham, NC: Duke University Press.

Stracke, E., Jones, J., Bramley, N., Csizér, K., & Magid, M. (2014). Investigating adult migrant ESL learners' language learning motivational profile in Australia: Towards a bicultural identity. In K. Csizér & M. Magid (Eds.), *The impact of self-concept on language learning* (pp. 155–170). Bristol: Multilingual Matters.

Stratton, J. (2011). Non-citizens in the exclusionary state: Citizenship, mitigated exclusion, and the Cronulla riots. *Continuum, 25*(3), 299–316. doi:10.1080/10304312.2011.565723.

Strömmer, M. (2016a). Affordances and constraints: Second language learning in cleaning work. *Multilingua, 35*(6), 697–721.

Strömmer, M. (2016b). Material scaffolding: Supporting the comprehension of migrant cleaners at work. *European Journal of Applied Linguistics, 4*(2), 239–274.

Stump, T. (2022). *The right fit: Attracting and retaining newcomers in regional towns.* Sydney: Multicultural NSW. Retrieved from https://multicultural.nsw.gov.au/wp-content/uploads/2022/11/TheRightFit_Talia-Stump.pdf.

Subtirelu, N. C. (2013). "English . . . it's part of our blood": Ideologies of language and nation in United States Congressional discourse. *Journal of Sociolinguistics, 17*(1), 37–65. doi:10.1111/josl.12016.

Subtirelu, N. C. (2015). "She does have an accent but . . .": Race and language ideology in students' evaluations of mathematics instructors on RateMyProfessors.com. *Language in Society, 44*(01), 35–62. doi:10.1017/S0047404514000736.

Sue, D. W. (2010). *Microaggressions in everyday life: Race, gender, and sexual orientation.* Hoboken, NJ: John Wiley & Sons.

Sue, D. W., Capodilupo, C. M., Torino, G. C., Bucceri, J. M., Holder, A. M. B., Nadal, K., & Esquilin, M. (2007). Racial microaggressions in everyday life: Implications for clinical practice. *American Psychologist, 62*(4), 271–286.

Sue, D. W., Nadal, K. L., Capodilupo, C. M., Lin, A. I., Torino, G. C., & Rivera, D. P. (2008). Racial microaggressions against Black Americans: Implications for counseling. *Journal of Counseling & Development, 86*(3), 330–338. doi:https://doi.org/10.1002/j.1556-6678.2008.tb00517.x.

Sullivan, C., Vaughan, C., & Wright, J. (2020). *Migrant and refugee women's mental health in Australia: A literature review.* Melbourne: Multicultural Centre for Women's Health. Retrieved from https://www.mcwh.com.au/wp-content/uploads/Lit-review_mental-health.pdf.

Sun, T., Schilpzand, P., & Liu, Y. (2023). Workplace gossip: An integrative review of its antecedents, functions, and consequences. *Journal of Organizational Behavior, 44*(2), 311–334. doi:https://doi.org/10.1002/job.2653.

Surova, S. (2018). National and ethnic identifications among the Slovak diaspora in Serbia: Stranded between state(s) and ethnicity? *Nationalities Papers, 46*(6), 1081–1100. doi:10.1080/00905992.2018.1488825.

The sustainable development goals report 2022. (2022). New York: United Nations. Retrieved from https://unstats.un.org/sdgs/report/2022/The-Sustainable-Development-Goals-Report-2022.pdf.

Tadesse, D. (2007). Gambella: The impact of local conflict on regional security. *Africa Portal.* Retrieved from https://www.africaportal.org/publications/gambella-the-impact-of-local-conflict-on-regional-security/.

Taibi, M., & Ozolins, U. (2016). *Community translation.* London: Bloomsbury.

Takahashi, K. (2013). *Language learning, gender and desire: Japanese women on the move.* Clevedon: Multilingual Matters.

Talmy, S. (2009). A very important lesson: Respect and the socialization of order(s) in high school ESL. *Linguistics and Education, 20*(3), 235–253. doi:https://doi.org/10.1016/j.linged.2008.10.002.

Tanasaldy, T. (2022). From official to grassroots racism: Transformation of anti-Chinese sentiment in Indonesia. *The Political Quarterly, 93*(3), 460–468. doi:https://doi.org/10.1111/1467-923X.13148.

Tankosić, A., & Dovchin, S. (2023). (C)overt linguistic racism: Eastern-European background immigrant women in the Australian workplace. *Ethnicities, 23*(5), 726–757. doi:10.1177/14687968211005104.

Tankosić, A., Dryden, S., & Dovchin, S. (2021). The link between linguistic subordination and linguistic inferiority complexes: English as a second language migrants in Australia. *International Journal of Bilingualism, 25*(6), 1782–1798. doi:10.1177/13670069211035561.

Tannen, D. (1984). *Conversational style: Analyzing talk among friends.* Norwood, NJ: Ablex.

Tannen, D. (1989). *Talking voices: Repetition, dialogue, and imagery in conversational discourse.* Cambridge: Cambridge University Press.

Tannen, D. (1994). *Gender and discourse.* Oxford: Oxford University Press.

Taronna, A. (2016). Translation, hospitality and conflict: Language mediators as an activist community of practice across the Mediterranean. *Linguistica Antverpiensia, New Series: Themes in Translation Studies, 15*, 282–302. doi:10.52034/lanstts.v15i.412.

Taylor, B. A. (1976). Towards a sociolinguistic analysis of "swearing" and the language of abuse in Australian English. In M. Clyne (Ed.), *Australia talks: Essays on the sociology of Australian immigrant and aboriginal languages* (pp. 43–62). Canberra: Pacific Linguistics.

Taylor, B. A. (1995). Offensive language: A linguistic and sociolinguistic perspective. In D. Eades (Ed.), *Language in evidence: Issues confronting Aboriginal and multicultural Australia* (pp. 219–258). Sydney: University of New South Wales Press.

Taylor, F. (2007). *The Berlin Wall, 13 August 1961–9 November 1989.* Berlin: Bloomsbury.

Teimouri, Y., Goetze, J., & Plonsky, L. (2019). Second language anxiety and achievement: A meta-analysis. *Studies in Second Language Acquisition, 41*(2), 363–387. doi:10.1017/S0272263118000311.

Tenedero, P. P. P. (2022). *Communication that counts: Language practice and ideology in globalized accounting.* Bristol: Multilingual Matters.

Teo, S. Y. (2003). Dreaming inside a walled city: Imagination, gender and the roots of immigration. *Asian and Pacific Migration Journal, 12*(4), 411–438.

Thomas, R. J. (2019). Sources of friendship and structurally induced homophily across the life course. *Sociological Perspectives, 62*(6), 822–843. doi:10.1177/0731121419828399.

Thomas, W. I., & Znaniecki, F. (1927). *The Polish peasant in Europe and America.* New York: Alfred Knopf.

Tilbury, F. (2007). "I feel I am a bird without wings": Discourses of sadness and loss among east Africans in western Australia. *Identities, 14*(4), 433–458. doi:10.1080/10702890701578464.

To, H., Grafton, R. Q., & Regan, S. (2017). Immigration and labour market outcomes in Australia: Findings from HILDA 2001–2014. *Economic Analysis and Policy, 55*, 1–13. doi:https://doi.org/10.1016/j.eap.2017.03.006

Torsh, H. (2020). *Linguistic intermarriage in Australia: Between pride and shame.* Basingstoke: Palgrave Macmillan.

Torsh, H. (2022). "Maybe if you talk to her about it": Intensive mothering expectations and heritage language maintenance. *Multilingua, 41*(5), 611–628. doi:10.1515/multi-2021-0105.

Tronvoll, K. (2022). The anatomy of Ethiopia's civil war. *Current History, 121*(835), 163–169. doi:10.1525/curh.2022.121.835.163.

Tsuda, T. (2003). *Strangers in the ethnic homeland: Japanese Brazilian return migration in transnational perspective.* New York: Columbia University Press.

Tusting, K. (2010). Eruptions of interruptions: Managing tensions between writing and other tasks in a textualised childcare workplace. In D. Barton & U. Papen (Eds.), *The anthropology of writing: Understanding textually mediated worlds* (pp. 67–89). London: Bloomsbury.

Ur, P. (2011). Grammar teaching: Research, theory, and practice. In E. Hinkel (Ed.), *Handbook of research in second language teaching and learning* (Vol. 2, pp. 507–522). London: Routledge.

The value of international education to Australia. (2015). Canberra: Australian Government. Retrieved from https://internationaleducation.gov.au/research/research-papers/Documents/ValueInternationalEd.pdf.

Vickers, C. H., & Deckert, S. K. (2013). Sewing empowerment: Examining multiple identity shifts as a Mexican immigrant woman develops expertise in a sewing cooperative community of practice. *Journal of Language, Identity & Education, 12*(2), 116–135. doi:10.1080/15348458.2013.775879.

Vidal, C. P., & Howard, M. (2012). Study abroad and language acquisition. *International Journal of Applied Linguistics, 22*(2), 279–280. doi:10.1111/j.1473-4192.2012.00320_2.x.

Village, A., Powell, R., & Pepper, M. (2017). Bonding and bridging among first generation Asian migrants in Australian Protestant churches. *Journal of Ethnic and Migration Studies, 43*(11), 1943–1963. doi:10.1080/1369183X.2016.1240027.

Viswanathan, M., Torelli, C., Yoon, S., & Riemer, H. (2010). "Fish out of water": Understanding decision-making and coping strategies of English as second language consumers through a situational literacy perspective. *Journal of Consumer Marketing, 27*(6), 524–533.

Walker, R., & Bantebya-Kyomuhendo, G. (2014). *The shame of poverty.* New York and Oxford: Oxford University Press.

Wang, Y. (2020). *The heritage language maintenance of Chinese migrant children and their families* (PhD dissertation). Macquarie University. Retrieved from https://figshare.mq.edu.au/articles/thesis/The_heritage_language_maintenance_of_Chinese_migrant_children_and_their_families/19435982.

Wang, Y. (2022). Speaking Chinese or no breakfast: Emotional challenges and experiences confronting Chinese immigrant families in heritage language maintenance. *International Journal of Bilingualism, 27*(2), 232–250. doi:10.1177/13670069221126043.

Wang, Y., & Piller, I. (2022). Christian bilingual practices and hybrid identities as vehicles of migrant integration. In R. Moloney & S. Mansour (Eds.), *Language and spirit: Exploring languages, religion and spirituality in Australia today* (pp. 307–326). Cham: Palgrave Macmillan.

Warriner, D. S. (2007). Language learning and the politics of belonging: Sudanese women refugees becoming and being "American." *Anthropology & Education Quarterly, 38*(4), 343–359.

Watkins, M., & Noble, G. (2019). Lazy multiculturalism: Cultural essentialism and the persistence of the Multicultural Day in Australian schools. *Ethnography and Education, 14*(3), 295–310. doi:10.1080/17457823.2019.1581821.

Watkins, P. G., Razee, H., & Richters, J. (2012). "I'm telling you . . . the language barrier is the most, the biggest challenge": Barriers to education among Karen refugee women in Australia. *Australian Journal of Education, 56*(2), 126–141. doi:10.1177/000494411205600203.

Watson, R. (Director). (1985–). *Neighbours* [TV series]. Australia, Fremantle.

Webb, S., Faine, M., Pardy, J., & Roy, R. (2017). The role of VET in the (dis) placing of migrants' skills in Australia. *Journal of Vocational Education & Training, 69*(3), 351–370.

Wen, L., & Maani, S. A. (2018). A panel study of immigrants' overeducation and earnings in Australia. *International Migration, 56*(2), 177–200. doi:10.1111/imig.12425.

Wenger, E. (1998). *Communities of practice: Learning, meaning, and identity.* Cambridge: Cambridge University Press.

West, C., & Zimmerman, D. H. (1987). Doing gender. *Gender and Society, 1*(2), 125–151.

Wienberg, J., Dutz, G., & Grotlüschen, A. (2021). Language learning of migrants: Empirical evidence from the German integration course system with a focus on literacy courses. In G. S. Levine & D. Mallows (Eds.), *Language learning of adult migrants in Europe: Theoretical, empirical, and pedagogical issues* (pp. 95–118). Cham: Springer International.

Wiese, H. (2015). "This migrants' babble is not a German dialect!": The interaction of standard language ideology and "us"/"them" dichotomies in the public discourse on a multiethnolect. *Language in Society, 44*(03), 341–368. doi:doi:10.1017/S0047404515000226.

Wilkinson, M. D., Dumontier, M., Aalbersberg, I. J., Appleton, G., Axton, M., Baak, A., . . . Mons, B. (2016). The FAIR Guiding Principles for scientific data management and stewardship. *Scientific Data, 3*(1), 160018. doi:10.1038/sdata.2016.18.

Williams Tetteh, V. (2015). *Language, education and settlement: A sociolinguistic ethnography on, with, and for Africans in Australia* (PhD dissertation). Macquarie University, Sydney. Retrieved from http://www.languageonthemove.com/wp-content/uploads/2015/07/Final-PhD-thesis_Vera-Williams-Tetteh.pdf.

Williamson, K., & Blench, R. (2000). Niger-Congo. In B. Heine & D. Nurse (Eds.), *African languages: An introduction* (pp. 11–42). Cambridge: Cambridge University Press.

Wills, S. (2008). Between the hostel and the detention centre: Possible trajectories of migrant pain and shame in Australia. In W. Logan & K. Reeves (Eds.), *Places of pain and shame* (pp. 277–294). London: Routledge.

Wilson, J., & Tonner, A. (2020). Doing family: The constructed meanings of family in family farms. *Journal of Rural Studies, 78*, 245–253. doi:https://doi.org/10.1016/j.jrurstud.2020.06.002.

Wilson, S. (2020). Family language policy through the eyes of bilingual children: The case of French heritage speakers in the UK. *Journal of Multilingual and Multicultural Development, 41*(2), 121–139. doi:10.1080/01434632.2019.1595633.

Wise, R. D. (2015). Migration and labour under neoliberal globalization. In C.-U. Schierup, R. Munck, B. Likić Brborić, & A. Neergaard (Eds.), *Migration, precarity, and global governance: Challenges and opportunities for labour* (pp. 25–45). Oxford: Oxford University Press.

Wong Fillmore, L. (1991). When learning a second language means losing the first. *Early Childhood Research Quarterly, 6*(3), 323–346.

Wotherspoon, G. (2016). *Gay Sydney: A history.* Sydney: NewSouth.

Wright, C. F., & Clibborn, S. (2020). A guest-worker state? The declining power and agency of migrant labour in Australia. *The Economic and Labour Relations Review, 31*(1), 34–58.

Wright, C. F., Clibborn, S., Piper, N., & Cini, N. (2022). *Economic migration and Australia in the 21st century.* Sydney: Lowy Institute. Retrieved from https://www.lowyinstitute.org/publications/economic-migration-australia-21st-century.

Wright, D., & Brookes, G. (2019). "This is England, speak English!": A corpus-assisted critical study of language ideologies in the right-leaning British press. *Critical Discourse Studies, 16*(1), 56–83. doi:10.1080/17405904.2018.1511439.

Wu, S., Renzaho, A. M. N., Hall, B. J., Shi, L., Ling, L., & Chen, W. (2021). Time-varying associations of pre-migration and post-migration stressors in refugees' mental health during resettlement: A longitudinal study in Australia. *The Lancet Psychiatry, 8*(1), 36–47. doi:https://doi.org/10.1016/S2215-0366(20)30422-3.

Xie, Y., & Peng, M. (2018). Attitudes toward homosexuality in China: Exploring the effects of religion, modernizing factors, and traditional culture. *Journal of Homosexuality, 65*(13), 1758–1787. doi:10.1080/00918369.2017.1386025.

Xu, X. (2020). Exploring the logic of name changes and identity construction: A reflective self-narration of assimilation expectations. *Names, 68*(1), 32–41. doi:10.1080/00277738.2018.1452937.

Yamanaka, K. (2003). "I will go home, but when?": Labor migration and circular diaspora formation by Japanese Brazilians in Japan. In M. Douglass & G. S. Roberts (Eds.), *Japan and global migration: Foreign workers and the advent of a multicultural society* (pp. 123–152). Honolulu: University of Hawai'i Press.

Yates, L., Ficorilli, L., Kim, S. H. O., Lising, L., McPherson, P., Taylor-Leech, K., . . . Williams, A. (2010). *Language training and settlement success: Are they related?* Sydney: Adult Migrant English Program (AMEP) Research Centre, Macquarie University.

Yates, L., Terraschke, A., Zielinski, B., Pryor, E., Wang, J., Major, G., . . . Williams Tetteh, V. (2015). *Adult Migrant English Program (AMEP) longitudinal study 2011–2014: Final report.* Sydney: Macquarie University. Retrieved from http://hdl.handle.net/1959.14/1184059.

Yeates, N. (2012). Global care chains: A state-of-the-art review and future directions in care transnationalization research. *Global Networks, 12*(2), 135–154.

Yeoh, B. S. A., Somaiah, B. C., Lam, T., & Acedera, K. F. (2020). Doing family in "times of migration": Care temporalities and gender politics in Southeast Asia. *Annals of the American Association of Geographers, 110*(6), 1709–1725. doi:10.1080/24694452.2020.1723397.

Yildiz, Y. (2012). *Beyond the mother tongue: The postmonolingual condition.* New York: Fordham University Press.

Yosso, T. J., Smith, W. A., Ceja, M., & Solórzano, D. G. (2009). Critical race theory, racial microaggressions, and campus racial climate for Latina/o undergraduates. *Harvard Educational Review, 79*(4), 659–691.

Yu, B., & Wright, E. (2016). Socio-cultural adaptation, academic adaptation and satisfaction of international higher degree research students in Australia. *Tertiary Education and Management, 22*(1), 49–64. doi:10.1080/13583883.2015.1127405.

Yu, Y., & Moskal, M. (2019). Why do Christian churches, and not universities, facilitate intercultural engagement for Chinese international students? *International Journal of Intercultural Relations, 68*, 1–12. doi:https://doi.org/10.1016/j.ijintrel.2018.10.006.

Zamora, J. (2022). *Solito: A memoir.* New York: Random House.

Zarb, K. (2022). Without China, how big is the global online ESL market in 2022? *Teach English Online.* Retrieved from https://teachenglishonline.com.au/global-online-esl-market-2021/.

Zecker, R. M. (2011). *Race and America's immigrant press: How the Slovaks were taught to think like White people.* London: Bloomsbury Academic.

Zentella, A. C. (1997). *Growing up bilingual: Puerto Rican children in New York.* Oxford: Blackwell.

Zhang, J. (2021). *Language policy and planning for the modern Olympic games.* Berlin and New York: De Gruyter.

Zhang, J., & Wu, Y. (2020). Providing multilingual logistics communication in COVID-19 disaster relief. *Multilingua, 39*(5), 517–528. doi:10.1515/multi-2020-0110.

Zhang, X. (2019). Foreign language anxiety and foreign language performance: A meta-analysis. *The Modern Language Journal, 103*(4), 763–781. doi:https://doi.org/10.1111/modl.12590.

Zheng, Y. (2020). Mobilizing foreign language students for multilingual crisis translation in Shanghai. *Multilingua, 39*(5), 587–595. doi:10.1515/multi-2020-0095.

Zhu, H. (2019). *Exploring intercultural communication: Language in action* (2nd ed.). London: Routledge.

Zogbaum, H. (2004). *Kisch in Australia: The untold story.* Melbourne: Scribe Publications.

Index

For the benefit of digital users, indexed terms that span two pages (e.g., 52–53) may, on occasion, appear on only one of those pages.